P9-DUY-652

Missing Children

MISSING CHILDREN

Rhetoric and Reality

by

MARTIN L. FORST

and

MARTHA-ELIN BLOMQUIST

LEXINGTON BOOKS
An Imprint of Macmillan, Inc.
NEW YORK

Maxwell Macmillan Canada
TORONTO

Maxwell Macmillan International
NEW YORK OXFORD SINGAPORE SYDNEY

Library of Congress Cataloging-in-Publication Data

Forst, Martin Lyle.
Missing children : rhetoric and reality / by Martin L. Forst and
Martha-Elin Blomquist.
p. cm.
Includes bibliographical references and index.
ISBN (invalid) 0-669-24418-X (alk. paper)
1. Missing children—United States. 2. Custody of children-
United States. I. Blomquist, Martha-Elin. II. Title.
HV6762.U5F67 1991
362.82'97'0973—dc20 91-9219
CIP

Lexington Books
An Imprint of Macmillan, Inc.
866 Third Avenue, New York, N. Y. 10022

Maxwell Macmillan Canada, Inc.
1200 Eglinton Avenue East
Suite 200
Don Mills, Ontario M3C 3NI

Macmillan, Inc. is part of the Maxwell Communication
Group of Companies.

Printed in the United States of America

printing number
1 2 3 4 5 6 7 8 9 10

To Our Parents

Contents

Introduction — *ix*

1. Missing Children: Who Are They? — 1
2. Counting Cases: The Extent of the Problem — 27
3. The Birth of a Social Problem — 55
4. The Politics of Missing Children — 83
5. Kidnapping: A Parent's Worst Nightmare — 115
6. Parental Abduction: Keeping It in the Family — 147
7. Runaways: Tragedies on the Installment Plan — 179
8. Law Enforcement and Missing Children — 213
9. Issues in Law Enforcement and Missing Children — 247
10. Conclusion: A Reappraisal of the Missing Children Problem — 281

Notes — 293

Index — 303

About the Authors — 307

Introduction

THE worst nightmare of any parent is having a son or daughter kidnapped by a stranger, never to be seen again. In recent years, media sensationalism about child kidnappings has helped to heighten these parental fears. High-profile child kidnap and murder cases receive a great deal of press and television coverage. They remind society of the vulnerability of children, and how impotent parents are to keep them safe at all times. A routine event in a child's daily life—walking to the corner store, taking a bus to school, playing in the front yard unsupervised—can lead to that one unforeseen, and sometimes deadly, encounter with a kidnapper.

Often, the sudden and unexplained disappearance of a child moves an entire community into action, especially when there are indications that the child may have been abducted by a stranger or be in physical danger. Volunteers of all kinds—relatives, neighbors, local merchants, members of churches or missing children organizations—join teams of law enforcement officers to search for the child, post photographs, offer the family emotional and financial support, and keep up hopes for the child's recovery.

During the past decade, increasing attention has been focused on "missing children"; legislators have passed new laws, police departments have adopted new procedures, and government officials have sponsored studies to determine how many missing children there really are. This attention has given rise to what might be called the missing children problem. But what exactly *is* the missing children problem? How accurate are the media portrayals of missing children? How many missing children are there in the United States each year, and what types of cases do they represent? How many missing children return home safely and how many are abused or never seen again?

After a decade of rhetoric, media hype, and political posturing, it's time for a sober analysis of the "problem" of missing children. This book presents an overview of the missing children phenomenon. We attempt to sort through the rhetoric and emotionalism of the topic to offer a realistic appraisal of missing children as both a problem and an agenda for social and political action. We describe the types of cases that make up the generic category of missing children, the most recent statistics on the numbers of children reported missing each year, the legal history of missing children, and the actions governmental agencies have taken or might take to address this issue.

Missing children constitute a complex problem with no single or easy solution. Indeed, the missing children cases that have traditionally received the least amount of attention from law enforcement agencies, politicians, and government agencies and are increasing in greatest numbers—parental abductions and runaways—pose the most complicated issues. They show the erosion in the structure of community and family life in the United States in the 1980s and 1990s. This weakening has occurred during the very period when governmental officials have paid great lipservice to the special place that "family" and "children" hold in American society.

Indeed, much of the "problem" of missing children is the problem of the status of children and the family in contemporary society. Preventing children from being lured into the cars of strangers, and arresting parents who abduct children are limited solutions. While these measures may have their place, they are not adequate substitutes for addressing the larger and more fundamental problems that affect the quality of life for growing numbers of Americans, young and old. While there are no clear or ready solutions to many of these problems—child abuse, high rates of divorce and family dissolution, substance abuse, poverty, and the like—two things are clear. First, doing something about missing children means doing something about a complicated problem. And second, doing anything significant or long lasting about missing children means improving some of the basic social institutions that affect the immediate and long-term welfare of all children—the family, the school system, and the neighborhood.

1

Missing Children

Who Are They?

MISSING CHILDREN is not a specific legal category. The term is a social creation, even a media invention, which has been used to describe a range of crimes or incidents. Governmental agencies—particularly law enforcement agencies—use various classifications for breaking down the broad category of missing children cases into specific types of situations. In large part, these classifications constitute the basis of investigative practices law enforcement agencies follow to recover children. It is important to emphasize at the outset that the classification of missing children cases is far from uniform throughout the country. States frequently use somewhat different legal definitions, and the categories that exist in one jurisdiction may not necessarily exist in another.

Nevertheless, there are some broadly accepted categorizations we use to organize this exploration of the phenomenon of missing children. The most typical scheme is founded on legal categories employed by state criminal and juvenile justice systems. It includes three legal categories: kidnapping, parental abduction, and running away from home. As we shall see in the next chapter, these categories also form the basis of statistics compiled on missing children. Another category sometimes used in law enforcement is the *unknown missing* child. Although there is no specific law against being *missing,* this term is used by law enforcement agencies when there is not enough evidence or information to place the case of a missing child into one of the other categories.

Later in this book, each of the categories is thoroughly discussed in its legal and social context. The purpose of this chapter is simply to review each of these categories to show the range of case types that come under the general rubric of missing children. The range is enormous—from the child who is kidnapped and killed by a stranger to the teenager who is simply a few minutes late coming home from school. Chapter 2 presents estimates of the numbers of cases falling into each category.

Kidnapping

The missing child category that arouses the most parental anxiety is kidnapping, which is sometimes called abduction by a stranger. As we shall see, an abduction does not have to be accomplished by a stranger to be considered a kidnapping.

Kidnapping has been a serious crime for hundreds of years. It was one of the original common law crimes; that is, it developed as a crime in England over a thousand years ago, before there was a legislature to codify it. Along with the rest of the common law, English colonists brought the law against kidnapping to this country in the seventeenth century. Since then, as will be detailed in chapter 5, the definition of kidnapping as used in the United States has greatly expanded.

Generally understood, kidnapping is the intentional taking of a person and compelling the person, either adult or child, to be detained against his or her will. The common law crime of kidnapping in England referred only to the act of taking a person by force out of the country. The definition of kidnapping has evolved in two significant ways in the United States. first, the person does not have to be taken out of the country; any movement, within a state or a county, is sufficient to constitute a kidnap. Second, force is not a necessary element of the crime; a person can be kidnapped through trickery or "inveiglement."

Every state in the country has a kidnapping statute broad enough to encompass the most common fact situations associated with this crime, including ransom, homicide or abuse, robbery, sexual assault, and long-term concealment.

Ransom

Perhaps the oldest reason for kidnapping is ransom. New York's kidnapping statute defines the elements of this type of kidnap:

> A person is guilty of kidnapping in the first degree when he abducts another person and when:
>
> 1. His intent is to compel a third person to pay or deliver money or property as ransom, or to engage in other particular conduct, or to refrain from engaging in particular conduct . . . .[1]

Similarly, Idaho's statute states in part:

> Every person who willfully: Seizes, confines, inveigles, leads, takes, entices away or kidnaps another against his will to extort money, property or any other thing of value or to obtain money, property or reward or any other thing of value for the return or disposition of such person is guilty of kidnapping. . . .[2]

The most famous kidnapping for ransom case in U.S. history is the Lindbergh abduction, called the crime of the century. Although some facts still remain in dispute, what happened to twenty-month-old baby Charles is clear. In the early evening of March 1, 1932, Charles's mother, Anne Lindbergh, and his nursemaid, Bety Gow, put baby Charles to bed in the new Lindbergh home in New Jersey. When the nursemaid went to check on the baby at 10 P.M., he was gone. Instead she found a ransom note on the window sill. After negotiating with the kidnappers through intermediaries, Charles Lindbergh paid $50,000 in cash. In exchange, he was told where the baby could be found. Unfortunately, baby Charles was not discovered there. Seven weeks later, the baby's body was found in the bushes about two miles from the Lindbergh home. Three years later, in 1935, Bruno Hauptman was tried and convicted for the kidnapping and murder of baby Charles.

Although infrequent, kidnappings for ransom still occur. In more recent times, the Chowchilla kidnapping case is perhaps the most widely known.

> In 1976 three young men hatched a plot to kidnap a busload of children to hold them for ransom. In July the men carried out a carefully detailed plan—they waylaid a bus near the small rural town of Chowchilla in central California. The three masked gunmen forced the twenty-six children riding on the bus (plus the busdriver) into two vans. The victims were driven for eleven hours without food or water, and were then transferred to another van that was already buried in the ground. The victims believed that they had been left to die. After struggling for sixteen hours, the children and the bus driver dug their way out of the underground tomb and called the police. The police found the kidnappers and searched their homes. In one of the homes, they found a draft of a ransom note demanding $5 million. The kidnappers did not have a chance to deliver the note because they were caught so soon after the crime. The three men were convicted and are still serving life sentences in prison.

Another kidnapping for ransom case took place in the San Francisco Bay Area in March 1990.

> A sixteen-year-old boy was abducted while on his way home after school. Shortly thereafter, the boy's parents received a telephone call from the kidnapper demanding $100,000 ransom to be paid in three days or their son would be killed. The parents notified local law enforcement officials, who, in turn, immediately called in the FBI to assist detectives in the investigation. Two agonizing weeks went by before the case broke—with a happy ending. The youth was found safe in a small apartment in a suburb just south of Los Angeles. He was located shortly after the two kidnappers were taken into custody following their attempt to pick up the ransom money. A former employee of the child's father was implicated in the abduction. Family joy reigned when the boy was returned home after his two-week ordeal.

Sometimes these cases have unique variations, in which the ransom is viewed by the perpetrator as an old and unpaid debt.

In June of 1990, two sisters—ages nine and eleven—were kidnapped in Los Angeles by two men who had smuggled the girls and their mother into the United States from Mexico. The mother had promised to pay the men a specified amount of money, but she was unable to raise the necessary amount. The men kidnapped the girls in order to induce the woman somehow to get the money and pay her debt. Before the scheme was completed, the two girls escaped, and the two men were arrested.

Robbery

Kidnapping for purposes of robbery has a long history in our legal system. Many states specifically list robbery in their kidnapping statutes, and some states prescribe more serious penalties for kidnapping for robbery. Part of California's penal code section on kidnapping states:

> Any person who kidnaps or carries away any individual to commit robbery shall be punished by imprisonment in the state prison for life with possibility of parole.[3]

Kidnappings for robbery commonly involve adult victims. Because they don't possess large sums of money, children are rarely victims of this type of kidnapping. Such cases do, however, happen on occasion, usually with a teenage victim.

In January 1990 two young men, ages nineteen and twenty, were arrested for kidnapping and false imprisonment. The two men had persuaded four girls, ages twelve and thirteen, to enter their car. The men had convinced the girls that they had mutual friends whom they would take the girls to see. Once in the car, it became clear that the men would not take them where they had promised to go. Three of the girls escaped at a park the men had driven to. The fourth girl escaped shortly thereafter. She told the police she had not been sexually assaulted, but that the men robbed her of $24.

Homicide or Abuse

Kidnapping can have tragic consequences, such as abuse, torture, or death.

Naturally, most kidnapping statutes address these acts. A section of New York's kidnapping statute states:

> A person is guilty of kidnapping in the first degree when he abducts another person when . . . [h]e restrains the person abducted for a period of more than twelve hours with the intent to . . . inflict physical injury upon him or violate or abuse him sexually. . . .[4]

Fortunately, homicide following a kidnapping is rare. One study conducted by the federal government found that only 2.8 percent of kidnappings involving children resulted in death.[5]

One incident involving kidnapping can constitute more than one crime. If a person is taken against his or her will (or is tricked), the crime of kidnapping has been committed. If the kidnapper then kills the victim, the incident becomes a homicide. The perpetrator can be charged with both crimes for that single incident.

Unfortunately, horror stories of abuse or homicide do occur, and these are the types of cases that are most likely to generate broad media coverage. Sometimes children—most commonly teenagers—fall victim to a serial killer.

> One of the most notorious cases in California history involved Gerald Gallego and his common-law wife, Charlene Williams. This team is responsible for kidnapping and killing as many as ten teenagers from 1978 to 1980. The pair plotted to kidnap young girls to serve as "love slaves" and then as sacrificial victims. A common tactic was for the team to approach teenage girls at shopping malls or fairs and tell them that they had the potential to be models or movie stars. The kidnappers lured the girls to a van where the victims would be tied up, sexually assaulted and then killed. These killers were eventually caught, tried and convicted. Gerald is now awaiting execution in San Quentin prison.

Similar incidents have taken place in other parts of the country.

In 1989 a family was vacationing in Las Vegas. The mother left her seven-year-old son for a couple of minutes in a video arcade of a casino. When the mother came back, the boy had vanished. Witnesses said thay saw a boy walking down the casino hallway hand-in-hand with an unidentified man. Nobody thought anything of it at the time since the man could easily have been the boy's father. An intense search and investigation took place after the disappearance. About a month passed when a gardener checking the sprinkler system in a local trailer park found the fully clothed body of the boy face down hidden from view under a mobile home. The police questioned many people, and some were considered suspects, but the police were never able to close the case with a conviction.

Sexual Abuse

Abuse of a kidnap victim does not necessarily have to end in homicide. Another crime that occurs with children involves sexual exploitation—either sexual abuse or rape. Sometimes younger children—ages three to ten—are abducted for these purposes. One study of kidnappings in two cities showed that over half (54 percent) of the victims had been sexually abused as part of the incident.[6]

One day in 1987, a six-year-old boy was walking home from school in his Chicago suburb. A man drove up slowly behind him. He called to the little boy, saying that he had lost his dog and asked the boy to help him search for the pet. The boy wasn't sure what to do, but when he went over to the car, the man dragged the boy inside. The man drove to an isolated country road where he pulled the boys pants down and fondled the boy's penis and forced the boy to fondle his penis. The man then dropped the boy off near where he had picked him up and told the boy that if he said anything about the incident, he would kill the boy's parents.

Teenage boys and girls also may be subject to kidnap and sexual assault.

> A sixteen-year-old girl was hitchhiking along a southern California highway on her way to the beach. A van with two young men pulled up and asked her if she wanted a ride. But they had no intention of taking her to the beach. They instead bound her hands, blindfolded her, and took her to an isolated spot in the hills. After raping the girl, the men left her in the hills. She was found not long thereafter by a passing motorist.

Desire to Have a Child

There is one set of circumstances in which the perpetrator has no desire to cause harm. This type of kidnapper takes a child—normally an infant—to love and care for as his or her own.

This situation is also observed by most state statutes. For example, Idaho's law provides:

> Every person who willfully . . . [l]eads, takes, entices away or detains a child under the age of sixteen (16) years, with intent to keep or conceal it from its custodial parent, guardian or other person having lawful care or control thereof, or with intent to steal any article upon the person of the child . . . is guilty of kidnapping.[7]

One of the most common situations of this type involves a person who takes a newborn from the maternity ward of a hospital. Such cases occur with sufficient frequency that law enforcement and hospital personnel have been able to develop a profile of the perpetrator. This type of kidnapper is generally a female without children. She wants an infant of her own; because she cannot have one she steals one from a maternity ward. The woman often deludes herself into thinking the child is really hers, and has every intention of raising it as her own.

A kidnapping with this motive does not have to take place in a maternity ward.

> In December 1980, a woman posing as a social worker came to the Newport News, Virginia, home of a woman

who had given birth to a healthy baby boy just fifteen days before. The woman told the new mother and the baby's grandmother that she wanted to take the infant and his two-year-old brother back to the hospital to attend the Christmas party. The mother nervously agreed. That afternoon, the older brother was discovered wandering around a shopping center in a nearby town. But the fake social worker and the infant had vanished. Neither has been seen or heard from since.

Unknown Motives

On occasion the motive for a kidnapping is unknown, usually because the crime has not been solved. In these cases, no ransom notes are sent, no communication is made with any parties—the child simply vanishes and is never heard from again. According to police standards, the only way law enforcement officials can be sure the case is a kidnapping is when one or more witnesses actually observed the abduction taking place.

On November 19, 1988, in a San Francisco suburb, a nine-year-old girl went to the grocery store one sunny Saturday morning with her girlfriend. The two girls traveled several blocks from their homes to the store on their skateboards. The girls left their skateboards in front of the store and went inside to get a treat. When they came back outside, one of the girl's skateboard was not in sight. When they glanced around, they saw it near a car in the parking lot. When the girl went to get it, a stranger opened the car door and pulled her inside and sped off. The other girl was standing nearby and witnessed the entire incident, but she could not get the license plate number. What happened to the abducted girl remains a total mystery. No ransom note, no nothing. The search goes on, and the motive for the abduction is totally unknown.

Hard-to-Categorize Cases

Some cases are so unusual they do not fit any pattern, although they still fall under the legal definition of kidnapping. A few such case examples will suffice to show the wide variety of cases—and the difficulty of using classifications to make generalizations.

> A four-year-old girl was abducted from in front of her apartment in Sacramento, California. She was discovered alive after spending forty-four days in a crawl space under a church altar, held captive there by the church's handyman. The kidnapper was caught—and the girl rescued—after the perpetrator attempted to kidnap another girl and a witness took the perpetrator's license plate number and called the police. No ransom was demanded and the girl had not been physically or sexually abused.

> A one-year-old boy was kidnapped by four men in Oakland, California, in what is believed to be a drug-related incident. The men broke into a home and told all of the residents to lie down on the floor. They abducted the child and told the residents that he was being taken in retaliation for something the boy's father had done to the four men. Fortunately, the perpetrators released the boy unharmed the next day.

As is the case with other crimes, the victim and the offender often know each other in some capacity.

> A sixteen-year-old girl from San Jose, California, was killed in a high-speed car crash after she was kidnapped at gunpoint by her spurned boyfriend. According to police records, the twenty-one-year-old boyfriend entered the girl's house, pulled a gun, and forced the girl into his car. A short while later, two highway patrol officers spotted the car and gave chase. The kidnapper lost control of the car, crashing and killing the girl.

Parental Abductions

Children are sometimes abducted by their own relatives—typically a parent in a custody dispute. Usually when a parent abducts his or her own child, the case is not classified as a kidnapping. Some states specifically exclude parental abductions from their kidnapping statutes. The federal law on kidnapping, for example, states:

> . . . Whoever unlawfully seizes, confines, inveigles, decoys, kidnaps, abducts, or carries away and holds for ransom or reward or otherwise any person, *except in the case of a minor by the parent thereof* . . . [is guilty of kidnapping].[8]

Many, if not most, states have now eliminated this exception with the passage of new laws specifically aimed at parents who take their child or children in a custody battle. These laws go by various names, and are discussed in detail in chapter 6. Suffice it to say at this point that officials handle parental abduction cases under various statutory names, such as custodial interference or child stealing.

Arizona's custodial interference law, for example, states:

> A person commits custodial interference if, knowing or having reason to know that he has no legal right to do so, such person knowingly takes, entices or keeps from lawful custody any child less than eighteen years of age or incompetent, entrusted by authority of law to the custody of another person or institution.[9]

As will be shown more clearly later, the specific wording of these statutes makes the crime difficult to prosecute. The most typical situation, however, occurs when one party has lost custody of the child following a divorce proceeding. For any one or more of a variety of reasons, and after having tried in varying degrees to gain lawful custody, the noncustodial parent takes the child or children from the parent having lawful custody.

Again, the specifics in these situations vary enormously. In some cases, the abductor takes the child out of the country, in others out of the state. Sometimes the abductor keeps the child within the same area, but attempts to conceal the child's whereabouts from the other parent. In some cases, the parent intends permanently to deprive the custodial parent of the child; in others the parent takes the child only for a limited period of time, for example, a weekend. In still other situations, the noncustodial parent may take the child out of a belief that the child is being abused by the custodial parent. There are also situations in which the noncustodial parent takes the child out of spite, to make the ex-spouse suffer.

Perhaps the most well-known parental abduction case in recent years involved Hillary Foretich.

> Shortly after Dr. Elizabeth Morgan gave birth to her daughter, Hillary, she separated from her husband, Dr. Eric Foretich. The parents, after trying to reconcile, divorced, and they agreed to a custody arrangement. The father had liberal visitation rights. When Hillary was about two years old, her mother asserts she began to make statements indicating that she was being sexually abused by the father. Allegations of sexual abuse were investigated by numerous people and agencies, and the results were inconclusive. The court, because of the lack of conclusive evidence, permitted the father to continue seeing the daughter. The mother finally decided the only way to secure her daughter's physical and mental health was to take the child out of the country and prevent the father from seeing her. With help from her parents, the mother arranged for the daughter to leave the country. By doing so, the mother was held in contempt of court; the judge sentenced her to jail until she revealed the location of the child. The mother refused to divulge the child's whereabouts for two years, during which time she was jailed. Finally Congress passed a law which in essence required the mother's release from confinement. The girl was finally found in New Zealand with her maternal grandparents. The father eventually decided not to pursue custody in the case.

It is not uncommon for parental abductions to involve allegations of child abuse, including sexual abuse. In part this is because in some jurisdictions the desire to protect a child against this type of harm constitutes a valid defense against the charge of parental abduction. Sometimes there are no allegations of child abuse. One parent simply wants to be with the child he or she would otherwise not get to see, or to see the child to a greater extent than the custody order permits.

> A twenty-four-year-old divorcee lived on a ranch near Tishomingo, Oklahoma, with her four-year-old son and her new husband. One day in July 1976, while the woman was shopping in town, four men drove to the ranch and abducted the boy. The little boy was struck with terror at first—and then he realized that one of the abductors was his natural father who had lost custody rights. Just then the mother came driving up and saw what was happening. She gave chase in her car. The abductor who was driving somehow lost control of the getaway car. The car went into a ditch and the boy was dead at the scene. The father died of injuries a few days later.

Other cases involve taking children across national boundaries when the custody of the child is in question.

> In 1975, A Fremont, California, couple went to Tijuana, Mexico, to adopt a baby. A one-day-old girl was carried out of the Tijuana hospital by the American couple. The facts were in dispute. They claim they had adopted the girl, but the mother claims she never put her baby up for adoption and that the girl was abducted. A Mexican court ruled in the mother's favor, saying that no legal adoption had taken place, and issued a warrant for the American man on kidnapping charges. The case went to the slow-moving American justice system. By the time the little girl was three years old, the American Immigration and Naturalization Service (INS) ruled that there was no legal adoption and that the girl should be deported. The couple fled to Florida with the girl. The Mexican mother traced the family to Florida and again filed a legal action. The INS again ordered the girl deported. The American couple appealed this ruling and the U.S. Court of Appeals held that the INS ruling was invalid because the little girl had not been represented by a lawyer. The child was placed in a foster home pending the legal outcome. By this time the little girl was six years old. One day the Mexican mother visited the girl in the foster home and took her out for a walk. They never returned. They sent

word through their lawyer that they were living happily in Mexico.

There are also cases in which the child is a pawn in a battle between two warring parents.

A Minneapolis couple had a bitter divorce. The woman, who had fallen in love with another man, was awarded custody of the couple's four-year-old son. The father, who did not want the divorce, got visitation on weekends. After brooding about his situation, the man decided not to return his son one Sunday night as required in the custody order. He wanted to get back at his wife, he wanted to see his son more, and he wanted to go back into court to have the custody order modified. The mother called the police. The police, in turn, called the man and told him that what he was doing was a violation of the criminal law, and that if he did not bring the child back immediately he would be subject to arrest. Reason prevailed over emotion, and he returned the child.

It is important to note that parental abductions do not always involve a custody battle with an ex-spouse.

A homeless woman in Chicago was charged with abduction after she secreted her twelve-year-old daughter out of a hospital. The juvenile court had taken wardship over the child because she was ill and needed medical attention. The mother, who was a Christian Scientist, thought the hospital might give the girl a blood transfusion, which was against the mother's religion, so she took her from the hospital.

Runaways

Runaways constitute the third category of missing children. In legal terminology, running away from home is what is called a *status offense.* It is a form of behavior that is not illegal if committed by an adult, but could be grounds for bringing a youth to the attention of the juvenile court authorities. In addition to running away, other common status offenses are truancy, curfew violation, and incorrigibility.

Runaway cases are so numerous and so varied as almost to defy description and generalization. The age range of runaways is broad—from the upper end of juvenile age jurisdiction (which in most states is eighteen years), down to children as young as five or six.

Some states specifically list running away from home as a form of behavior for which a juvenile can be arrested and be made a ward of the juvenile court. For example, Nevada's Juvenile Code states:

> Except as otherwise provided in this chapter, the court has exclusive jurisdiction in proceedings . . . [c]oncerning any child living or found within the county who is in need of supervision because he . . . [d]eserts, abandons or runs away from his home or usual place of abode. . . .[10]

Other states do not specifically list running away as a proscribed form of behavior. In these states, the juvenile laws are written in a more general way so that it is implicit that running away is not legally permissible. In California, for example, the welfare and institutions code, which contains laws governing juveniles, provides that the juvenile court can assume wardship over a juvenile who is "beyond the control of his parents or guardian."[11] The California appellate courts have interpreted this phrase to include running away from home.

A romantic image of running away has popped up in American culture and literature. Tom Sawyer and Huckleberry Finn ran away from home and had adventures on the Mississippi River. And the adventures of young boys running away to join the circus—recounted as "coming of age" stories—are often idealized.

In reality, most runaway episodes are not nearly so romantic. Many are prompted by instances of some type of abuse at home—physical, sexual, or emotional. Youths who run away often then face abuse and exploitation in their new life on the streets.

> A child prostitution ring was recently broken up near the San Francisco International Airport. The ring provided

> Asian girls, as young as twelve years old, to Asian businessmen. The ringleader recruited runaway girls in need of money and a place to stay, and introduced them to the world of prostitution. The probe began after an anonymous tip focused attention on frequent visits of the young girls and their clients to a motel near the airport. A raid resulted in the arrest of one of the "johns," and a twelve-year-old girl was also taken into custody. Other arrests followed.

A relatively large percentage of runaways run from some sort of facility for juveniles, such as a group home. Often these children have been abandoned or neglected, and have been in and out of public or private facilities all of their young lives.

> A sixteen-year-old boy in Boston had been living in foster homes and group homes for the past three years, since the juvenile court judge made him a ward of the court and took him away from his alcoholic parents. The boy had a history of minor delinquencies, including drug abuse, and had run away from his court-ordered placements at least ten times. On the most recent runaway episode, the boy and three of his friends at the group home wanted to hang out down town late one Saturday night. The counselor of the group home wouldn't let them, so they snuck out the back door and went down town anyway. The counselor reported the boys missing when he couldn't find them during a room check. The police presumably looked for the boys, but they came home on their own about 2:00 the next morning after their night on the town.

For many youths, running away is triggered by some family incident, such as when the parents and child have an argument and the child leaves the house in an emotional burst. The fight may have been about the rock concert that the parents would not allow the child to attend, about the poor grades the youth is getting in school, or about the late hours the youth is keeping with his or her current romantic interest. Canadian police have a realistic yet cute name for this type of case—an *affaire-of-the-heart.*

In some cases, the child remains away from home for long periods of time—sometimes never returning. These are the youths who populate sections of large cities, such as Times Square in New York, the Hollywood area of Los Angeles, and the Polk Gulch area of San Francisco. They become street kids who survive by various means—often illegal and harmful to their well-being—such as theft, prostitution, drug sales, or pornography.

> The New York City police arrested a fourteen-year-old girl for prostitution. After an investigation, the police learned that the girl had run away from Minneapolis when she was twelve and made her way to New York. Because she could not work at a regular job and had no other skills to survive on the streets, she turned to prostitution. She quickly came under the control of a pimp. When she grew tired of the pimp's abuse, she went back to the streets; when that became too stressful, she went back to the pimp. The girl had been arrested as a runaway on several occasions, but she simply ran away from the shelter or other places she was sent to live. The police felt that there was little they could do to change the girl's life.

Unknown Missing

This fourth category of missing children, also called *otherwise missing* by some experts, is not a legal category per se. Instead, it is sometimes used administratively by police and other governmental agencies in those instances when there is insufficient information or evidence to fit the case into one of the three legal categories.

When a person makes a report of a missing child, law enforcement investigators consider the facts and evidence and make a tentative case categorization. Sometimes this process is easy, because the evidence is plentiful. For example, on occasion a witness sees a child pulled into a car by force, or a relative hears a person discuss his plan to abduct his children from his ex-wife's home. Sometimes a juvenile leaves a note before she runs away from home.

A problem arises when adequate evidence is lacking. Suppose the police receive a call at 4:30 in the afternoon and the parent reports that her thirteen-year-old daughter has not come home from school. What type of case is this? It could be a kidnapping by a stranger. Maybe the child ran away from home because of bad grades. If the parents are divorced and having a custody dispute, maybe the child's father abducted her. Maybe the girl was hit by a car and fell unconscious into a ditch. It is also likely that a child of this age may well have stopped off at a friend's house or at a nearby shopping mall and is simply forty-five minutes late coming home. Without evidence that would clearly permit the identification of a missing child into a particular legal category, law enforcement agencies will initially classify such a case as *unknown missing*.

> In March 1990, a seventeen-year-old girl was reported missing by her mother after the girl failed to return home from her visit with a friend. The girl's car was found about half way across the San Francisco Bay Bridge when another motorist ran into it. The facts of the case are sketchy. The girl appears to have had car trouble. She may have taken a ride with a stranger who abducted her. She could have stopped the car there to commit suicide. One witness thought he saw a girl on the bridge near the car about this time. Police think the girl may have been standing in front of the car waiting for help, when a motorist ran into her car and knocked her over the guard rail and into the bay. A search was made of the bay, but no body was ever found. Sadly, the mother told the press that she hoped that her daughter had been kidnapped because that way she might still be alive.

A similar case from San Francisco presents a number of possible inferences.

> A twelve-year-old boy visited a local beach—known for its strong undertow—with his mother, stepfather and the family dog. The boy had a history of running away from home, and he seemed plagued by school and family problems. His natural father lived in the area, and the divorce had been less than amicable. The boy and the dog were playing near the water, and the mother and stepfather

walked back to the car. A while later, the dog ran up to them without the boy. The mother and stepfather went to look for the boy, but he was nowhere to be found. They called the police immediately, and a search was conducted. The police thought the boy could have been swept into the ocean and drowned. He could also have run away, as he had done on several previous occasions. He could have been taken by his natural father, or he could have been kidnapped by a stranger. The boy was never found, and the case remains open.

Sometimes the facts lead the authorities, and particularly the parents, to believe that a child's disappearance is the result of foul play.

On September 5, 1982, in West Des Moines, Iowa, a twelve-year-old boy left home to do his regular morning paper route. His miniature dachshund, Gretchen, accompanied him. Later that morning, Gretchen came home, but the boy did not. He had vanished without a trace. Since he had never run away in the past, the parents were convinced he had been kidnapped, and persuaded the police to conclude the same. But there were no witnesses of any kind, and no evidence whatsoever. The case remains unsolved.

Confronted with an ambiguous situation, law enforcement investigators use a process of deductive reasoning, guided by several considerations, to classify a missing child case. The age of the missing child is of utmost importance. Generally speaking, young children are less likely to run away than older children; teenagers are less likely to be abducted by a parent. Another important factor is the child's school performance. Poor grades and behavioral problems at school are often predictors of running away from home. Family problems are also often a precursor of running away. The custody status of the child may be a relevant variable. Is the child living with his or her natural parents, or has a custody dispute been in progress?

Police agencies around the country use different criteria in deciding when sufficient evidence is present to classify a case. Some police agencies are more willing to classify a case as a kidnapping solely based on a process of deduction. In general, however, law enforcement agencies tend to be rather cautious when classifying missing children cases, particularly as kidnappings by a stranger. Unless there is a witness to the abduction or clear physical evidence, police are reluctant to change an unknown missing case to a kidnap case.

The category of unknown missing usually includes children who are lost or have been the victims of accidents. In June 1990, terrible flooding swept through parts of the mid-west. Flash floods hit Shadyside, Ohio, and numerous people were swept away. Three children were reported missing, presumably drowned by the raging waters.

Small children sometimes get themselves in precarious predicaments when playing. They climb trees, wander into unknown areas, play in dangerous waters, and explore caves and mines. Sometimes this exploration leads to tragic consequences.

> In Livermore, California, a four-year-old boy went out in the back yard to play. He wandered around the yard, and eventually made his way into the garage where his curiosity was aroused by all of the intriguing things he saw. But on this July 1990 day, his curiosity got the best of him. His mother couldn't find him, so she called the police. About 150 people helped search for the boy, along with the police dogs and a helicopter. Late that afternoon, the boy's dead body was found inside a camping cooler fitted with a latch that locked automatically when the lid dropped. The boy was declared dead upon arrival at the local hospital.

Fortunately, most cases of lost children do not end in the death of the child, although parents may face hours of agony before the child is located.

> Late one September afternoon in 1982, a mother left her three children in front of their house in Bedford, Virginia, near the Blue Ridge Mountains, while she went inside to cook dinner. The oldest child, an eight-year-old girl, was playing with her two brothers, one five years of age and the other who was not quite two years old. The mother set

her kitchen timer for ten minutes, so she could check on the kids after a short time inside the house. When she came out, the toddler was gone, and the two older children did not know where he was. Since the boy was always inquisitive, the mother figured that he had wandered off into the six acres of forest surrounding the home. The mother searched by herself at first. She checked the four lane road that ran in front of the house, and then she started exploring the forest. With no immediate results, she called the local law enforcement agency, which arrived with a search dog. A search party worked all through the night, and then about 5:00 A.M. they located the boy in the forest unharmed.

Most of the time, when small children wander away from home, they are not in particular danger and they are found quickly. Many times the child is found before the police car reaches the scene, or the child is found by the police shortly thereafter. Many of these cases are resolved so quickly that they are not even logged as statistics of missing children.

A frantic mother called the Indianapolis, Indiana, police one afternoon to report that her three-year-old daughter was missing. The worst fears rushed through the mother's mind—her child had been kidnapped or fallen victim to a terrible accident. She gave the description of the girl, and told the police dispatcher that the girl was wearing green shorts. The police dispatcher transmitted this call to a patrol car that was in the neighborhood. On the way to the woman's house, the police spotted the little girl playing with several other children about two blocks from home. The police picked up the girl and had her back with her mother within five minutes of the initial call.

Sometimes there is a difference of opinion as to what happened to the child. Parents often assume their child has been kidnapped; police are more cynical, particularly when teenagers are involved, and often assume the child is a runaway. Case classifications may change as new information surfaces.

In July 1990, a frantic father reported his fifteen-year-old Chinese American daughter missing. The girl, a budding tennis star, had gone to a local bus stop in Berkeley, California, to attend a nearby tennis tournament. That was the last anybody saw her. The father was convinced she had been kidnapped; he appeared on local TV and pleaded with her captors to release her. The police checked into the matter and found that the girl was unhappy and under tremendous pressure from her parents to succeed in school as well as on the tennis court. The police speculated that the girl had run away. About six days later, the girl called her parents from Connecticut to say she had run away. Police in Connecticut arranged for her return home.

Throwaways

The term *throwaway* is being used with increasing frequency to describe those youths who are abandoned by their parents or kicked out of the house. (Scholars also use the terms *thrownaways, pushouts,* and *castouts.*) There is some debate whether this category should be included in the general designation of missing children, because their parents generally do not report their departure to the police, and these youths are usually able to survive by themselves on the streets.

Throwaway children often exhibit common background characteristics. Many throwaways come from dysfunctional families in which one or both parents are substance abusers. These parents can hardly provide the basic necessities of life for themselves, let alone their children. Viewing their children as an intolerable burden, they tell them to leave home.

In other instances the parents are getting through life relatively well, but the child—usually a teenager—constantly gets into trouble. Throwaways in this group have been in trouble with the law on numerous occasions, may abuse drugs themselves, and generally cause their parents untold misery. Finally, the parents have had it to the limit and refuse to allow the child back into the house.

In a small, rural community in Colorado, a sixteen-year-old boy told his Mexican migrant parents that he was gay. As devout Catholics, the parents were horrified, thinking the boy was possessed by the devil. They couldn't tolerate the thought of having a gay son, so they told him to leave. He hitched a ride to Denver, and he has lived on the streets ever since, residing sometimes in shelters, sometimes in the park, and sometimes with men who pick him up. He earns money by turning tricks and panhandling, and he hangs around with other kids in similar situations.

Variations in Definitions of Missing Children

It is important to note that there remains much variation in how missing children cases are defined. This variation, in turn, has implications for how statistics are kept and how the missing children problem is perceived.

Although it is common to place all types of cases into a general missing children category, this is not done in all jurisdictions. In some jurisdictions, the term *missing* child means that the authorities do not know what happened to the child, similar to the category of *unknown missing* used in this book. In this more limited definition, therefore, law enforcement agencies do not count cases in which they believe they know what happened to the child. A law enforcement officer might say something like "Johnny So-and-So is not 'missing'; he ran away from home with two of his friends." Or "Sally So-and-So isn't 'missing'; her mother took her in violation of a custody order." Those jurisdictions that use the more limited definition of missing children report fewer cases.

When we start to think about the varying definitions of missing children, it raises the question of what it means to be missing. Consider two case scenarios. First, a father takes his son in a custody dispute. The father leaves a note as to where he and the child will be. Second, a sixteen-year-old girl runs away from home because she feels abused by her new stepfather. Each week she calls her mother and tells her she is fine, but that she does not want to come home. Are the children in these two cases missing? It depends on how one looks at it. If one's conception of missing children is of children who are not where they are supposed to be, then the two children are missing. But if one's conception of missing children is of children whose whereabouts are unknown, then the two children might not be considered missing. In reality, parents and the police know where many missing children are.

Consider also the problem of defining a runaway. For example, how long does a child have to be away from home to be considered a runaway? Some authorities believe that a child should be counted as a runaway no matter how short a time the child is gone, if it is clear that the child in fact has run away. Other authorities believe that a youth should not be counted as a runaway unless he or she is gone at least overnight.

For example, the King County (Seattle) Runaway Network defines a runaway as any "youth absent from [his or her] legal residence."[12] If the child's absence is of short duration (for example, a half hour or so away from home), it would include an enormous number of children, particularly teenagers, who come home after some specified time.

Similarly, Gray Davis, a prominent California politician and founder of the California Foundation for the Protection of Children, believes that any child seventeen years old or younger whose parents are unaware of his or her whereabouts should be considered missing. Missing children figures would really be inflated if that were the case, because many children—especially teenagers—roam around without their parents knowing where they are.

In short, the definition of missing children remains confused and in need of clarification. A recent report on missing children, discussed in detail in the next chapter, concludes, "because of definitional controversies, and confusion about the concept of missing children, public policy still needs to clarify the domain of this problem."[13]

As we shall see in the next chapter, these varying definitions of missing children have consequences for estimating the number of missing children in the country. There are many instances in which law enforcement authorities know what happened to a child, and perhaps even where the child is located. How law enforcement agencies record such cases therefore affects the numbers of cases reported to the media.

Conclusion

We have presented these case descriptions to make one general point: the types of cases that fall into the rubric of missing children are so broad and varied that generalizations about them are difficult to make. Even cases within the various categories of kidnap, parental abduction, and runaway show enormous variation. The common conception of missing children as youngsters who have been snatched by strangers lurking in the park or around school grounds is limited, if not inaccurate. As the following chapters show, the public's misconception of missing children cases has been due, in large part, to media sensationalism and political posturing.

2

Counting Cases

The Extent of the Problem

No one knows how many children are missing. Accurate information does not exist. This is due in part to inadequate record-keeping procedures and to the confusion surrounding the definition of missing children. Experts are currently limited to educated guesses of the numbers, based on fragmented law enforcement data from around the country, and on a handful of social scientific studies that use inconsistent methodologies. This chapter first explains the inadequacies in the traditional methods of counting criminal cases, and then reviews studies that have estimated the number of missing children—both in the United States and Canada. The chapter concludes by comparing the missing children problem with other social and crime problems, such as child abuse, homicide, and rape.

The Inadequacies of Official Statistics

The Traditional Methods of Counting Crimes

Determining how many crimes are committed each year nationwide is primarily the responsibility of law enforcement agencies. Yet counting crimes is a much more difficult undertaking than first meets the eye. States often define crimes differently or use inconsistent data collection methods; securing comparable crime data for the entire nation remains problematic.

It became abundantly clear by the end of the 1920s that the nation's crime statistics were woefully inadequate. Police officials nationwide did not know the annual number of murders, or any type of crime for that matter. A consensus emerged in the law enforcement community on the need to improve the nation's method of keeping crime data. The International Association of Chiefs of Police (IACP) appointed a committee in 1928 to develop a system of comprehensive and uniform crime reporting applicable to law enforcement agencies throughout the country. The committee evaluated various crimes on the basis of their seriousness, frequency of occurrence, pervasiveness in all geographic areas of the country, and likelihood of being reported to law enforcement. It eventually created a system—still in use today—called the Uniform Crime Reports (UCR).

The IACP committee realized that keeping track of each separate crime would be unwieldy, because there are literally thousands of different criminal offenses. The UCR therefore concentrates only on eight crimes, called Index offenses. These Index offenses include murder and nonnegligent manslaughter, forcible rape, robbery, aggravated assault, burglary, larceny (theft), motor vehicle theft, and arson.

The Federal Bureau of Investigation (FBI) began implementing the UCR system in 1930 and assumed responsibility for compiling and publishing all crime data annually. Currently over sixteen thousand law enforcement agencies in the United States report crimes to the FBI.[1]

Although the FBI has relatively complete information on the index offenses, the data are much less comprehensive and reliable for all other crimes. All nonindex offenses are placed into eighteen other general crime categories, called Part II offenses. Surprisingly, both kidnapping and parental abduction are coded into more general Part II crime categories, such as "all other offenses" and "offenses against family and children." Because other crimes are lumped into these categories, it is impossible to determine specifically how many stranger kidnappings or parental abductions there are.

Determining the annual number of runaways from the UCR presents a slightly different problem. The UCR Handbook instructs law enforcement agencies to count only those runaways apprehended by a law enforcement officer. Considering that only a small, but unknown, percentage of all runaways are apprehended by the police, the number of runaways reported in the UCR is much lower than the actual number of cases that occur each year (that is, those youths who run away but are not taken into custody).

Alternative Measures

It is important to note that the inadequacies of national statistics are not unique to the problem of missing children. Accurate data are also in short supply regarding child abuse, wife battering, incest, consumer fraud, and hundreds of other offenses—particularly those that take place in the privacy of the home.

None of this is news to those who work in the field of social research. Criminologists have been frustrated for years in their attempts to get a handle on the number of crimes committed each year. Social scientists have therefore developed a variety of alternative (or supplemental) measures to make better estimates of the extent of crime and other social problems in the United States. Several of these methodologies are briefly reviewed here, so that subsequent discussions of estimates of missing children will be more comprehensible.

First, the routine collection of supplemental data sometimes may be mandated by state legislatures. The most prominent example is the required reporting of child abuse by medical professionals to child protective services agencies. This type of data is explored in greater detail at the end of this chapter. Second, some large-scale studies have been mandated by Congress and have received special funding to ensure that the data collected are exhaustive. These large-scale studies often provide the most complete sets of data regarding various social problems. In recent years, Congress has made missing children the subject of such special research efforts.

Third, a method gaining wide currency is the victimization survey. In this type of research, a sample of people are asked if they have been the victim of different types of crime. The proportions of people claiming to have been victimized are then generalized to the entire population. The best example of this research method is the National Crime Survey. This survey, conducted by the federal Bureau of Justice Statistics (of the Department of

Justice), surveys up to 136,000 people across the country each year. Their responses to questions about crime and victimization are extrapolated to the rest of the country's population. Interestingly, kidnapping is specifically exempted from the National Crime Survey, which is the largest victimization survey in the country. Less ambitious versions of this methodology are used by individual researchers. They interview smaller, usually representative, samples of the general public about a social issue of interest—for example, family violence, drug abuse, sexual behavior, AIDS, and the like—in order to get estimates of behaviors or incidents that are not adequately documented in official records.[2]

Early Estimates of the Number of Missing Children

Estimates of the number of missing children vary widely for both the total number missing per year and the number within each of the various categories of missing children. Particularly at the end of the 1970s and beginning of the 1980s, there was a great deal of confusion and debate over the figures, where they came from, and how they should be interpreted. In large part this was due to the fact that initially researchers lumped all categories together for one single estimate, rather than examining each category separately.

In 1983, for example, the U.S. Department of Health and Human Services estimated the number of missing children at 1.5 million a year.[3] This was a general figure on missing children, which meant *all categories* of missing children. The relative proportions of types of cases—for instance stranger kidnappings or parental abductions—were not given. As we shall see in the next chapter, these aggregated figures were used by many private missing children's groups or missing children advocates as a means to inflate their claims about the extent of the abduction problem. The statistics were used as a tool to urge lawmakers and citizens to take political and social action.

Soon after researchers first began to estimate the number of missing children cases, it became evident that they needed to consider the statistics of each type of missing child category separately.

Kidnapping

Beginning in the mid-1980s, the first attempt at estimating stranger kidnappings yielded quite different figures; some of the statistics for this category of missing child cases appear to have been quite inflated.

In 1985, Jay Howell, then executive director of the National Center for Missing and Exploited Children, estimated that between four thousand and twenty thousand children were kidnapped by a stranger each year. Some estimates in the popular media were set as high as fifty thousand children a year kidnapped by strangers. Where these figures came from remains unclear.[4]

Many experts, including those in law enforcement, disputed these early claims. For example, in that same year, the executive director of the Washington-based American Youth Work Center set the figure closer to one hundred stranger abductions per year.[5] To many law enforcement personnel working in the field, these initial figures appeared exaggerated. In their everyday patrol and investigation assignments, officers seldom encountered a kidnapping case. Moreover, one FBI spokesperson in 1985 said the fifty thousand figure seemed quite inflated. He pointed out that the United States lost fifty thousand troups in the Vietnam War. Most everyone knew someone who died there. But, he asked, "How many of us know someone who has had a child abducted?"[6]

The FBI's own data tend to bear out the notion that there are relatively few child kidnappings by strangers—at least the serious type of case in which the FBI would assist a local law enforcement agency. For example, in 1981, the FBI investigated only thirty-five child kidnappings. The figures are comparable for other years as well—forty-nine cases investigated in 1982, sixty-seven in 1983, sixty-eight in 1984, fifty-three in 1985, and fifty-seven in 1986.[7] Why would the FBI investigate only fifty-three cases in 1985 if, as the executive director of the National Center for Missing and Exploited Children suggested, there were up to twenty thousand stranger kidnappings?

The federal government became increasingly interested in missing children by the mid-1980s. One of the first priorities was to secure more comprehensive and accurate data on the nature and extent of the various types of missing children. A number of small-scale studies were undertaken both to determine the number of kidnappings and to look at the characteristics of this crime in greater detail.[8] The National Center for Missing and Exploited Children, an agency created by Congress in 1984 to help recover and conduct research on missing children, undertook one of the early studies. (This agency, often called the National Center, will be discussed in detail in subsequent chapters.)[9]

The findings of the National Center's study, "An Evaluation of the Crime of Kidnapping As It Is Committed against Children by Non-family Members," were published in 1986. Center researchers examined records maintained by two police departments, Jacksonville, Florida, and Houston, Texas. Researchers also examined those cases that were reported to the National Center. In addition, they reviewed newspaper reports of non-family kidnappings from throughout the country. A total of 1,299 cases were included in the study, but only 211 of these were from actual police records in the two cities.[10] It is these cases that most likely provide a more representative portrait of kidnap cases, because the media cases were, almost by definition, of a more sensational nature.

The purpose of the National Center's study was not to provide a national estimate of the number of kidnap cases. That would have been difficult because only two police departments were involved in the study. Some social science purists would question how representative these departments are, because there are approximately sixteen thousand full-service law enforcement agencies in the United States. Rather, the study was to learn more about the characteristics of kidnap victims and the circumstances of the offense.

However, the figure of 211 kidnappings in only two cities is quite surprising. This is a large figure, considering the fact that the FBI investigated only fifty-three cases in the entire United States in 1985. How could the FBI investigate so few cases when law enforcement agencies listed so many? The apparent anomaly revolves around the definition of "kidnapping" and "missing children" and the relationship between the two.

It is often assumed that kidnapping is synonymous with missing children, or with being missing. In fact, the majority of children who are kidnapped in the legal sense of the term are not missing. In most states, kidnapping includes the act of luring or enticing away a child for the purpose of committing another crime, such as sexual abuse, no matter how short a distance the person is moved or how limited the time the victim is with the perpetrator. In most child kidnapping cases, the perpetrator has possession of the victim for a brief period, and the victim is released after some form of sexual abuse. Typically, the victim returns home and relates the incident to the parent, who in turn calls the police. The police consider the case a sexual assault and a kidnapping for legal and statistical purposes. However, the child is already home. No missing child report is filed and no missing child investigation is conducted, obviously, because the child is back with his or her parents. In the National Center's study, researchers found that "virtually all law-enfocement records (97.6 percent) reported children as kidnapped and missing under 24 hours."[11] Thus, a typical kidnap case is not synonymous with a missing child case, that is, a case in which the child's whereabouts are not known for some period of time.

This study reported several other findings of interest.

- More than half (54 percent) of the victims of kidnap were sexually assaulted.
- Law enforcement records showed that 62.4 percent of the children kidnapped were between the ages of eleven and seventeen.
- Younger children tended to be kidnapped less frequently. Infants constituted only four-tenths of 1 percent of the kidnap victims.
- According to the police records, the majority of kidnap victims (88 percent) were girls.
- A small percentage (2.8 percent) of the kidnap victims were killed in the incident.

Parental Abductions

Until recently, data on parental abductions have been almost nonexistent. That is, there were some early estimates in the 1970s, but they were crude guesses at best. Hard law enforcement data did not exist. In many states, law enforcement agencies did not concern themselves because parental abduction was not considered a crime. And no comprehensive or reliable studies, at least at the national level, had been undertaken. As a result, the estimates varied substantially.

For example, in a story in the October 18, 1976, issue of *Newsweek,* the number of parental abduction cases was estimated to be about twenty-five thousand per year throughout the country.[12] This figure contrasted with the statistic reported one year later, by Children's Rights, Inc., a nationwide clearinghouse for parental abduction cases, of about 200,000 parental abductions per year.[13]

In fact, in the 1970s and 1980s, nobody had any reliable or accurate data. What is amazing about these estimates is that "experts" made them in the absence of any sound or recognized data collection procedures of methods.

Runaways

When interest groups first began to draw attention to missing children cases in the mid-1970s, there were two sources of data regarding runaways: UCR crime data and special studies.

The UCR collects limited statistics on runaways. It is a curious record-keeping system. For runaways, the UCR does not collect data on *reported* cases of runaways, but only on those runaways *arrested.* The UCR figures indicate that about 125,000 runaways are taken into custody each year in the entire country. This figure grossly underestimates the number of runaways because the police do not take action with all the runaways they encounter. For reasons that are explained in detail in chapters 8 and 9, police in most states do not routinely arrest runaways.

Some city law enforcement agencies keep statistics on *reports* of runaways, but these figures are not given to the FBI or any other national statistics keeping system. Thus, only sporadic figures from various cities are available. For example, San Francisco has about 250 reported runaways each month (for a total of about three thousand per year). These are only the youths who ran away from their residences in San Francisco and were reported as runaways by their parents. The figures do not include all of those juveniles who run away from other cities and come to San Francisco to live on the streets. Some cities provide estimates of all runaways, no matter where they come from. Officials in Los Angeles, for example, estimate that roughly ten thousand runaways come to Hollywood during any given year.

Runaways became a political and social issue in the 1970s, for reasons that are discussed in detail in chapter 7. Lawmakers in Congress wanted to get better estimates of the number of runaways. At that time, runaways were viewed as a social problem rather than a crime problem. Congress therefore gave responsibility to the Department of Health and Human Services for producing estimates of the numbers of runaways within the United States. The *National Statistical Survey of Runaway Youth* was conducted in 1975 (published in 1976). Estimates of the numbers of runaways depended on the definition used. When counting youths who remained away from home at least on night, the researchers concluded that 733,000 youths ran away from home in 1975. When the shorter-term incidents were included, the total figure came to about 1 million runaways a year.[14]

The estimates of runaway cases from the social services sector have been relatively stable over the past ten to fifteen years—ranging from 1 million to 1.5 million per year. In February 1990, Dr. Wade Horn, the commissioner for the Administration of Children, Youths and Families, testified before a U.S. Senate Subcommittee that runaways remain a problem to the present time.

> We estimate that there are approximately one million youths who run away from home in the course of a year, and who stay away at least one night. This estimate is based on a survey conducted in 1976. No comparable national study has been conducted since that time.[15]

Recent and Comprehensive Estimates

As the topic of missing children has become a more prominent political and social issue in recent years, the demand for more accurate and comprehensive data has increased. Politicians and social science researchers have desired up-dated, detailed statistics on missing children cases. Several research projects—differing in scope and methodology—have been undertaken in recent years. The most comprehensive of these have been the National Incidence Studies.

The National Incidence Studies

Congress passed the Missing Children's Assistance Act in 1984, which authorized the U.S. Department of Justice, through its Office of Juvenile Justice and Delinquency Prevention, to fund a study to determine the annual number of missing children in all categories. Eventually, a contract to conduct the studies was awarded jointly to the University of New Hampshire Family Research Lab and the research institute of Westat, Inc., in Rockville, Maryland. Officially called the National Incidence Studies of Missing, Abducted, Runaway, and Thrownaway Children (NISMART), the research has been more commonly referred to as the National Institute Studies. This series of studies, costing approximately $1.6 million and released in 1990, provides the most complete and accurate estimate of the numbers of missing children to date; the findings are reviewed here in detail.

The National Incidence Studies used a variety of approaches to secure their estimates.

- A review of records in approximately one-hundred law enforcement agencies nationwide. This part of the study was designed to obtain the total number and types of stranger (and other nonfamily) kidnappings, including those incidents that do not result in homicide
- A study of five years of data from the FBI's Supplemental Homicide Reports to determine the number of children murdered each year after being kidnapped
- A telephone survey of thirty-thousand randomly selected households throughout the country. In-depth interviews with

parents were conducted to produce estimates of the total numbers of all types of missing children

- Follow-up interviews with runaways who had returned home to provide more detailed information about their experiences while they were away
- Analyses of statistics on thrownaways reported in the National Study of the Incidence of Child Abuse and Neglect to provide estimates and profiles of youths who are abandoned or kicked out of their homes by parents or guardians

The researchers divided missing children cases into five separate categories:

nonfamily abduction

family abduction

runaways

lost, injured, or otherwise missing

thrownaways[16]

The National Incidence Studies collected revealing data on the various types of missing children. From these data, researchers made estimates for 1988 only; however, it is reasonable to assume the 1988 figures are comparable for other recent years.

Anticipating that definitional problems regarding the various categories of missing children would make developing valid estimates problematic, the Incidence Studies researchers developed two definitions. They generated two sets of estimates—a low and a high estimate—for each of the five categories of cases.

The first, more general definition of cases used by the researchers was called *broad scope*. This definition applied to all incidents covered in the legal definition of each category of missing child case; it encompassed all "minor" incidents as well as the more serious cases. The second and more restrictive definition—policy focal—pertained to a more limited number of cases. These were defined as "episodes of a more serious nature, where children are at risk and there is need for immediate intervention."[17] The policy focal cases were thus a subset of the broad scope cases.

Nonfamily Abductions. The broad scope definition of nonfamily abduction consisted of all legal elements of kidnapping, including luring a child for the purpose of committing another crime. The researchers stated, "Many short-term abductions that took place in the course of other crimes like sexual assault were counted under this definition."[18] This could include, for example, the case of a person enticing a child ten feet behind a bush for the purpose of a sexual assault. As noted earlier, however, child victims in such cases may not actually be considered missing.

Using the broad scope definition, the researchers estimated that there were between 3,200 and 4,600 child kidnap cases in the United States in 1988. The researchers also pointed out that these estimates might be low, because they were based on official records, and not all crimes are reported to the police.

Researchers classified cases as policy focal kidnappings—also referred to as *stereotypical kidnappings*—if they met at least one of five criteria: the child was gone over night, was killed, was transported a distance of fifty miles or more, was ransomed, or the perpetrator intended to keep the child permanently. Based on the data collected, the researchers estimated that there were between two-hundred and three-hundred of these more serious cases in the United States in 1988. This is obviously a much smaller figure than the early estimates of thousands of cases, and more closely approximates the number of cases investigated by the FBI.

It is also interesting to note that the National Incidence Studies use the term *non*family kidnapping instead of *stranger* kidnapping. This is most likely because many kidnappings, like other crimes, are committed by people who know the victim in some capacity. Frequently the offender is the disgruntled boyfriend of the child's mother. Sometimes the perpetrator is a babysitter and some times a friend or neighbor. Total stranger kidnappings are rare.

Children Murdered by Strangers. Part of the Incidence Studies consisted of an analysis of homicide data found in the FBI's Comparative Homicide computer file. As part of the UCR system, this file contains specific information from the Supplemental Homicide Reports submitted to the FBI by police departments across the country. Unfortunately, specific information about kidnapping was often not available in the computer records, and the researchers had to make inferences from the data.

The researchers found a total of 260 homicides occurred between 1980 and 1984 (an average of fifty-two per year), in which a stranger killed a child and the circumstances of the homicide involved some sexual or other felony offense. Research staff assumed that kidnapping was an element of these types of killings (with sexual overtones). However, it is possible this assumption was incorrect; some unknown number of these cases in fact may have entailed sexual assault and homicide *without* kidnapping.

During that same five-year period, the researchers also discovered an additional 530 cases (an average of 106 per year) occurred in which a stranger killed a child and the circumstances of the homicide were unknown. It was impossible to determine how many of these cases involved kidnapping.

Putting these two findings together, the researchers concluded that the number of children kidnapped and murdered by strangers ranges from 52 per year (the conservative estimate) to 158 per year (52 plus 106), which represents the more liberal or outside estimate. If we split the difference between those conservative and outside estimates, we arrive at a figure of 105 such cases of stranger kidnapping/murder per year for purposes of this discussion.

A few additional findings are worth noting. Older children (ages fourteen to seventeen) were found to be more at risk of the crime of kidnapping combined with homicide than were younger children (ages zero to nine). Specifically, while the chances of the older group being kidnapped and murdered are approximately seven per million children, the chances for the younger category are less than one in a million. Moreover, girls are at higher risk than boys and racial minorities are at greater risk than whites of being kidnapped and murdered.

Family Abductions. Cases under the broad scope definition of family abduction included situations in which a family member took a child in violation of a custody agreement or decree, or a relative failed to return a child at the end of an agreed-on visit, with the child being away at least overnight. Using this definition, the researchers estimated that there were 354,100 such cases in the U.S. in 1988.

Cases classified as policy focal family abductions were more serious and involved at least one of three additional aggravating circumstances: (1) an attempt was made to conceal the taking or the whereabouts of the child, or to prevent the other parent's contact with the child; (2) the child was transported out of state; or (3) there was evidence that the abductor had the intent to keep the child indefinitely or to permanently alter custodial privileges. Under this definition, researchers estimated that there were 163,200 such cases nationwide in 1988.

Several other interesting findings emerged regarding the characteristics of family abduction cases.

- Family abductions are most likely to occur in January and August, because these are the months when school vacations end and visitations are exchanged.
- Most episodes last two days to a week; 10 percent of the cases last a month or more.
- Based on the analyses of victimization data, the Incidence Studies researchers found that in four of ten cases, the caretaking (custodial) parent contacted the police. (In other words, the police were *not* contacted in 60 percent of the cases.) In five out of ten cases, the caretaking parent contacted a lawyer.
- Although sexual abuse is a feared aspect of family abduction, it is rare, occurring in less than 1 percent of the cases.
- In at least half of the episodes, the caretaking parent knew where the child was most of the time; the problem was getting the child returned.

Runaways. Cases classified as broad scope runaways were children who left home without permission and stayed away at least overnight. Researchers also counted children as broad scope runaways if they met a combination of age and time away criteria—for example, if they were already away from home at the time of the study; if they were at least fifteen years old and had been away for two nights; if they were fourteen years or younger and had been away for one night. The number of such cases was estimated at 450,700 throughout the United States in 1988. As a subset of broad scope runaways, researchers defined policy focal runaways as children who were without a secure and familiar place to stay during the episode. There were an estimated 133,500 such cases in 1988.[19]

Both of these figures are substantially less than the million or so cases estimated by other surveys. However, the researchers in the Incidence Studies claimed that the discrepancies were related to methodology and definition. They asserted that if their methods and case classification scheme had been used in earlier efforts, such as the one conducted by the Department of Health and Human Services in 1975, other inquiries would have yielded essentially the same figures.

Lost, Injured, or Otherwise Missing. This category consists of a variety of different types of cases—generally those that did not fit into the other categories. Under this classification, broad scope cases consisted of children missing for varying periods of time, depending on the child's age, disability, and whether the absence was due to an injury. For example, to fall into this category, a child between the ages of eleven and thirteen years would have to be absent from home for at least eight hours, but a child between seven and ten would only have to be gone four hours. Researchers estimated there were 438,200 such broad scope cases in 1988. Policy focal cases were broad scope episodes that were serious enough for the police to be called. There were an estimated 139,100 policy focal cases in 1988.

Most of the cases in this general category were young children (under four years of age) who were lost, and older juveniles (sixteen and seventeen year olds) who were independent and did not keep in touch with their parents or guardians. The largest subgroup consisted of children who lost track of time or misunderstood when they were supposed to be home. Injured children made up only 6 percent of the total group.

Thrownaways. The Incidence Studies also included a final category of cases that the researchers termed *thrownaways*. Broad scope thrownaways were defined as children in one of the following situations: they were told to leave home by their parents; they were abandoned; or they were not allowed to return home once gone. Research staff estimated that there were 127,100 such children nationwide in 1988. Policy focal thrownaways were cases of children who were without a secure and familiar place to stay during some portion of the episode. There were an estimated 59,200 of these cases in 1988.

The Incidence Studies suggest that thrownaways were formally lumped together with runaways in previous estimates. But the current studies separated the two types of cases; researchers claim that thrownaways constituted 22 percent of the pooled group of thrownaways and runaways.

There has been some debate as to how this group relates to the designation of missing children. The issue is whether thrownaways should be considered missing. If a parent kicks a child out of the house, it is likely that the parent will *not* report the child as missing. For statistical purposes, at any rate, the child is not a missing child. The child may be on the streets alone, but because no one is looking for him or her, the youth is not missing.

National Law Enforcement Study

A recently completed study of law enforcement agencies provides additional data about missing children cases, particularly kidnappings. This multi-year project was conducted in several phases, focusing on missing children incidents that took place in 1986.[20]

In the first phase of the study, researchers conducted a mail survey with 791 randomly selected law enforcement agencies throughout the country. These agencies were representative of law enforcement agencies in the United States—from the smallest to the largest. Of these 791 agencies, 95 percent reported *no* stranger kidnappings for the entire year of 1986. Only a small number of the larger police departments reported investigating even one kidnapping case that year. The median number (similar to the average) of kidnappings for all departments was zero.

During the third phase of this study, researchers examined actual police records over a three-month period in six law enforcement agencies around the nation. The police files in those six agencies contained eleven nonfamily kidnappings. Of those, almost half were perpetrated by the boyfriend of the mother.

The eleven victims were, generally speaking, not away from home long.

- Eight of the children were gone two hours or less.
- One child was gone for fourteen hours.
- One child was gone three days.
- One child was gone three months.

The findings included other facts of interest.

- One case involved a seventeen-year-old female kidnapped by a twenty-one-year-old acquaintance. The victim was kept in a motel room for three days before being returned by the offender.
- Three cases involved girls (ages eight, eight, and fifteen) who were taken from the street and sexually molested. All three were gone for a short period, and the incident was reported to the police *after* the children had returned home.
- In the case of the victim who was gone for three months, the offender was known by the parent.

Summary

To summarize the findings of these recent studies, only a small percentage of all missing children cases are abduction cases. And of this number, only a small percentage are stranger kidnapping cases. Stranger kidnappings constitute less than 1 percent of all missing children. Of those children kidnapped, most are older juveniles—teenagers. Most kidnapped kids are not missing in the technical sense of the term, because they are already back home. And of the small number of kidnapped and missing cases, 2.8 percent end in a homicide.

Canadian Statistics

The Canadian government has also recently attempted to determine the number of missing children in its jurisdiction. In large part, the concern expressed about missing children by the Canadian government arose out of the same social pressures operating in the United States.

The Ministry of the Solicitor General of Canada started the Missing Children Research Project (M.C.R.P.) in December 1985 as one of four components of an initiative focusing on missing children. The thrust of the M.C.R.P. was to collect statistics on the number and types of missing children cases in Canada. Canadian crime statistics suffer from the same general problems of spotty and inadequate reporting procedures that affect crime statistics in the United States. The M.C.R.P. was intended to create a more comprehensive description of the various types of missing children in Canada.

Because of the high cost of collecting data from every law enforcement agency in Canada, the researchers limited the scope of their inquiry to a sample of four cities. Three of the cities were large—Toronto, Montreal, and Edmonton. Surrey, a small city, was the fourth site. These four cities constitute approximately 29 percent of the Canadian population. M.C.R.P. research staff collected information on 12,446 cases over the twelve-month period—between December 1, 1986 and November 30, 1987. They extracted data from law enforcement files on all types of missing children cases, their characteristics, and their disposition (that is, whether the child was recovered).

The cases were classified in a manner similar to the case classification system used by American researchers—kidnapping, parental abduction, runaway, and other. Of the 12,446 cases, nine were deemed to be stranger abductions. Thus, less than 1 percent (specifically seven-one-hundredths of 1 percent) were stranger abductions. As mentioned, the study collected specific information on these cases. Of the nine cases, three involved males (one aged twelve and two aged fifteen), and six involved females, ranging in age from nine to sixteen years. Of the six females, a thirteen-year-old girl was reported as a runaway on two previous and three subsequent occasions. A 15-year-old male was subsequently reported as a runaway. All but one of the nine were found either on the same day or the next day. The outstanding case involved a twelve-year-old boy who left the house with his father and did not return. The father was found dead, and the child is presumed kidnapped by his father's assailant.

Canadian researchers counted 314 nonstranger abductions, primarily parental abductions; these cases constituted about 3 percent of the total of 12,446 cases. The nonstranger abduction category was specifically broken down into parental abduction when a custody order had been secured (63 cases), parental abduction when no custody order had been secured (234 cases), abduction by other relatives (7 cases), and abduction by a person known to the victim, other than a relative (10 cases). Thus, out of all *abduction* cases (323), less than 3 percent were by a stranger.

The vast majority of missing children cases analyzed in the M.C.R.P. study—86 percent—were runaways. Of the 10,696 runaway cases, the majority (5,832) of children ran away from their own home. The second largest category (4,024) constituted those youths who ran away from some form of institution. And finally, 840 of the youths in this category ran away from a foster home.

In the final category of cases, the classification *other,* served as a catch-all for hard-to-classify cases. There were 1,427 cases in this category, and these cases were broken down into four subcategories. First, 381 children were considered lost. Second, 178 children were found who had never been reported missing. Third, 23 children were classified as unknown missing, which means that there was not enough information to place the case into one of the categories. And finally, 845 cases were placed into a subcategory called *miscellaneous,* which included children who were overdue, throwaway children, invalid complaints, and affaires-of-the heart.

In sum, the Canadian data paint a statistical picture of missing children that is very similar to that in the United States. The vast majority of missing children are runaways. Of those children abducted, the vast majority are taken by a parent or relative. Only a small fraction (less than 1 percent) of the total number of missing children are abducted by a stranger.

Comparisons

The foregoing figures suggest that there are large numbers of missing children, at least for some subcategories of cases. While we now have more accurate statistics on various categories of missing children, to assess the significance of these numbers, we must consider how they compare with the magnitude of other social or criminal behavior. In this section, we first compare missing children cases, and particularly kidnapping, with other major crime categories. We then make a comparison between kidnapping and domestic child abuse, that is, abuse of children by their parents or guardians.

Comparisons with Other Major Crime Categories

If even one child is kidnapped in the United States, that is one too many. And if 105 or so children are kidnapped and murdered each year, that is 105 too many. If the 105 kidnapping/homicide figure is correct, this means that approximately one such case occurs every third day somewhere in the United States.

On the surface, this seems shocking. Yet, compared with other major crime categories (that is, crimes against the person recorded in the Uniform Crime Reports), the number of children kidnapped and harmed by strangers is small. Consider the most serious crime category—criminal homicide. Although the figures fluctuate slightly from year to year, generally about twenty thousand criminal homicides are committed annually in the United States. (Criminal homicide is defined by the UCR as first and second degree murder and nonnegligent manslaughter.) According to the FBI's "Crime Clock," one homicide takes place about every twenty-five minutes somewhere in the United States. Only about seven-tenths of 1 percent of the homicides in the country are perpetrated by strangers against children.

While the number of reported homicides appears large, it is actually an infrequently occurring crime when compared with other crimes against the person. According to the Uniform Crime Reports, roughly ninety thousand rapes are *reported* each year in this country. That equals one rape every six minutes somewhere in the United States. Moreover, many rapes are never reported. Estimates vary as to the number of unreported rapes, but the true figure is probably several times the number reported. Some researchers have placed the number of rapes between two hundred thousand and four hundred thousand per year.

Another Index offense is robbery, which is defined by the UCR as the taking or attempting to take anything of value from the care, custody, or control of a person or persons by force, threat of force or violence and/or by putting the victim in fear. Thus, robbery (as opposed to burglary) can be considered a crime against the person, because the taking of property must be from the person directly by force or fear of force. Approximately five hundred thousand robberies are reported annually in the United States—or one robbery every minute of every day. Again, many robberies are never reported to the police, so the actual number is likely to be much higher.

The final crime against the person reported as an Index offense in the UCR is aggravated assault, which is defined as the unlawful attack by one person on another for the purpose of inflicting severe or aggravated bodily injury. This is the most common crime against the person, with roughly nine hundred thousand reported annually in the United States. Thus, there is one aggravated assault every thirty-five seconds in the country.

In short, although the intentional harm of even one child is a serious matter, the "problem" of stranger kidnapping is small compared with other crime categories in which a victim is physically harmed—or even killed.

Comparisons with Domestic Child Abuse and Neglect

Perhaps it would be more appropriate to compare abductions—both by a stranger and a parent—with other forms of abuse that take place within the family setting.

It may be helpful first to describe the extent of child abuse and its specific manifestations. Many of the problems existing with data on missing children have historically been true of child abuse cases as well. Early attempts to determine the extent of child abuse were hampered by the same record-keeping problems that have plagued missing children statistics. Attempts to use UCR data proved fruitless, because child abuse is not a specific Index offense on which careful records are kept. Rather, it is lumped into a greater category called "offenses against family and children," which includes several other crimes, for example, spousal abuse. It therefore has been impossible to separate child abuse incidents from the other crimes.

Recognizing this, some social scientists and medical personnel attempted to make independent assessments of the extent of child abuse. In 1962, for example, the American Humane Association undertook one of the first studies to determine the number of child abuse incidents in the United States. Because of the lack of official data, the American Humane Association primarily used newspaper articles to make its assessment. The study documented on 662 cases of child abuse in the entire country in 1962.[21]

Relatively speaking, this is a small number of incidents. It would have been easy to downplay the problem of child abuse and let it rest. But other events were taking place at the same time. Most important, in 1962 Dr. C. Henry Kempe and his colleagues published an article in the *Journal of American Medical Association* describing serious incidents of child abuse that took a discernible pattern. They called this phenomenon the "battered child syndrome," and showed first that abuse was much more prevalent than had been believed, and second, that it often goes unnoticed and unreported.[22]

It became clear that a major problem—for the abused child as well as for government agencies responsible for collecting accurate statistics—was that doctors and other people who work closely with children did not report child abuse to the authorities. As a result, in 1962 the Children's Bureau of the U.S. Department of Health, Education, and Welfare held a conference on child abuse. The participants recommended that model child abuse legislation be drafted that would require certain types of professionals (for example, doctors, nurses, teachers) to report known cases of child abuse and neglect to social service agencies or to the police.

State legislatures around the country began to act. Only five years later, in 1967, every state in the country and the District of Columbia had enacted child abuse reporting laws. California's statute is typical:

> . . . [A]ny child care custodian, medical practitioner, non-medical practitioner, or employee of a child protective agency who has knowledge of or observes a child in his or her professional capacity or within the scope of his or her employment whom he or she knows or reasonably suspects has been the victim of child abuse shall report the known or suspected instance of child abuse to a child protective agency immediately or as soon as practically possible by telephone and shall prepare and send a written report thereof within thirty-six hours of receiving information concerning the incident.[23]

More recently, some states have modified their laws to require photo development companies to report suspected cases of child pornography.

Since 1962 and that first study by the American Humane Association, the number of reported child abuse cases has skyrocketed. Debate continues among the experts as to whether the ballooning figures represent an increase in the actual extent of child abuse, or simply an increased awareness and reporting of what has gone on for generations.

In any event, child abuse statistics are staggering as well as shocking. By 1976, over half a million cases were reported. In 1982, the American Humane Association estimated nearly one million cases of abuse or neglect. By 1985, nearly two million cases were reported. By 1987, the figure rose to two and one-quarter million cases. A special report released in June 1990 disclosed that there were two and one-half million cases the previous year. Responding to the study, Louis Sullivan, Secretary of the U.S. Department of Health and Human Services, called the incidence of child abuse in the country a "national tragedy."[24]

It is important to emphasize, moreover, that these figures are based on those cases *reported* to the authorities. How many more cases are never reported? Researchers have attempted to determine this figure, mainly by asking a random sample of people about abuse in their families, and then projecting the results to the national population. For example, one national authority on abuse in the family, Richard Gelles, conducted a study involving 2,143 families and concluded that child abuse is more prevalent than originally thought. He found that about 80 percent of the parents used physical punishment on their children. But the study also showed more extreme abuse. Twenty percent of the parents, for example, had hit a child with some object, and 4 percent stated that they had "beaten up" the child. Shockingly, about 3 percent of the parents indicated that they had used a knife or a gun on their children. Applying these rates to the general population of children aged three to seventeen, Gelles estimated that there were about 1,200,000 children whose parents had at some time in their lives *attacked them with a lethal weapon.*[25]

Just as with missing children, officials categorize child abuse cases into different types. Of particular relevance to our discussion are child sexual abuse and child abuse cases involving homicide.

Child Sexual Abuse. Measuring the extent of child sexual abuse is difficult for the same reasons we have discussed: the victim or the victim's family fails to report it. Nevertheless, studies have shown in general, that between 25 and 28 percent of American women—that is, roughly one out of four—are sexually molested or abused by the time they reach fourteen years of age.

Even the most insidious cases of sexual abuse, such as incest, are large in number. One estimate puts the number of incest cases at five thousand per year. Diana Russell, an authority on the subject, estimates that sixteen thousand daughters aged five to seventeen experience sexual activity with their father each year.[26] In Illinois, 8,397 children were allegedly sexually abused by a parent or a parent figure in 1986. Investigators found clear evidence of sexual abuse in 4,902 of these cases.[27]

Two important points about these figures are worth noting. First, the reported figures underrepresent the true figure of sexual abuse. Because of embarrassment, fear, and other reasons, most cases of sexual abuse, particularly those that occur within the family, are not reported to the authorities. Diana Russell's study on this issue concluded that only 2 percent of the cases of child sexual abuse occurring within the family are reported.

Thus, the actual number of cases is much higher, and even more shocking.[28]

Second, the thousands of incidents of child sexual abuse each year are not committed simply by strangers—dirty old men lurking around parks and school grounds. On the contrary, most incidents of child sexual abuse are committed by someone known to the victim. Approximately 70 to 80 percent of the abusers know their victims; moreover, 40 to 50 percent of the abusers are family members. Two prominent researchers, Lucy Berliner and Mary Kay Barbieri, found that strangers constitute only a small percentage of child sexual abusers. They conclude, "Parents and parent surrogates account for a substantial portion of offenders in reported cases."[29]

Child Abuse Homicide. Tragically, some incidents of child abuse are so severe that they result in the child's death, that is, homicide at the hands of a parent or caretaker. Although estimates vary also on the number of cases of fatal child abuse, figures do exist. The National Committee on Prevention of Child Abuse estimates that for 1987, about 1,100 cases of child abuse resulted in homicide. This figure was 25 percent higher than just two years previously.[30] In 1980, the National Committee on Prevention of Child Abuse reported that there were 1,225 cases of child abuse homicide. Moreover, about as many children were killed by their parents or caretakers in 1986 *in New York alone* (112), as were kidnapped and killed by strangers *in the entire country*.[31]

The most recent statistics are even more dramatic. Another National Commission, which submitted its final report to President Bush in June 1990, estimated the number of child abuse deaths may be as high as five thousand per year.[32] Thus, the number of child deaths at the hands of parents and guardians (using a conservative figure of 1,225) is about twelve times greater than the number of kidnapping/homicide cases (105) perpetrated by strangers.

A study of childhood mortality published in 1983 in the *American Journal of Diseases of Children* shed further light on fatal child abuse. The study revealed that homicide is one of the five leading causes of death in children in the United States. About 5.1 percent of all deaths of children are the result of homicide.[33] Since 1925, the rate of homicide for children one to four years of age has increased four-fold. And who is killing all of these children? Considering all children—from birth to age eighteen—strangers account for about 10 percent of the homicides. However, mothers are responsible for 13 percent and fathers for another 10 percent. Other family members and acquaintances account for another 44 percent. Thus, the majority of homicides against children are perpetrated by parents, other relatives, or acquaintances. The younger the child, the greater the proportion of homicides committed by natural parents, and the smaller the proportion committed by strangers.

Consequences. To this point, our discussion of child abuse has been intended to offer a comparative yardstick for assessing the magnitude of the problem of missing children. However, there may be an additional relationship between child abuse and missing children. Specifically, there may be a causal relationship between child abuse and running away from home. Studies have documented that children, especially teenagers, who have been abused or neglected by their parents turn to dysfunctional behaviors—delinquency, suicide, and running away from home—to cope with their predicament. Abuse and its connection to runaways is explored in detail in chapter 7.

Conclusion: The Bogey Man Lives at Home

As we noted in the first chapter, the popular conception of the missing child is of one who is forcibly kidnapped by a stranger and then physically abused or killed. The "problem" of missing children, according to this conception, is one of strangers perpetrating heinous crimes against innocent young children. The more realistic picture is such crimes do occur, but they are extremely rare. Fortunately, stranger kidnappings represent less than 1 percent of all missing children—both in the United States and in Canada. Of the cases of *abduction* that do take place, the majority involve the taking of a child by his or her natural parent. Only about 3 percent of all abductions are perpetrated by a stranger.

The vast majority of missing children are runaways, most of whom are teenagers who return home on their own within forty-eight hours. Teenage runaways are also the victims of abuse, but they are more likely to be abused by their parents at home than by strangers after they have run away from home.

Thus, it appears that focusing attention on strangers as constituting the greatest threat to children is misplaced. In actuality, the problem of child abuse, in all of its forms, dwarfs the problem of missing children. Although there may be a million or so runaway incidents each year, approximately two and one-half million incidents of child abuse and neglect occur in the United States annually. And while estimates suggest 105 children are kidnapped and killed by strangers each year, at least twelve times that amount are killed by their own parents or caretakers.

In the foreword to the Executive Summary of the Incidence Studies Report, Robert Sweet, Jr., administrator of the Office of Juvenile Justice and Delinquency Prevention of the U.S. Department of Justice, states, ". . . the incidence of missing children is composed of different social problems greatly stemming from the weakening of the American family."[34]

The problem of missing children should be viewed more accurately as a family problem rather than a crime problem. As Jay Howell, former executive director of the National Center for Missing and Exploited Children stated, "The most dangerous place for a child in this country is in his or her own home."[35]

3

The Birth of a Social Problem

CHILD abduction has always aroused great public concern, but only in recent times has it received such keen attention. The birth of the missing children problem is the subject of this chapter. The creation and development of this social problem, like others, resulted from a curious combination of social forces: media attention given to a few spectacular cases, political pressure from influential lobbyists, and a ground swell of sympathy and concern from individuals around the country for victims and families. This chapter is limited primarily to chronicling the efforts of various groups within the private sector—specifically the media and private organizations—to call attention to missing children and to have missing children treated as a serious national problem. The next chapter describes how governmental entities responded to the sense of alarm fostered by the private sector's claims about the nature and extent of the missing children problem.

Constructing the Problem

At the end of the 1970s and beginning of the 1980s, several sensational crimes involving children launched the nation's concern about missing children. Some of these cases involved the kidnapping of children, followed by homicide. In other cases, children were killed, but it was unclear whether they had been kidnapped. Many of these early cases also involved sexual abuse. Although these cases were different, they were somehow melded together and considered missing children cases. Many of the victims' families and communities saw these cases as the beginning of a new crime wave that appeared to be threatening the safety of children everywhere. Only some of the cases that generated fear over missing children are presented here.

In 1976, a tragedy of multiple slayings occurred near Detroit in Oakland County, Michigan. Over the course of a fourteen-month period, residents were terrorized by a childkiller who took the lives of four children. Two of the victims were boys (ages eleven and twelve), who had been sexually molested before being slain; neither of the two girl victims had been molested. In each incident the killer used a similar modus operandi (MO). Although all of the incidents involved kidnapping, no ransom note accompanied the abductions. In each case, the body of the child was found, laid out as if set to rest at a funeral, dressed in clean clothes and meticulously scrubbed. To date, the individual responsible for these homicides has not been caught.

During 1977 and 1978, residents of Sacramento, California, were shocked by the crime spree of the so-called vampire killer. During this two-year period, the vampire killer took the lives of numerous victims. The deaths were particularly grisly; the victims' bodies were cut up and parts were removed. Blood was found splattered throughout the rooms of the victims' homes. The killings were worse than those shown in such movies as *Nightmare on Elm Street* or *The Texas Chainsaw Massacre.* In one of his last crimes, the vampire killer broke into a home and tortured several family members, including children. When the police arrived, one of the children was missing. They eventually found the child, mutilated and dead. The killer, Richard Chase, was eventually caught and convicted.

One of the most highly publicized cases of the decade claimed the lives of victims from several states. The perpetrator, Ted Bundy, was suspected of killing as many as forty women between 1974 and 1978. Of the twenty-five victims that have been clearly linked to Bundy, five were less than eighteen years of age, the youngest being twelve years old. One set of victims were members of Chi Omega Sorority at Florida State University. In mid-January 1978, Bundy went into the sorority house and clubbed two coeds to death and injured several others. Bundy also kidnapped and killed a twelve-year-old girl from Lake City, Florida six days before he was arrested for the Chi Omega killings. Forensic experts suggested that the girl's throat had been slit and that Bundy used a knife on her genitals. He then left her body in an abandoned hog shed. Bundy was finally caught and arrested in Florida on February 15, 1978, for the murders of the college girls and the twelve year old; he was later convicted and sentenced to death.

In 1979, the residents of the Los Angeles area were shocked by the brutal killings of four teenage girls by two men, Lawrence Bittaker and Roy Norris. In each case the girl was sexually assaulted and tortured before being killed. Of the four victims, one sixteen-year-old girl had been forcibly abducted into the killers' van as she was walking home one evening. The other three victims got into the men's van voluntarily and were later killed.

That same year, the case of John Wayne Gacy horrified parents in Chicago and around the country. There had been several reports of missing juveniles in the area, and the police were finally led to Gacy's house in the Chicago suburb of Norwood Park. The police searched under Gacy's house and under the floor of his garage. They found rows of skeletons and decomposing bodies. Gacy told the police that he had sexually molested and strangled roughly thirty-two boys at his house. He could not remember the exact number, and several of the bodies (about five) had been dumped in the Des Plaines River instead of buried under the house. These crimes took place over a three-year period. Many of the victims were runaways. Many others had been lured to his house and subsequently reported as missing. But because the youths reported missing had all been older teenage boys, the police assumed they had run away from home.

Between 1979 and 1981, the Atlanta child murders captivated the nation's attention. During that time, at least twenty-eight bodies of dead children—all African-American—were found in the Atlanta area. Fear struck parents in the area; literally dozens of articles appeared in national magazines. Finally, the police caught a twenty-four-year-old African-American man named Wayne Williams, who was eventually convicted of asphyxiating two of the twenty-eight slain children. The mother of one of the murdered boys, Yusef Hawkins, later testified before Congress about missing children.

Another example is the case of Etan Patz. On May 25, 1979, this five-year-old New York boy walked to the bus stop one morning—and has not been seen since. His mother, Julie Patz, would later be named to a national task force on missing children.

The Adam Walsh case is the most well-known among the cases of younger missing children. On July 27, 1981, six-year-old Adam and his mother were in a shopping center in Hollywood, Florida. His mother left him alone for a few minutes; when she returned, Adam had disappeared. Law enforcement officials and citizens participated in a massive search, but he was not immediately located. Finally, after about two weeks, the remains of Adam's body were found in a ditch about one hundred miles from where he disappeared. His abductor has never been caught.

The case of Kevin Collins caused alarm for residents of San Francisco. On the afternoon of February 10, 1984, ten-year-old Kevin vanished after attending basketball practice. He was on his way home, and was last seen at a bus stop near his school. In the years since, there have been a few sightings of Kevin; some people thought they spotted him around the city. The police have followed up on these leads—but Kevin remains missing to this day.

While these cases involved actual situations and victims, the fears they generated of unknown abuses and potential, lurking malefactors have given rise to rumors connecting young children to a wide range of harms. For example, in the late 1970s and the 1980s, Satanism, or devil worship, became linked with some criminal activities that injured children. Most of these crimes—ritualistic sacrifices and abuse—did not involve *missing* children; rather youngsters were claimed to have been victimized by individuals who otherwise had lawful authority over them—such as, preschool teachers—or who were relatives or neighbors known to the children. Although most of the prominent cases linked to Satanism did not include kidnapping, the association was made anyway. Rumors began to circulate that children were being kidnapped for Satanic sacrifices. Other rumors told of children who were kidnapped and sold into prostitution by the Mafia or were sold into white slavery in Middle Eastern countries, or who were kidnapped and sold to childless couples by Mexican immigrants in this country. These rumors have linked perpetrators of harm to children with individuals or groups who are generally viewed as criminal types or socially undesirable.

Interestingly, rumors of mass child kidnapping surfaced in other countries as well. For the past few years, many parents in Mexico have feared that their children are being kidnapped, smuggled to the United States, and butchered for their body parts by rich Americans who need organ transplants. The Mexican media may have spread these stories, but there are no documented cases of such atrocities.

Media Coverage

Many of the well-known cases involving missing or exploited children have been isolated or random events perpetrated by individuals in a particular locale. Other cases have duly caused regional or national panic because they involved perpetrators who traveled into several states and claimed their victims from different communities; some engaged in a crime spree that victimized an entire community. We know about the Adam Walsh case, the Ted Bundy slayings, and the vampire killer tragedies in large part because of the attention which the media—TV, radio, newspapers, and popular magazines—have given them. The media have played an important role in not only informing us of factual events associated with specific cases of missing children, but also in shaping our awareness of and reactions to them. Some social scientists who study social problems view the media's role in drawing attention to an event and framing it in a specific way as a key ingredient in elevating a human interest story to the status of a social problem.

Americans have long been fascinated with crime and mysteries, and the media have cultivated and catered to this fascination. With their graphic portrayals of crime, journalists, authors, filmmakers, and TV producers have helped to make crime sensationalism an integral part of American life and culture. Mystery novels sell like hot cakes. Entire sections of book stores include the true crime genre in which writers describe the more violent and bizarre crimes of our time. Books on the Charles Manson cult killings, Son of Sam (David Berkowitz), and Ted Bundy abound.

Crime fiction and mystery stories also do well at the box office; *The Godfather, The Untouchables,* and *Fatal Attraction* are but a few examples of popular movies on the subject. An entire film genre has developed around crime thrillers. In addition, nonfictionalized crime has recently become the subject of a new genre of television series. These shows, such as *America's Most Wanted*, dramatize actual crimes in which the offender is still at large, and invite home viewers to assist authorities in locating the perpetrator by reporting sightings or other information that would help close the case.

The crime reports shown on the television news or printed in the morning newspaper each day are more than simply reports of the news. These stories are given media prominence because news personnel believe they are what people want to know about. These stories have a natural psychological fascination. Psychologists say people need to have a way to integrate gory, lurid, crime stories (and other random catastrophic events or tragedies) into their ordinary life experiences—to make sense of their social reality. Whatever the reason, as a media subject, crime—and particularly violent crime linked with sex—"sells." Sex and violence increase TV ratings, as well as newspaper and magazine circulation.

True crime stories have long enjoyed popularity. The Leopold and Loeb case in 1924, for example, captivated the American public for decades. Nathan F. Leopold, Jr., and Richard A. Loeb had been neighbors and childhood friends; they were also both child prodigies. At the time they committed their infamous crime, Loeb had graduated from the University of Michigan at a relatively young age, and Leopold was a graduate student at the University of Chicago. Motivated by the desire to prove their "intellectual superiority," the two young men formulated a plan to commit the perfect unsolvable crime.

As planned, they kidnapped and killed a fourteen-year-old boy named Robert Franks who lived in their Chicago neighborhood. Their "perfect" plan went awry when one of the killers accidentally dropped his glasses at the scene of the crime. Leopold and Loeb were eventually caught and tried for the boy's murder. At the time, the penalty for murder was execution. The famous attorney Clarence Darrow defended the pair. At the trial it became clear that the two young men had committed the crime but Darrow convinced the court to spare their lives. Instead, they received life imprisonment. This case was later dramatized in the 1959 feature film *Compulsion,* starring Orson Wells as Clarence Darrow.

The Lindbergh kidnapping is another example of a true crime story that captured the media and public attention for weeks. News reports referred to the case as the crime of the century. Over the years, the case has given rise to numerous books; recent recounts question whether Bruno Hauptman, convicted in 1935, was really the guilty party or whether he was wrongfully convicted on circumstantial evidence because of the prejudicial and passionate feelings of the public and the jury.

The Media and Missing Children

Runaways were the first category of missing children to receive attention from the media, but coverage was limited. A few books and documentary films provided accounts of the hopelessness and despair that children who run away to large cities experience. For example, Robin Lloyd, an investigative reporter, chronicled the lives of boy prostitutes in his book *For Money or Love,* published in 1976. This compelling, but distressing book documented the experiences of young "chickens" (boy prostitutes) and the "chickenhawks" (the adult men) who prey on them. Lloyd's descriptions of this exploitation were then—and remain—an eye-opener for the American public. Unfortunately, the attention Lloyd gave to the problem of runaways did not stimulate coverage by other writers or news reporters; but the subject of runaways did attract some cinematic interest.

Released in 1985, the movie *Streetwise* documented the life of runaways and street youths in Seattle, Washington. The film portrayed the lives of lonely, mixed-up teens who, without skills, jobs, or money panhandled for spare change, "dumpster dived" for old food, and "turned dates" (engaged in prostitution) for money to survive. The documentary showed city life for runaways as a fearful and brutal struggle for a survival that stripped these youngsters of childlike naiveté or trust. In depicting the daily difficulties and exploitative situations runaway youths encountered in the city, the film implicitly invited social inquiry into the broader circumstances of these youths—specifically, the chaos of the home life from which they had run away such that they would prefer street life to home, and the paucity of services to help these youths make a healthy transition to independent living and self-sufficiency.

Interestingly, although the experiences of runaway children and the circumstances that led to their flight clearly constituted tragic human interest stories that affected large numbers of youngsters nationwide, TV newscasters, newspapers, or popular magazines did not feature articles about them. Rather, most media forums overlooked the plight of runaway youths; they did not present the topic as a newsworthy issue or develop it as a problem that warranted widespread social concern or recognition. Those who were interested in reading or writing about runaways were limited to professionals in the social services, and academics and researchers in the social sciences, who saw the problems of runaways as involving complex economic, sociological, medical, and psychological issues.

In the early 1980s, broad-scale media attention began to be focused on the tragedies of a different group of missing children—those who were victims of abductions. Stories of missing children began appearing in popular magazines, such as *Ladies' Home Journal, Reader's Digest,* and *Redbook,* which appealed to a much larger audience than documentary films or nonfiction books. Most of the early magazine articles were about parental abductions, not kidnapping by strangers. Eventually, magazines carried stories of all types of missing children, including runaways. Using standard journalistic techniques, authors of these magazine articles made their stories good reads by using catchy headlines, or by presenting a horrifying scenario in the first paragraph of their article in order to hook the reader.

Articles about children missing as the result of parental or stranger kidnapping had been infrequent up through the beginning of the 1980s. Because these articles on missing children were rare, they were listed under abduction or kidnapping in the *Reader's Guide to Periodical Literature.* It wasn't until 1983/1984 that such articles were given their own subject matter heading: missing children.

The popular magazine's approach to the subject of missing children—especially of abducted children—was very different from the earlier coverage of runaway children. While Lloyd's book delved into the complex social problems raised by youth prostitution, the articles in the popular magazines depicted abduction cases in sensational and simplistic terms. The broader social and legal issues surrounding these cases received cursory treatment; authors failed to research or otherwise substantiate sweeping claims made by spokespersons for victims and their families regarding the nature or the extent of cases involving parental abduction or stranger kidnapping. The articles largely addressed the subject through anecdotes or cited statistics that suggested kidnappings were frequent occurrences, and involved large numbers of youngsters.

One example of this coverage is found in the July 1982 issue of *Reader's Digest.* An article entitled "Missing: 100,000 Children a Year," contained the subheading ". . . thousands are murdered annually. . . ."[1] (As more recent data suggest, the figure is really closer to one hundred a year.) Another example is found in the October 24, 1983, issue of *U.S. News and World Report.* Entitled "The Tragedy of America's Missing Children," the article, as most such articles, began with a heart-wrenching story about a twelve-year-old girl, a piano virtuoso and Russian emigré, who had disappeared without a trace from a shopping center near her home in Louisville, Kentucky. The article sited several similar cases and then claimed ". . . 20,000 to 50,000 children are snatched by strangers—most never to be seen again."[2] In December 1985, *Parents Magazine* ran an article entitled "Kids and Kidnapping." The article contained language sure to ignite the fears of parents across the country: "There's a fever sweeping our country—fear of kidnapping."[3] The article claimed that no one knows how many children are kidnapped by strangers each year, "but estimates range from 4,000 to 20,000."[4]

Many of these articles appeared to be informative. Yet, in light of the more recent and accurate estimates, the figures presented in most were grossly exaggerated; the reports and stories were more alarming than they were informative. Indeed, because no accurate data on various types of abduction cases existed in the early 1980s, it is unclear from where writers derived some of their figures. The hyperbole of their claims was certain to make readers anxious over the safety of children and thus receptive to measures that increased the safety of their family. Some articles offered parents strategies for safeguarding their youngsters. Such strategies implied that the problem of disappearing or abducted children was one that was widely prevalent and could disrupt *any* family or community, but it was also a problem that could be prevented and solved. In fact, the impressions given were far from accurate. Other articles encouraged parents to get involved in local, state, or national efforts to recover missing children and to contact public officials about their concerns.

Interestingly, the popular magazine coverage of the subject of missing children did not merely present missing children as human interest stories, news, or a problem communities could take action about. The magazines became an integral part of some of the cases of missing children. In at least two instances, stories of missing children run in magazines led to the children's recovery, and these recovery stories appeared in subsequent issues of the same magazines.

A *Ladies' Home Journal* article about parental abduction provides the first example. The April 1981 issue ran an article entitled "Child Snatching: Cruelest Crime," which told the story of several children abducted by their parents. The hook was the story of six men forcibly abducting a boy—one of the men was the boy's father. Seven stories were told and seven pictures were presented of missing children, all abducted by a parent. One of the children had been abducted two and one-half years before the article was published. Despite the time lag, a person recognized the boy and called the police, and the boy was later reunited with his mother. The story of the recovery and reunion was recounted in another article published in the August 1981 issue of *Ladies' Home Journal.*

A similar example is found in the July 1982 issue of *Reader's Digest,* which contained an article about several missing children. Part of the article told the story of a sixteen-year-old girl who had run away from her family in Florida two years earlier. The girl had traveled to various places, but had settled down with a boyfriend and a new baby in a small town in Georgia. A fourteen-year-old girl in that town read the article and thought she recognized the girl in the article as a new employee who worked with her mother. The girl showed the article to her mother who agreed to look into the matter. Eventually, the runaway girl was reunited with her family, and the story of the reunion was developed into a separate article in the November 1982 issue of the *Reader's Digest.*

Clearly, the coverage popular magazines gave of missing children cases played an important role in bringing the tragedy of children who are abducted or simply disappear to the attention of the general public. Had the coverage of cases involving parental or stranger abductions been limited to the more objective journalistic reporting or documentary accounts of runaway children that appeared in the 1970s, the subject of missing children would have likely remained a topic of interest to a small circle of academics or social service practitioners. However, by casting the plight of missing children in dramatic, simplistic, and sympathetic terms, popular magazines helped to generate broad awareness of these cases. More important, they also helped to shape the public's perceptions of the nature and significance of these cases. Through popular magazines, Americans began to acquire a consciousness of missing children as a distinct and important social problem that appeared to affect thousands of children; it was also a problem that could be solved if more government resources were devoted to locating and recovering missing children and to prosecuting those who abducted or exploited them.

Following the lead of popular magazines, electronic media picked up the subject of missing children around 1982. Stories about missing children were aired on several national television news specials and talk shows, including *60 Minutes, Donahue, Geraldo, 20/20,* and *Sally Jessy Raphael.*

TV became a powerful medium through which the public's consciousness of missing children was heightened; by reaching millions of American households across the country, TV drew viewers into the problems faced by families trying to recover their children, and the sorrow and despair they felt by their lack of success. Talk shows, news reports, docudramas, and movie specials put the faces of missing children within view of all of America, and reminded audiences of the special vulnerability of children.

The best-known and most widely viewed television show on missing children was the docudrama called "Adam," based on the Adam Walsh case. The show first aired on TV October 10, 1983. The movie stars Daniel J. Travanti—well known for his leading role in the popular TV police serial, "Hill Street Blues"—and tells the tragic story of Adam Walsh, his abduction and murder. Part of the film depicts the efforts of Adam's parents, John and Reve Walsh, to organize searches, work with the police, and do everything humanly possible to find their son. John Walsh eventually emerged as a dynamic force, lobbying for legislative reform and changes in law enforcement policies and procedures.

As with magazine articles, TV news programs, talk shows, and movie specials actually aided the recovery of some missing children. For example, at the end of "Adam," the producers showed the photographs of fifty-five missing children, and asked the viewing public to call local authorities if they had any information on the whereabouts of these children. Fourteen children were located as a result of this television presentation.

There have been at least three airings of "Adam," the third appearing on April 29, 1985. (A sequel called "Adam: His Song Continues" was broadcast in 1986.) Again, the photos of about fifty children were displayed at the end of each show. One girl was Melissa Klein of Springfield, Ohio, who had been reported missing the previous June when her father did not bring her home after his designated visitation period. A short time after "Adam" played the third time, the police received an anonymous tip that the girl was living in Sacramento, California, with her father. The police quickly located them and returned the girl to her mother.

In addition, missing children was the subject of at least one popular film that played in movie theaters across the country in 1983. The movie, *Without a Trace,* was based on the novel *Still Missing* by Beth Gutcheon, which was a story similar to the real-life case of Etan Patz. In the film, a mother leaves her house early one morning with her six-year-old son and drops him off for his short, two-block walk to school in Brooklyn. The mother returns home from her university teaching job in the afternoon and waits for her son. But he doesn't come back.

The mother calls a neighbor, whose daughter is in the same class as her son, and learns that her son had not been in school all day. Fearing the worst, she immediately calls the police, but they initially have doubts that the boy was kidnapped. They ask if the boy has run away before, or if the father spanked the boy to make him unhappy at home. The mother informs the police that she is separated from her husband. The police then think the father abducted the child, since statistically speaking, this is a much more likely occurrence than a stranger abduction. After this assumption proved erroneous, the police came to believe the boy was kidnapped. They install a bank of phones in the mother's house and wait for a ransom demand—or some indication of a kidnapping. But none comes.

The police search, and they wait; they search, and they wait. After a few weeks, the police return to the station house to resume their regular assignments; they have other, more current, and pressing cases to investigate. The case is kept open and active, but the police investigators do not look as hard as they did at first. The mother is disgusted because she feels the police are giving up. Finally, after four months, the police receive a tip that the boy is in Connecticut. But unlike the case of Etan Patz who has not been seen since his disappearance in 1979, the film story has a happy ending—the police locate the boy, unharmed, and reunite him with his mother.

The showing of "Adam" marked the transformation of missing children from being the subject of human interest stories and isolated personal tragedies to being a national cause. With its several presentations, "Adam" gave enormous puplic exposure to the plight of kidnapped children. Approximately 85 million people have seen the movie on television, and reportedly thirty-eight parentally abducted children and one child kidnapped by a stranger have been recovered as a result of these shows.

The electronic media's interest in missing children was significant for two reasons: it captured the attention of audiences in a way other media forms could not; it also reached more people. Through television exposure, the actual or fictionalized accounts of missing children were brought into American homes across the country. TV coverage made the personal tragedies of otherwise unknown victims and their families real and familiar.

Although producers of TV programs select topics to entertain and, to a lesser extent, inform audiences, they also make their selection based on commercial requirements. Except for the few publicly owned TV broadcasting companies, all major TV companies compete for advertising dollars. High ratings are essential to attract companies who are willing to pay top dollar for product advertising. Under pressure to package subjects in a way that attracts and sustains the attention of millions of people, commercial television gravitates toward stories that sell—that is, those that have the potential for heavy emotionalism. It downplays the objective, complex, or critical treatment of subjects. Missing children was a topic that fit the criteria for high viewer appeal.

Perceptions of a Widespread and Growing Problem

Sociologists suggest that there are two basic requirements for a condition or situation to achieve the status of a social problem. First, in order for individuals or groups to get others to view their cause as a significant problem, they must convince the public that the condition or situation affects, or could affect, a significant number of people. Second, there must be a perception that the condition or situation is getting worse. In their claims about the nature and the extent of the problem of missing children, spokespersons and missing children organizations successfully met both of these requirements.

The horror stories depicted in the media did not create a social problem by themselves. Spokespersons for missing children had to show that these horror stories and tragedies were not just isolated incidents. It is here that some of the early estimates of missing children discussed in the last chapter take on special and practical significance.

Despite the absence of hard statistical data, lobbyists were not afraid to venture estimates of the number of children kidnapped each year. The figures they gave were shocking. The statements of parents and spokespersons for missing children were also shocking. For example, John Walsh, Adam Walsh's father, asserted, "This country is littered with mutilated, decapitated, raped, strangled children."[5] Michael Agopian, an expert on parental abductions, added, "We are all aware of the Adam Walsh case, but please recognize that there are tens of thousands of additional Adams that are not so prominently reported by the media."[6] Then Representative Paul Simon of Illinois stated, ". . . the most conservative estimate is that 50,000 young people disappear each year because of stranger kidnappings."[7]

Even the National Center for Missing and Exploited Children, in one of its early publications, estimated the number of stranger kidnappings as high as fifty thousand per year. This figure was later revised to be between four thousand and twenty thousand.[8] These high estimates would later come back to haunt the National Center.

As a strategy to get the attention of government officials and to generate widespread support for their cause, lobbyists and organizations painted the stranger kidnapping of children as a serious problem affecting large numbers of youngsters and families. Indeed, their claims made it seem as if there was an epidemic raging through the country. To create this impression, spokespersons and lobbyists lumped the numbers of different categories of missing children cases together.

In actuality, the numbers of stranger kidnappings were relatively small (and while comparatively speaking, parental abductions constituted a larger group of missing children, that number was also quite small when compared with runaways). However, by including the numbers of the most common type of missing child case—voluntary runaway—in their statistics on the most serious (and least common) type of case—abduction by a stranger—lobbyists successfully created the illusion that the kidnapping of children was a massive social problem. What appeared in the press were the total numbers from all categories—a million or more missing children. By grouping all cases into the generic category of missing children and suggesting most missing children were victims of kidnaps, spokespersons established missing children as a social problem with dimensions that could not be ignored.

Spokespersons of the missing children cause also needed to create the impression that the problem of missing children was getting worse over time. This impression was particularly crucial in order to motivate public or governmental officials to take action. If things were getting better, clearly there would be little or no need for governmental involvement. However, whether there are actually more cases now than in other historical periods is difficult to establish because of two problems. To the extent historical data do exist, they are insufficient to draw firm conclusions. As was shown in the last chapter, crime statistics on any type of missing children are woefully inadequate—and they always have been. Moreover, although recent studies have used research methods that have produced more accurate and inclusive counts, these studies do not provide comparable information for previous decades. Thus, it is impossible to determine whether crimes involving children are on the increase—and specifically whether there has been an increase in the number of missing children. It is feasible—even likely—that the perceived increase in numbers of cases is due to an increase in public awareness and publicity about the cases. This phenomenon of increased awareness has confused statistical inference about other crimes much in the public eye in the 1980s—for example, rape, child abuse, spousal abuse, and the like.

Yet, even without hard data, some reasonable conclusions can be drawn. It seems likely that the rate of parental abduction is higher in the 1980s than in earlier decades, since the divorce rate is higher and child custody disputes occur more frequently. It is also possible that the number of runaways is higher in the 1970s and 1980s than in earlier decades. As will be discussed in chapter 7, many states relaxed or curtailed legal restrictions of runaways in the mid-1970s. Those legal changes made it easier for runaways to remain on the streets with less fear of intervention by the police. However, the number of runaways has probably not increased since the 1975 national survey. Indeed, the rate of runaway cases may have gone down. As a statistic, the rate is a function of the number of young people in the population at any given time capable of this behavior (for example, ages ten to seventeen). To the extent the overall population of individuals under seventeen has declined in recent years as the baby boom generation has aged, there are fewer youngsters "at risk" of running away than there were ten or fifteen years ago.

Stranger kidnappings are another story. No reliable evidence exists to suggest that the number of stranger kidnappings is higher today than at any other point in history. Compared with other types of missing children—voluntary runaways and parental abductions—the perception that stranger kidnappings are on the rise is most likely the result of media attention, not an increase in the actual number of such cases.

In part, we base this inference on the history of an analogous problem in the 1920s and 1930s when the molestation of children was perceived as a growing problem. At that time, a seeming rash of child molestations aroused public fear and indignation and prompted lawmakers around the country to pass sexual psychopath laws to put convicted (or even suspected) child molesters in mental hospitals for an indeterminate period of time, possibly for life. These laws were enacted not because an actual increase in such cases had occurred, but because a few tragic cases sensationalized by the media created pressure on public officials to take some kind of action.

In the history of missing children, the occurrence of just one case of a child's disappearance was sufficient to galvanize public concern and governmental action. For example, the Lindbergh case of 1932 brought about major changes in legislation regarding kidnapping.

Naming the Problem

Joel Best, a sociologist who has studied the issue, claims that the term *missing children* was coined in 1981 and was first used in testimony before Congress.[9] One category of missing children—victims of parental abductions—was the subject of Congressional hearings at the end of the 1970s when interest groups pressured federal lawmakers to make the investigative resources of the FBI available to help prosecute parents who abducted their children. At these hearings, the term *missing child* was bandied about, but it initially referred only to child-snatching, or parental abduction. It was not used to apply to runaways or to children kidnapped by strangers.

But by the time the Senate Judiciary Committee conducted hearings on exploited children in 1981 and 1982, references to missing children included children abducted by strangers. Other interest groups and spokespersons specifically concerned with the recovery of children abducted by their parents found it in their best interest to relate victims of parental abduction with missing children who were victims of stranger kidnappings, because the latter category had become the spotlight of media and legislative attention.

By calling them missing children, spokespersons for children kidnapped by strangers helped their cause because they used terminology that already had special connotations. For example, the phrases *missing in action,* or *missing at sea* in time of war suggest an individual is in grave danger or that he or she may be dead, never to be seen again by family and friends. The term *missing* conjures up the tragedy of a person whose body may never be found and given a proper funeral; it also suggests ongoing suffering for family members who are unable to confirm and accept their loss, complete the grieving process, or put the tragedy in the past. While a loved one is missing, family members are unwilling to give up hope of recovery, or to give up searching.

Rallying behind a National Cause

By the mid-1980s, intensive media coverage made missing children a *cause célèbre* around which millions of people across the country rallied. Thanks to testimony presented at the Congressional hearings, missing children largely had become synonymous with children kidnapped by strangers. Through docudramas, TV talk shows, and magazine articles, missing children groups received the media's help in launching a national campaign to publicize the names, faces, and descriptive statistics of missing children. The goals of this campaign were to prevent the abduction of children and to secure the return of those youngsters who had been the victims of kidnapping. Initially, groups and individuals in the private sector began to develop networks, strategies, and products to further this campaign. These private sector activities eventually stimulated political and governmental entities to take action as well.

Private Industry Initiatives

One of the most visible strategies organized by private companies involved putting the photographs of missing children on a variety of products. A Chicago dairyman named Walter Woodbury was the first person to put the now familiar photographs of missing children on milk cartons. Woodbury had a fervent desire to help, and he declared, "I will hit the moon when one kid is returned."[10] One week later, his wish came true. Ironically, the recovered child had not been kidnapped by a stranger, or even a parent. Rather, the first beneficiary of the milk carton program was a runaway; a thirteen-year-old girl saw her picture on a milk carton and returned home after having run away two months before.

Woodbury began putting photographs of missing children on milk cartons at his Midwestern dairy in December 1984. By January 1985, about four hundred dairies around the country were participating in this program. Eventually, more than seven hundred dairies put pictures of missing children on their milk cartons.

The milk carton strategy prompted other industries to place photos of missing children on their products—paper plates, cereal boxes, grocery bags, egg cartons, film envelopes—and to place displays of these photos in a variety of locations—at over thirteen thousand supermarkets, as well as in airports, post offices, subway cars, municipal buses, moving vans, vending machines, on benches at bus stops, and in utility bills and junk mail coupons. Photos of missing children also appeared on numerous scoreboards at large sports stadiums, such as the DiamondVision screen at the Pittsburgh Pirates baseball games.

Many organizations became involved in the effort to publicize the identities of children reported to law enforcement as missing. The National Child Safety Council, the nation's oldest and largest nonprofit child safety council, was particularly influential in promoting this work. It is credited with leading a campaign that by 1985 put pictures of missing children on 2.5 billion milk cartons, 20 billion grocery bags, and 45 to 50 billion pieces of mail. According to then National Child Safety Council President, H.R. Wilkinson, these pictures helped find eleven children.

California has been one state where a network of private firms and companies has been responsible for displaying the pictures of children reported missing. By 1986, pictures of thirty children in all had been placed on 50 million grocery bags, 35 million milk cartons, 3 million fast food cups, 700,000 egg cartons, and in 30,000 vending machines. Only thirty children were selected for this exposure on the theory that it would be easier for the public to become familiar with their names and faces. As a result of this exposure, thirteen of these children have reportedly returned home or been reunited with parents.

Since 1982, more than a thousand private companies or corporations have donated their services to assist the missing children campaign. In addition to putting pictures on products, private industry has sponsored other measures to aid parents in safeguarding their children. For example, some companies, such as Texize, which manufactures household products, have funded missing children education and prevention programs. Other companies have incorporated services to prevent or recover missing children into their regular business operations. For example, one successful effort was the Operation Home Free program run by Trailways Bus Corporation. This program provided free rides to runaways who wanted to return home. As of 1985, more than four thousand runaways and their families had benefited from this service.

Safety First

Since the mid-1980s, local nonprofit agencies and public agencies have joined together to promote massive safety efforts to protect children, especially from stranger kidnapping. Scores of brochures have been published by PTAs, law enforcement, and nonprofit organizations, and distributed at schools, county fairs, malls, and the like. A number of local school districts and law enforcement agencies have instituted fingerprint programs sponsored by state funds. To date, thirty-five states operate fingerprint programs for elementary school children. In addition, many schools have also implemented child protection or self defense programs to help children protect themselves if confronted by a potential abduction.

A number of private companies and nonprofit organizations designed identification kits that parents could purchase to assist in the recovery of their child, in the event he or she disappeared. For example, Californians for Missing Children, a nonprofit organization based in San Francisco, sells an identification kit for a nominal fee ($3). The identification kit includes twelve pages, with places for fingerprints, hair, dental records, and the like.

While many of these measures may have helped parents feel better able to keep their children safe from harm, they do little to actually prevent kidnappings. These activities are much like locking the barn door after the horses are gone. The identification kits create search tools that are largely useful for identifying and recovering a child *after* he or she had disappeared.

Private industry appeared to be rallying behind an important social cause; yet the effect of this attention was to generate a certain degree of hysteria and hype. More families became fearful for their children's safety as they were made aware of the potential for their children to be abducted. They did not know that their perception of a kidnapping threat was much larger than its actual likelihood. Ironically, the public service activities of private industry did not make neighbors and parents feel safe or give them a sense of control over the problem. Rather, in many communities, these well-meaning efforts created an undue atmosphere of fear and anxiety.

High Technology

Concern for missing children created a new, growth industry of its own. Individuals and companies promoted products related to missing children. Some of these promotions were altruistic and some were designed to make money.

Enterprising individuals saw new applications for computer technology in the prevention and recovery of missing children. A dentist in Denver, for example, proposed implanting microdots into the teeth of children so that they could be identified—if they were found dead, if they were too young to give information, or perhaps if they were found years later and looked different.

Another computer application was developed to project changes in the physical appearance of young children over time. Two medical illustrators—Scott Barrows and Lewis Sadler—were responsible for developing a computer program that can show from a photograph how a child's face will change over the years.

Working in their University of Chicago laboratories, these two scientists developed a computer simulation system in 1989 that ages the faces of children in a matter of minutes. Barrows and Sadler found in their research that there are thirty-nine key facial dimensions needed in age simulation. The distance from the bridge of the nose to the base of the chin, for example, typically increases by 12 percent between the ages of six and thirteen.

The computer system has a laser scanner to create a copy of an original photograph. The computer then digitizes the image, and it is displayed on a monitor along with a list of the thirty-nine facial measurements. The program divides the face into a map of about one hundred pieces and applies the normal growth pattern for each part. The program can then generate new photographs of what a child would look like at any time period after his or her disappearance. One executive at the National Center for Missing and Exploited Children stated, "If there's been a single revolutionary leap in my 20 years of experience with [missing children], this is probably it."[11]

The videotaping industry has also benefited from the missing children campaign by being able to expand its applications and markets. Many private studios have offered videotaping services to parents who want a visual and audio record to help identify their children. Some companies charge a handsome fee; others offer these services free as part of a good will promotion. For example, Blockbuster Video, the nation's largest video rental chain, has a setup where parents can videotape their children at no charge.

The electronic industry has been working on devices that can alert parents about a potential abduction; one anti-kidnapping device has been developed that is similar to the electronic transmitter retail stores attach to clothing to prevent thefts of merchandise. If someone tries to shoplift an article of clothing, a signal sounds to alert the store personnel of the attempted theft when the person passes through a detector set up at the store's exits and entrances. The retail and mail-order company, The Sharper Image, advertised a product called *Guardian Angel,* which operates much like the clothing store device—it consists of a transmitter that can be attached to the child's clothing. The transmitter keeps track of the child and sounds an alarm if the child ventures out of a specified area.

High-tech companies have been working with hospital security personnel to develop an electronic device that may be attached to a newborn's ankle or wrist, and would operate on the same principle as the retail clothing transmitter. In the hospital setting, the detector is located at the main door of the nursery; a loud alarm sounds, alerting security personnal of an attempted abduction if an unauthorized person tries to carry an infant wearing the device out of the nursery.

Missing Children Organizations

The national campaign on missing children also promoted the emergence and growth of private, nonprofit organizations whose purpose was to help find missing children—or to prevent victimization in the first place. By 1985, an estimated one hundred such organizations nationwide had come into existence. These organizations provided a variety of services. Most functioned as coordinators of volunteer efforts by the media, community residents, and public officials to recover children reported missing. Many also served as fund-raisers to help defray the costs to families of publicizing the disappearance of their children and sustaining long-term searches for their children. Several of these organizations also provided despairing parents with a support system. Child Find, Vanished Children's Alliance, Adam Walsh Resource Center, Children of the Night, and the Kevin Collins Foundation are but a few of the more prominent nonprofit organizations that came into being to help the missing children cause.

Many of these organizations were started by parents whose children had been abducted, or were still missing. Many of these parents expended enormous personal resources—financial as well as emotional—to set up organizations to help others in similar situations.

One such parent was Gloria Yerkovich, whose daughter was abducted by her ex-spouse in 1974 when the daughter was six years old. The daughter has not yet been found. Ms. Yerkovich wanted to do something constructive regarding child snatching, so she created Child Find, a nonprofit organization dedicated to helping parents and children involved in child snatching cases. Similarly, Harold Miltsch of Rochester, New York, founded Stop Parental Kidnapping following the abduction of his stepdaughter. Stop Parental Kidnapping distributes newsletters and flyers with the pictures of abducted children on them. This organization sends information on missing children to schools, hospitals, and medical personnel, such as pediatricians and orthodontists.

Another organization, Children's Rights, Inc., was founded by

Arnold I. Miller. Miller searched for five years for his son, and finally a picture in a national magazine led to the boy's reunion with his family. Children's Rights, Inc., has over ninety chapters throughout the country. The organization publishes a quarterly newsletter, and provides a hot-line and other support services for parents of missing children, particularly those abducted.

An organization called Find the Children was established by the producer of the docudrama "Adam." Find the Children performs a variety of services: it distributes photos of missing children and acts as a liaison between families of missing children and investigators. Having roots in Hollywood, it also raises money for missing children activities with an annual celebrity auction.

Another parent's search for her missing child resulted in the founding of the Vanished Children's Alliance. Georgia Hilgeman's agony turned her into a crusader for others in her situation. In 1976, Hilgeman's ex-husband, Juan Rios, took their daughter, Monica, who was then thirteen months old, for a regular visitation. Rios then reported that over the weekend, Monica had disappeared while they were visiting Oakland, California. Finally, after five years of searching, Hilgeman found Monica in Mexico with relatives of Rios. Rios was later arrested and convicted of falsely imprisoning his own child, which was the first conviction for this offense in California history.

News that Monica was found led to parents calling Hilgeman and asking for help. These pleas motivated her to establish the Vanished Children's Alliance in 1980. This organization is one of the oldest missing children organizations in the country, and it predates the Adam Walsh case by one year. It has a distinguished board of directors, advisory board, and honorary board members, including politicians, media personalities, psychologists, judicial and legal personnel, and business leaders.

Some of the specific services offered by Vanished Children's Alliance include the registration of a missing child by the victim parent; providing victim parents with assistance to determine the location of their missing child; assisting the recovery of a missing child once located; providing victim parents with emotional support through telephone communications and group meetings in various locales in California; disseminating pictures of (and information about) missing children through the media; accepting sightings of missing children; conducting awareness workshops on the subject of missing children; training law enforcement, social service, educational, and community groups in preventative techniques; publishing a newsletter on current activities, recoveries, meetings, and legislation to members; and networking with various other reputable missing children's groups in this country and internationally.

The Adam Walsh Resource Center is perhaps the most well-known missing children organization in this country. The Center grew directly out of the efforts of John and Reve Walsh to find their son Adam. When he began the search for his missing child, John Walsh realized that media exposure would improve Adam's chances of being discovered and returned to his family. On August 10, 1981, he went on ABC's "Good Morning America" to discuss his son's case. This media exposure proved instrumental in mobilizing the entire missing children's movement.

As a result of John Walsh's TV appearance and other organizational efforts, the Adam Walsh Center was born in the fall of 1981. In 1982 the Center merged with the Child Advocacy Board of Broward County (Florida), and became the Adam Walsh Resource Center. The Resource Center is based in Florida, but has branch offices in other locales such as New York and Orange County, California. In the early days of the organization, much of the efforts were put into lobbying or political activities. The Center's work with legislators and other public officials was intended to bring about changes in state and federal laws as well as in the local policies of agencies.

The Adam Walsh Resource Center provides many of the same services as other missing children's organizations. Staff members work closely with law enforcement agencies to maintain a liaison with parents. They help parents collect the necessary materials to help the police conduct searches. For example, they secure photos of the children and get them published. Staff members also advise family members in stress—depending on the type of case at hand. For example, staff members refer parents whose children were taken by an ex-spouse to private investigators and attorneys.

As the number of missing children organizations grew during the 1980s, the competition for funding grew as well. The scramble for scarce dollars has become fierce. Most organizations use standard solicitations, for example, through the mail and the media. In their mail solicitations, many of these organizations seek new members for specific dollar amounts; in exchange for membership the contributor receives a newsletter or some type of recognition. Other organizations go further by using more sophisticated or aggressive fund-raising tactics. For example, the Vanished Children's Alliance offers donors the option of donating real estate and stocks, or making the Vanished Children's Alliance a beneficiary of the person's estate.

The Unscrupulous and Their Scams

Unfortunately, unscrupulous con artists have used the missing children cause as an opportunity to run various scams for making fast money by preying on people concerned about innocent children being victimized. They have exploited the reputations of legitimate nonprofit missing children organizations.

Many of these con artist scams follow a similar pattern. Typically, after arriving in a new locale, the con artist rents a small apartment and a post office box, obtains a bank of phones and several local telephone books, and hires a crew of callers for a minimal hourly rate to solicit money. Following a script prepared by the con artist, the callers dial residential phone numbers at random. They tell respondents they are calling on behalf of an organization concerned with recovering missing children. The respondent is asked to make a contribution to the cause in the form of a check, which is to be mailed in to the post office box. To motivate people to send checks, the callers play on their sympathy and fears. After a short period of time—from a few days to a few months—the con artist cashes in the checks and leaves town to set up the operation in a new location.

One case of a solicitation scam under the guise of helping missing children ended in the prosecution of the perpetrator. In 1984, a con man formed a fund-raising program called Kids for Missing Kids in Mesa, Arizona. Until the authorities began to ask questions about the use of the funds, he had been successful in defrauding the town's residents of a considerable sum of money. When local law enforcement began to investigate his solicitation activities, the man fled across state lines. Eventually police caught up with him; he was tried, convicted, and sentenced to serve fourteen years in prison for fraud.

Another type of fraud or exploitation of the missing children campaign has involved individuals claiming some sort of expertise or interest that helps parents recover a missing child. Private detectives, psychics, would-be authors—alerted to the disappearance of the child and the family's request for assistance from the news or posters—contact the parents with an offer to help. Unfortunately, the publicity about a missing child often attracts imposters who do not have the abilities they claim or whose offer of help is largely motivated by the desire to make a quick dollar by taking advantage of a distressed family. In one case in California, a Nazi group volunteered to pass out flyers of a kidnapped girl if the group could put its swastika logo on each flyer.

Conclusion

If the Lindbergh case was the crime of the century, then the Adam Walsh case was certainly the crime of the decade. These cases shared two important characteristics. Both involved the kidnapping and murder of a child. And both set off a ground swell of public indignation.

Over the years many other kidnappings have occurred that have involved more heinous or brutal acts—for example, the torture of the victim or the slayings of multiple victims. What distinguished the Lindbergh and Walsh cases from other kidnappings was not simply the gravity of the crime or the fact that the perpetrators took child victims. Rather, they affected the American public. These two cases became the subject of intensive and ongoing media attention; they triggered widespread concern and anxiety throughout the country about what suddenly appeared to be a terrible crime problem that was on the rise. It was perceived as a crime problem that threatened the safety and well-being of larger numbers of children.

The birth of the missing children problem shared the same course of awareness, definition, and development as other issues that have come to be viewed as social problems in recent years. Spokespersons for particular missing children cases and groups concerned with recovering missing children made claims that growing numbers of these incidents were victimizing children in all sectors of society. The media helped to give a name to the problem; they also drew attention to actual and potential missing children cases by dramatizing the cases and by treating the claims of concerned parents and spokespersons about the nature and extent of the missing children problem as if these were uncontrovertible facts.

Such media coverage generated a wave of social concern and the desire to do something about missing children. Much of the initial action on missing children was taken at the local level—by affected parents, private individuals, and organizations—to recover specific cases of missing children. Some parents looking for their missing children also brought their plight to the attention of public officials. These parents became political activitists; they put the recovery of their children on the political agendas of state and federal lawmakers. The campaign to make missing children a political issue is described in the next chapter.

4

The Politics of Missing Children

THE media coverage on missing children and the national concern it triggered did not merely put children's faces on milk cartons and grocery bags. The campaign to prevent and recover missing children extended into political action and pressure for legislation. Individual parents as well as spokespersons for missing children organizations became forceful lobbyists in getting missing children on the legislative agenda in Washington, D.C., as well as in state capitols across the nation. Interest groups attracted the attention of a few key members of Congress who were willing to draft legislation and enlist the support of their colleagues in the Senate and House. These political activities ensured that missing children would be treated as a social problem in an arena where individuals with power, prestige, and resources could make decisions that would have far-reaching effects. As a topic of legislative hearings and national lawmaking, missing children had truly arrived as a significant social problem of the 1980s. While groups and companies in the private sector were coordinating volunteer efforts to prevent and recover missing children, enterprising individuals like John Walsh were waging a successful political campaign to get more governmental resources directed toward solving the problem of missing children.

Although lawmakers passed legislation to address the situation of runaways and victims of parental abductions, the interest generated in these two groups of children was relatively minor compared with the concern shown when a missing child became typified as a young child kidnapped by a stranger and abused or killed. As noted in the last chapter, it was mutually advantageous for advocates of the different categories of missing children to foster this typification. It was useful for lobbyists for victims of stranger abductions to associate their cause with runaways and parent abduction cases because these other types of cases were more numerous and made the problem of missing children seem larger than it otherwise was.

Interestingly, the same individuals and groups lobbied for bills addressing the different categories of missing children. For example, spokespersons for the families of parental abductions and runaways also testified at hearings on missing children. Indeed, while witnesses testified about stranger kidnappings and sexual exploitation, much of the Congressional testimony about missing children was about the plight of runaways and victims of parental abduction.

The responses by politicians to pressure from missing children spokespersons and organizations were varied. Some helped enact national legislation, others succeeded in modifying state laws, and still others changed policies and procedures used by local law enforcement agencies. This chapter concentrates on political events at the national level—specifically the lobbying that ensued at the beginning of the 1980s and resulted in major pieces of federal legislation. Our discussion is limited to the laws that were passed regarding missing children in general—that is, laws that were to apply to all categories of missing children. Federal and state legislation specifically governing runaways and parental abductions is addressed later in this book.

Lobbying for Missing Children

Senate hearings on missing children (other than runaways and parental abductions) began toward the end of 1981. The first hearing on the specific topic of missing children was held on October 6, 1981, before the Subcommittee on Investigations and General Oversight of the Committee on Labor and Human

Resources. The hearing was held before this particular subcommittee in large part because the senator who introduced a bill to help missing children, Paula Hawkins, was a member of it. Paula Hawkins was also a first term Republican senator from Florida who had become interested and involved in the Adam Walsh case a few months earlier.

Among those present at the hearing were Edward Kennedy (D-Mass.) and Jay Howell, who was chief counsel for the Committee. (Howell would later become head of the National Center for Missing and Exploited Children.) Numerous witnesses also testified before the Committee, including the parents of three young children who had been kidnapped and killed or who disappeared without a trace. Two law enforcement officers also presented information to the Subcommittee.

The opening statement of the hearing was made by Senator Paula Hawkins, who talked about the problem of missing children as a national disgrace.

> In years past, we all became accustomed to the late evening question from our television set saying, "It is 11 P.M. Do you know where your children are?" Most of us were lucky; we knew where are children were. But today, *hundreds of thousands* of American parents cannot answer that simple question. Their children are lost, and with that loss comes an ordeal of unimagined horrors, unknown and unseen, but as real and heartfelt as any tragedy facing the American family. . . .
>
> No one among us can even accurately describe the extent of the problem. We simply do not know how many children disappear from their families each year. The estimates are as high as 1.8 million children per year.
>
> The children of this Nation are its most valuable and vulnerable and unprotected resource. Many of these children who disappear from their families are victims of crime. It is also true that hundreds of these children are runaways who safely return to their families.[1]

As was the pattern in most of the missing hearings to come, this one began with the telling of tragic stories by the parents who had to live through the nightmares. The first parent to testify was Julie Patz, mother of Etan Patz.

> My son disappeared on the morning of May 25, 1979. At 10 minutes to 8 o'clock on that morning, I walked him to the sidewalk in front of our home in New York City. It would have been the first morning he was to walk the 1 1/2 blocks to the schoolbus by himself.
>
> The schoolbus was clearly visible from the front of our home; there were other children and parents waiting there. I discussed procedure one last time with my son, Etan; watched him walk the first half block with only one block left to go; turned and went back into my home; and that was the last time I saw my son.[2]

The dramatic testimony was followed by another heartbreaking story—the disappearance and killing of Adam Walsh. Both of Adam's parents, John and Reve Walsh, appeared at the hearing, but it was John who related their story.

> On July 27, 1981, at approximately 12:30 P.M., our only beloved son, Adam John Walsh, was abducted from the Hollywood Mall in Hollywood, Fla. He and his mother had been shopping in the Hollywood Mall and he was in the toy department while his mother was approximately three aisles away. In the matter of less than ten minutes, he vanished. What proceeded has been called the largest manhunt in south Florida history.[3]

John Walsh continued to tell the full story of his son's disappearance and the recovery of Adam's decapitated head two weeks later, as well as what the police did and did not do during Adam's disappearance.

Next to testify was Camille Bell, the mother of one of the children murdered in the Atlanta child killings of 1979.

> Madam Chairman, On October 21, 1979, Yusuf, my nine-year-old son, was asked by a neighbor to go to the store. She was an elderly lady and could not pay him for going, and none of the other children in the neighborhood would go for nothing, and he would; that is why he was asked.
>
> He left at around 4 o'clock, going to a store that was three blocks away—a store that he had gone to almost daily since he was seven. He got to the store, he bought what he was sent for, started home, and he did not get back. By 5 o'clock, we were very concerned because it was not like Yusuf to loiter and not come

> back, especially when he was on an errand for someone else; he was a relatively responsible child.
>
> We called the police at a little after 6, and by 6:45 they were there. They took a report. One of the policemen remembered seeing him because even though it was October, it was in the upper 80's and Yusuf was wearing a pair of brown shorts and no shoes and no shirt. And the policeman saw him going to the store and said that he reminded him of the last days of summer.
>
> Yusuf did not turn up, and I pulled together a search. The police department could not do a search; they did not have the manpower, or they said they did not. I got the ROTC of Smith High School to get together with me and the two missing persons police officers who were assigned to the case, and we did a search of the community about one week later. At that point, we did not find anything.
>
> Things went on for a while, and on November 8, Yusuf's body was found in an abandoned school that should have been boarded up but was not. . . . Finally, when he was found, the community did rally quite a bit and there was help that came from within the community. That was a little late; Yusuf had been strangled, and things went on, and things go on now.[4]

Mrs. Bell's testimony was followed by that of a couple of law enforcement officers, who described their procedures for handling missing children cases. Also testifying was Kristin Cole, information director for Child Find of New Platz, New York, an organization founded to help find children who had been abducted by a parent.

The next Senate hearing was held on November 5, 1981. The subject of that hearing was exploited children, but the link between missing children and exploited children was beginning to be made. This hearing was held before the Juvenile Justice Subcommittee of the Committee on the Judiciary. (Most of the hearings on missing children would be held before this subcommittee.) Senator Arlen Specter (R-Penn.), Chairperson of the Subcommittee, reigned over the hearing; he introduced and heard the testimony of a variety of persons interested in or knowledgeable about the exploitation of children. Interestingly, the vast majority of this testimony related to the exploitation, particularly the sexual exploitation, of older juveniles, who were frequently runaways or homeless youth.

The November 5 hearing began with testimony from a boy

named David who had been involved in child prostitution in Louisville, Kentucky. David was introduced to Senator Specter by John Rabun, then manager of the Exploited Child Unit of the Jefferson County (Louisville), Kentucky Department of Human Services. John Rabun had been active in studying runaways and child exploitation in Kentucky for some time. (He, too, later became the head of the National Center for Missing and Exploited Children.)

What follows is an extensive quote of the questions and responses that conveys the tone of these hearings, the direction of the discussion, and the particular language in which the issues were presented.

> MR. RABUN: David has just turned seventeen years old. He was a victim, as a young child, of physical and sexual abuse by his own family and friends of the family at the age of seven. Later he learned he could use sexual acts to survive on the streets. That became an important part of his history.
>
> SENATOR SPECTER: Mr. Rabun, could you give us a little bit of background as to the form of sexual abuse David was subjected to at the age of seven?
>
> MR. RABUN: Yes; it was adult male friends of the family who—can I mention the actual sex acts, Senator?
>
> SENATOR SPECTER: I think we can deal with the problem only if we understand it, and to the extent you can be subtle and diplomatic, fine. But we have to communicate.
>
> MR. RABUN: Surely. The sex acts involved fondling and oral sex from the adult onto the child. Obviously at that point the child did not understand what was going on nor the severity or seriousness of the acts themselves. The physical abuse has to do more with beatings, being thrown up against walls—that sort of things.
>
> SENATOR SPECTER: And, Mr. Rabun, over how long a period of time was David subjected to that kind of sexual abuse?
>
> MR. RABUN: A couple of times, starting at seven, and then maybe 1 year or so later. It would be sporadic incidents arising out of situations, perhaps overzealousness in discipline, that type of thing.

> David is not gay. I say that up front because he calls himself a hustler. By definition, a hustler is a boy prostitute. Girls use the term *prostitute;* boys use the term *hustler.* Most boy hustlers are not gay. David is not gay.
>
> David is, by his own admission, drug-dependent since the age of twelve. He will be able to explain to you a progression in the juvenile justice system in his life from seven years old, being a dependent child in front of the juvenile justice system, based upon the physical sexual abuse as a child to an eleven- to twelve-year-old age where he became a status offender, a runaway, ungovernable behavior, and then, at the age of fourteen or fifteen, got into the juvenile delinquency area of the juvenile justice system, being involved in drug usage and drug pushing, burglary, some minor forms of robbery, prostitution, and carrying concealed deadly weapons for the purpose of safety.[5]

It is interesting that the bulk of the testimony given by David, as a result of direct questioning by Senator Specter, related to his prostitution, drug abuse, and crime, and not to the physical and sexual abuse he suffered at the hands of his own family and friends of the family.

Another witness at the hearing was Terry Sullivan, who was the former prosecutor for the state of Illinois, and a member of the team that prosecuted John Wayne Gacy for the multiple murders of teenagers in the Chicago area. In order to get a better idea of the types of children who fell victim to Gacy, Senator Specter asked:

> Mr. Sullivan, as best you can piece it together from the evidence you have, give us a typical scenario of what happened with any one of the victims of John Gacy, from the point of leaving home, contact with Gacy to the extent you know it, exploitation if any.
>
> MR. SULLIVAN: . . . we still have some seven or eight victims who are unidentified to this day, which I think brings more into focus the real problems of the runaways, especially in identification and cooperation with law enforcement. . . . But when you are talking about the typical

> scenario, usually the individuals, the youths who would have left the homes, left them because of the fact that they did not get along with their parents or they were beaten or their parents abandoned them or their parents were alcoholics. Whatever it was that drove them from their homes as victims, they ended up drifting to a place where they thought they could exist and get away from their home life.[6]

Another witness was Father Bruce Ritter, founder and president of Covenant House in New York City. Father Ritter, as we shall see, has been a major player in the field of providing services for runaway and homeless youth since 1968.

Father Ritter's testimony centered around the runaway and homeless kids (street kids) he and his organization serve in New York.

> FATHER RITTER: About one thousand kids a month come to our program. Two-thirds of them are boys. Forty-five percent come from New York State, the rest from all over the country. Two-thirds have been involved in prostitution and pornography. Eighty percent of these kids come from one-parent families with a history of alcoholism, child abuse, plus. There are very few mysteries about why children run away from home. Very few children leave a warm, loving, and supportive family.
>
> As I am sure most of you know, Times Square has become the center for prostitution and pornography in the United States. Everyday hundreds and hundreds of boys and girls, young men and young women, make their living there as prostitutes in the ten blocks around where our center is located and where I live on Eighth Avenue.
>
> The sex industry is at least a $1 billion a year business. The police have identified hundreds of pimps who work that neighborhood, controlling literally thousands of young people.[7]

All of the testimony at the November 5 hearing related primarily to the sexual exploitation of older juveniles, typically runaways who left home voluntarily as a result of parental abuse. This picture is a far cry from the typification of the missing child that came later—that of a small child forcibly kidnapped by a stranger and killed.

At the next Senate hearing, on April 1, 1982, two very different visions of the missing children problem were melded. This hearing was on exploited and missing children, two separate subjects. Seven witnesses testified. The first five dealt with a continuation of the November 5, 1981, hearing. The last two witnesses focused on a specific piece of federal legislation aimed at the more narrow typification: child victims of stranger kidnapping.

In his introduction, Senator Specter summarized the testimony that had been presented at the previous hearings:

> Last November 5 we commenced in this committee the investigation into the sexual exploitation of juveniles in connection with our general concerns about the problems of juvenile delinquency and the impact on juveniles of the kind of activity affecting later criminal conduct. One aspect of great concern is the issue of child pornography, that it has become a multimillion dollar business and has affected the loss of thousands of children having been exposed to photography and incidental abuse.
>
> The Federal laws that prohibit the production of child pornography and the distribution of child pornography and transportation of minors across state lines are fields where existing legislation is not strong enough. Today we are going to be moving into that area.
>
> Our first witness is an ordained minister and former high school teacher who recently entered a guilty plea in State court on twelve counts of sexual activity involving thirteen- to fifteen-year old boys. He has begun his probationary sentence and is making an effort to pull his life together.[8]

This person, called simply the witness during his testimony, talked with great candor about his exploitation of teenage boys.

> SENATOR SPECTER: What specific crimes were you charged with that you pleaded guilty to?
>
> THE WITNESS: I think I recall eleven counts of sodomy in different degrees and then three other charges relating to distribution of literature, distribution of alcohol, and marihuana.

SENATOR SPECTER: What kind of literature did you distribute; was it pornographic?

THE WITNESS: Actually I only did that on one occasion and it was pornographic. I describe them as girly magazines.

SENATOR SPECTER: Whom did you distribute the girly magazines and pornographic literature to?

THE WITNESS: To the boys that I picked up.

SENATOR SPECTER: How many boys were involved, as you say, you picked up?

THE WITNESS: It seems to me that the counts, the eleven counts—or the fourteen counts would deal with I think four or five boys. There had been others.

SENATOR SPECTER: How many others had there been?

THE WITNESS: I really cannot answer that because I do not really know.

SENATOR SPECTER: Can you give me an estimate?

THE WITNESS: Quite a few.

SENATOR SPECTER: Several dozen?

THE WITNESS: Several dozen.

SENATOR SPECTER: Fifty?

THE WITNESS: Several dozen I think might be more accurate and in the various cities.

SENATOR SPECTER: Are you willing to identify the cities?

THE WITNESS: Yes, if that would be helpful.

SENATOR SPECTER: Yes.

THE WITNESS: In no order, St. Louis, Cincinnati, Indianapolis, Louisville, Cleveland.

SENATOR SPECTER: What was the youngest of the boys?

THE WITNESS: The youngest boy turned out to be thirteen.

SENATOR SPECTER: In the incident that you were suspected of, entered the guilty plea to?

THE WITNESS: Yes, sir.

SENATOR SPECTER: How old was the oldest of the boys involved in the guilty pleas?

THE WITNESS: I think sixteen. Almost one year—nine months went by and it seems to me one might have been fifteen moving to sixteen. I am not quite sure. Let us say thirteen to sixteen.

> SENATOR SPECTER: What was the specific conduct that you were involved in that led to this guilty plea?
>
> THE WITNESS: Well, all of the boys that I did have sex with or some kind of relationship with were street hustlers. That is, they were out on the streets and were picked up that way.[9]

Again, what emerged from this testimony, and more like it, is a very different picture of the missing and exploited child than has been projected in the contemporary view of missing children. The bulk of the testimony at this hearing concerned older juveniles—teenagers—who had run away from home because of abuse and were exploited on the streets by other adults.

However, the sixth and seventh witnesses at this hearing switched gears, and focused attention on another type of case. The first of these two witnesses was Paula Hawkins, the first-term senator from Florida, who introduced the bill about which the testimony was directed. The bill, eventually enacted by Congress in somewhat modified form as the Missing Children Act of 1982, dealt with expanding the federal computer system to keep track of missing children and unidentified dead bodies, both adults and children. Interestingly, one of the agencies to be affected by the legislation—the Department of Justice—objected to some of the bill's provisions. Specifically, the Department opposed language that would have allowed individual citizens to contact the FBI directly and enter a missing child's name into the FBI computer system. Eventually, some compromises in the Hawkins bill were reached; the bill was modified to enable parents to receive FBI assistance through requests made by local law enforcement agencies.

In her introductory remarks, Senator Hawkins, who would play a key role in other federal missing children legislation, changed, with interesting word juxtaposition, the topic at hand to missing and exploited children.

> SENATOR HAWKINS: Mr. Chairman, I am happy to be here to testify on a subject of grave concern to this entire country, our children.
>
> I commend you for addressing this subcommittee's attention to what we now know is a true national tragedy, our missing and exploited children.

> I want to express my appreciation to you for your important role as one of the original co-sponsors of the legislation which I introduced before the committee to begin to address the problem of missing children and unidentified dead in this country. I am most grateful for your continued help in this important endeavor.[10]

Senator Hawkins then outlined the reasons why her proposed legislation was needed, and addressed the specific objections to the bill by the Department of Justice. She concluded with a plea for the bill:

> I know that your subcommittee has heard testimony today and on past occasions which *dramatize highly the true scope of this national tragedy* [emphasis added].
>
> Consideration of the legislation before you today is an important step forward in the work of this Congress to insure the safety of this Nation's children. Your efforts are appreciated by all families and all Members of this Congress.[11]

Senator Hawkins then introduced the person who became a key spokesperson for missing children and for legislation regarding missing children: John Walsh, father of Adam. Once again, Mr. Walsh summarized the tragic experience that befell his family; he then related his experiences—and disappointment—with law enforcement agencies involved in the case. Walsh then stated that he did not want his son's death to be in vain. He wanted to work to get law enforcement and other governmental agencies to be more responsive to the problem of missing children.

> We [Walsh and his wife, Reve] have determined that although we would never be able to find any answers to Adam's death, that in our minds, he would not die in vain. We thought that the best way to deal with our grief was to do something for the rest of the missing children in the United States. With the donations that we received, we set up the Adam Walsh Outreach Center for Missing Children and proceeded to tell the story of missing children to a nation that is obviously unaware that this problem exists.[12]

Walsh then pointed out what he viewed as a serious problem with the country.

> It is certainly evident the priorities of this great country are in some disorder. A country that can launch a space shuttle that can return to the Earth and take off again, a country that can allocate millions of dollars to save a small fish, threatened with extinction, in the Tennessee Valley River, but does not have a centralized reporting system or a nationwide search system for missing children, certainly needs to reaffirm the very principles that this country was founded on, namely, personal freedom.[13]

Walsh then presented some facts and figures on missing children.

> After contacting and speaking with many of the twenty or so individual missing children agencies throughout the country, it appears that statistics indicate that there are over one hundred and fifty thousand individual children missing each year. Approximately one hundred thousand of them are runaways, and children snatched by ex-parents. *The unbelievable and unaccounted-for figure of fifty thousand children disappear annually, and are abducted for reasons of foul play* [emphasis added].[14]

Finally, Walsh expressed his dismay that the Department of Justice had opposed the bill introduced by Senator Hawkins.

> Having been an active registered voter, a Republican, and a strong believer in the American way, you can imagine my feelings and the tears that came to my eyes when I read that letter and the words "therefore the department [of Justice] recommends against enactment of this bill."

Missing Children Act of 1982

The Missing Children Act of 1982 was the first piece of federal legislation related to missing children in general. This legislation was rather simple in content, although potentially far-reaching in implication. Federal law already existed authorizing the Attorney General of the United States (through the appropriate federal agencies) to keep various records on criminals and crimes, particularly related to criminal identification. The 1982 legislation added one new section to existing law that directed the Attorney General to keep records on missing children and to disseminate those records to state and local agencies. The new language stated:

> The Attorney General shall—
> . . . (3) acquire, collect, classify, and preserve any information which would assist in the location of any missing person (including an unemancipated person as defined by the laws of the place of residence of such person) and provide confirmation as to any entry for such a person to the parent, legal guardian, or next of kin of that person (and the Attorney General may acquire, collect, classify, and preserve such information from such parent, guardian, or next of kin). . . .[16]

National Crime Information Center

The practical effect of the new law was to change slightly the operation of the National Crime Information Center, or NCIC as it is called in law enforcement circles.

Established by the FBI in 1967, the NCIC is a nationwide computerized communications and information system. Since its creation, the NCIC's mission has been to serve as a national index and network for state law enforcement information systems throughout the country. The NCIC permits users to access millions of criminal justice records instantaneously through its on-line computer system. (Off-line inquiries can also be made.) Over sixty-four thousand agencies currently participate in the NCIC network, which is located in Washington, D.C., but has connecting terminals throughout the United States, Canada, Puerto Rico, and the U.S. Virgin Islands.

The central idea behind the NCIC is to enable law enforcement agencies across the country to share information for solving crimes, catching criminals, and identifying missing persons or stolen property. In a large country with many opportunities for easy and quick travel, criminals can readily cross state lines to elude local law enforcement personnel. The problem of ready mobility is not a new concern for law enforcement authorities. As far back as 1875, the state of Texas published a *List of Fugitives from Justice,* in order to alert law enforcement agencies of criminals who fled justice and should be caught and returned to the place where they committed a crime. With the NCIC system, such alerts and requests for assistance can be communicated around the country in a matter of seconds. These days, law enforcement agencies request information from the national computers on the average of five hundred thousand times a day, and it takes only about two seconds to access any record.

At the time the Missing Children Act was passed in 1982, the NCIC system contained several separate computer files. These files included the vehicle file (for registering stolen vehicles), boat file (for registering stolen boats), gun file (for registering stolen guns), and a wanted person file (for persons with an outstanding arrest warrant). All of the files were used in a similar way. If, for example, a person stole a car in Nebraska and drove it to Louisiana, the police in New Orleans would otherwise have no way of knowing the car in their jurisdiction had been stolen. But if the police in New Orleans saw an abandoned car or stopped the driver for a traffic violation, they could run a check through the NCIC system. When the officer discovered that the police in Nebraska had listed the car as stolen, the officer in New Orleans could detain the driver and take possession of the car, bringing about its return to the rightful owner.

In addition to the files pertaining to missing or stolen property, by 1975 the NCIC system had a file for registering missing persons. The missing persons file operated according to the same principle as the stolen car file. On taking the report of a missing child, a local law enforcement agency could enter the child's name and other vital information into the NCIC computer. If a law enforcement agency in another jurisdiction found the youngster and determined the child's identity, the officer could run the child's name and date of birth through the system. If the inquiry made a "hit," it meant that the child had been reported missing in another jurisdiction. The law enforcement agency could then hold the child and arrange for his or her return home.

The operational details of the NCIC system and its utilization by local authorities is described in greater detail in the chapter on police investigation. Suffice it to say here, although the computerized registry and inquiry system for missing persons was similar to the computerized system for identifying and recovering stolen property, its functions were more complicated—it is relatively easy for humans to conceal their identities. Inquiries that could generate a hit in runaway cases, for example, were dependent on youngsters giving correct identifying information to the officer. However, given their age and the fact that many of them do not want to be found and returned home, many runaways do not carry any identification or are unwilling to reveal their true names and dates of birth. Thus, such youths could not be found listed in the system even if another police agency had actually logged in their names as reported missing by parents.

The above discussion provides a background for understanding the actual impact of the Missing Children Act, which had been so heavily lobbied for by individuals such as John Walsh, Paula Hawkins, and Arlen Specter. What did this act do? Very little, relatively speaking. At the time of the bill's passage, the NCIC system already had twelve files, one of which was a missing persons file (established seven years before the new act). The new act was largely symbolic. It was the first federal bill to refer specifically to missing children. It was a public statement affirming the national government's interest in missing children.

Prior to the 1982 Missing Children Act, local law enforcement agencies were filing reports of missing children to NCIC. Between 1975 and 1982, the NCIC's Missing Persons File had accumulated 791,403 records of missing persons reports, and had an average of 10,555 of such cases per month. Of these, approximately 76 percent were in the juvenile category. Specifically, there were 601,446 records for missing juveniles, with a monthly average of 8,020. Thus, the majority of entries into the missing persons file *before* passage of the 1982 Missing Children Act were of missing children; at the time the act was passed, there was a system already in place to record such cases and to help law enforcement identify them.

Clearly, the problem with the NCIC system was not that the federal government did not have a missing persons file or that it did not offer resources to assist the investigation or recovery of missing children. It did both. Rather, the problem was that local law enforcement agencies underutilized existing federal capacities and resources. For example, in 1982, there were approximately one million runaways reported to local law enforcement agencies. However, there were only 114,000 juvenile records entered (or about 11 percent of all runaways) into the missing persons file. What was needed was a statutory mandate at the *state level* to require local law enforcement agencies to put the names of missing children into the NCIC system. Eventually, many states did enact legislation that mandated law enforcement officers make such reports.

Ironically, the only practical effect of the 1982 Act was to create one new file—the thirteenth—called the Unidentified Bodies File. This new file collected information largely unrelated to the identification or recovery of missing children. Rather, it was set up to maintain a register of deceased individuals around the country—the majority of whom are adults—who could not otherwise be identified.

The Hearings of 1983

Concern for missing children—especially victims of stranger kidnapping—did not die down with the passage of the 1982 Missing Children Act. Spokespersons for missing children organizations continued to lobby federal legislators to keep missing children on the legislative agenda. Senator Paula Hawkins continued to be the legislative entrepreneur for the missing children cause. She was instrumental in arranging for hearings on missing children before the Senate Judiciary Committee (Subcommittee on Juvenile Justice) in 1983. The first, held on February 2, 1983, was specifically related to missing children. Part of the purpose of the hearing was, again, to dramatize the problem of missing children, but also to focus attention on FBI policy regarding missing children cases. As we shall see, some witnesses were critical of the FBI for not taking a more active role in the investigation of kidnap cases that originated at the local level. Senator Paula Hawkins introduced the problem.

> The criminal abduction of children has become an all too familiar tragedy, *visited upon countless homes and communities throughout our entire country* [emphasis added].
>
> The cases that we are going to address today do not involve the kidnapping of a child by his or her parent. Today we are examining ten cases involving the disappearance of children nine years of age or younger. Too often, the consequences of such cases are severe. Families are destroyed, law enforcement professionals are frustrated, and an awful sense of fear grips the hearts of every community in which these tragedies occur.[17]

In her remarks, Senator Hawkins criticized the apparent reluctance of the FBI to become involved in some local child kidnapping cases. To dramatize her point about the lack of sufficient concern with kidnapped children and the FBI's priorities for allocating resources to the investigation of different types of cases, Senator Hawkins described the FBI's efforts to assist in the recovery of a stolen item that involved great monetary value and notoriety.

> The kind of investigation we are seeking did occur when Fanfreluche, ten, disappeared from her home in Kentucky. The FBI became immediately involved in the case, bringing in special agents from two states and several field offices to participate in a successful search to locate her. She was found, still in the State of Kentucky, and was returned to her home. Franfreluche was a racehorse who was in foal to Triple Crown winner, Secretariat.[18]

The February 2 hearing attracted testimony from some lawmakers new to the cause of missing children, who wanted to lend their influence to bringing about federal action—and who in turn could benefit politically from appearing to do something about the problem of missing children. For example, Orrin Hatch, senator from Utah, provided a statement that was entered into the record. He noted concern about the problem of missing children, concern for children and their families, and support for federal legislation. Interestingly, Hatch's statement also emphasized the need for local communities to take action "without federal intervention."[19]

To punctuate his concern, Senator Hatch called attention to the extent of the problem of missing children. He referred to statistics that had been previously quoted by John Walsh and others about the numbers of missing children cases, although these figures still had no clear source or empirical basis.

> I would like to thank the Judiciary Committee for beginning hearings on the tragedy of child kidnapping and victimization. The Department of Health and Human Resources has estimated that 1.8 million children disappear each year. A significant number do not leave of their own accord. In fact, last year the

> Federal Bureau of Investigation approximated the number of children abducted by strangers to be fifty-thousand.[20]

Also among the witnesses who testified at the February 2 hearings were parents who told the tragic stories of their children being kidnapped or disappearing. Mrs. Helen Burton of Breckenridge, Texas, related the story of how her three-year-old child disappeared. Frank Papesh of Bedford Heights, Ohio, testified how his daughter, Tiffany, was kidnapped for ransom when she was eight years old. John Walsh testified again, and recounted the kidnapping of his son Adam. Much of the testimony was critical of the police, and particularly the FBI.

Testimony was also given by Paul Simon, then representative in Congress (now senator) from Illinois. While Paula Hawkins was the champion of the missing children cause in the Senate, Representative Simon came to serve that role in the House. In part, Simon's interest was prompted by the numbers of children whom he had heard experts claim as victims of stranger abductions; like Hatch, Simon included in his testimony the figure of fifty-thousand children kidnapped by strangers. At the February 2 hearing, Simon's remarks were directed at the FBI, as well, stating that the "FBI's record on missing children has been a spotty one."[21]

A spokesperson from the FBI addressed this hearing on behalf of the agency. Oliver B. Revell, assistant director of the Criminal Investigative Division of the FBI, testified about the Bureau's policies and practices in responding to missing children cases. He spent the bulk of his testimony defending the agency's policies and pointed out the difficulties the Bureau faced in deciding when to enter a missing child case.

> I know of no subject that is more compelling or heartrending than the kidnapping or assault or murder of children. I would also point out that there is no federal statute against the murder of children, and there are thousands of murders every year. There is no federal statute against the assault or the sexual abuse of children. We have no jurisdiction in those areas, either. We do have jurisdiction when there is an abduction of a child and the interstate transportation of that child, and we do a very effective job in those cases. I could sit here and cite you case

after case we have solved, we have recovered the child, in many instances, we have returned the child to the parent, and we have obtained the conviction of the offender.

Our dilemma is that many children, including young children, are not abducted. They wander off, they are lost, they are taken by relatives, or there is some other type of situation that occurs that clearly is not within the statute or the mandate of the federal kidnapping statute.

I would simply point out that where we have an indication that a child has been abducted or taken, and where we have an indication of a federal violation, the resources and the expertise that the Bureau can offer and can invoke in these cases are put into full play, and we work these cases at a very high priority.

We do not have the capability or the jurisdiction to search for each missing child. *I do not known the accurate statistics; I do not think anyone does* [emphasis added]. But some reports I have seen indicate that there are one million children a year who at one time or other are reported missing.[22]

During this testimony, Senator Specter questioned Revell's knowledge of the numbers of cases of children reported as missing. Revell informed the Subcommittee that there were approximately sixteen thousand children in the NCIC missing persons file. Further, Revell himself questioned the figure of fifty thousand abducted children referred to by Senator Hatch and others. He said he did not know the source or validity of that statistic. This mysterious fifty thousand figure of stranger abductions would continue to surface at subsequent hearings.

Interest groups and sympathic lawmakers kept missing children in the limelight in 1983. Yet another Congressional hearing was scheduled in July. The hearing of July 12 dealt with the serious topic of serial murders. It is curious that a hearing on serial murder was held before the Subcommittee on Juvenile Justice, because most of the examples given in testimony were of murderers who killed adults, not children. In her introductory remarks, for example, Senator Hawkins referred to the case of Gerald Eugene Stano who "cut a path of murder and bloodshed across the State of Florida from 1973 until 1983."[23] Stano reportedly admitted to the murder of thirty-nine *women.*

One of the individuals who testified was Ann Rule, journalist and author from Washington state. She had studied and written about serial killers for some years. Among her books was *Small Sacrifices,* the true story of a woman in Oregon who shot her children, took them to a local hospital, and blamed the shooting on a "shaggy bearded stranger."[24] The story frightened local residents because they feared the killer was still on the loose. Eventually the police determined the woman, Diane Downs, shot the children herself. She was convicted and sent to prison. Well-known actress Farrah Fawcett later starred in a TV docudrama about the case.

The discussion of serial murder and missing children—particularly those involving murder and violence—at the same hearing clearly gave the message that the two were linked. Testimony on the by-now familiar case of Adam Walsh was once again included in the hearing, although there was no evidence to link Adam's murder with any serial killer. Senator Hawkins prefaced John Walsh's testimony with these remarks:

> Today we will again hear from my good friend, John Walsh, of Hollywood, Fla., whose son, Adam, was brutally murdered in the summer of 1981 in south Florida. Since that time, John and I have worked together continuously to increase this country's awareness of the tragedy of missing and murdered children and to try to correct the gaps that we found in our law enforcement system.[25]

Although not a peace officer himself or an expert in crime investigations, police training or operations, Mr. Walsh stated that serial killers often struck in more than one state, and that law enforcement authorities were not equipped to coordinate cases that take place in different states, either as serial murders or child kidnapping. He expressed his frustration with the failure of law enforcement officials to coordinate a multi-state investigation of his son's case.

In part, Walsh's testimony was to encourage the Subcommittee to consider passing some legislation that would create a centralized computer record-keeping system that would help keep track of homicides that take place in different states. He stated such a system would provide the technology to pull together in one place information on "some of these five thousand unidentified dead bodies throughout the country with similar types of mutilation, similar types of murder, and once and for all, county coroners and homicide detectives in Utah can say we have ten bodies here that were similarly killed to ten bodies in Florida."[26]

When Senator Specter next asked John Walsh about the connection between his son's disappearance and death and the hearing topic of serial murder, Walsh treated the question as an opportunity to make a general point about the circumstances and evils that threatened missing children everywhere. Walsh claimed such children were invariably the victims of serial killers and sexual molestation. He based this claim on "impressions" and fears of parents with whom he had spoken, rather than on specific evidence in his son's case, or any other case within his knowledge.

> SENATOR SPECTER: Mr. Walsh, did you have any reason to believe that your son was the victim of a serial killer?
>
> MR. WALSH: . . . after meeting thousands of parents of missing children, interviewing police chiefs, interviewing coroners, interviewing prosecuting attorneys, et cetera, . . . [Adam] may well have been [the victim of a serial killer]. That 90 percent of the murderers of children, when a relative is not arrested, it is these types of losers, as the police use the term, where no one is a suspect, can be the result of serial murderers that prey on children, and they are normally child molesters that may molest twenty, thirty. The average child molester, according to *Newsweek* and *Time* magazines, molests six to eight children before he is ever caught. You know that. I mean I speak to somewhat experts here. And that when they do find the child that feels will threaten them or tell someone, they often quote their terms—I have heard three child molesters testify, one before your committee before—snuff the victim, so Adam very well could have been the result of a multiple child murderer that roamed throughout the State.[27]

Like so much other testimony from spokespersons on missing children, Walsh's claims about the number, circumstances, and similarities of missing children cases were based on speculation. Senator Specter was curious about the discrepancy and conflicting figures being cited by the various witnesses. He pressed other witnesses on the numbers issue.

> We are having a short debate on how many unsolved murders there were last year. We have heard the figure 3,600 so-called random murders and 20,000 unsolved murders. There is always difficulty surrounding statistical data.[28]

Senator Specter asked another witness, Pierce Brooks, a former police chief in two different departments and a member of the law enforcement community for over thirty-five years, if he knew how many unsolved murders there were in the country. Brooks gave a revealing answer, which contrasted markedly with the testimony offered by Walsh and other missing children spokespersons.

> If I told you, it would be just an honest guess. I was asked by a person in the news media: "How many of these murders are there?" I said maybe five hundred or one thousand, and some of my colleagues just came down on top of me because they said it was thousands and thousands.[29]

In his concluding remarks at the hearing, Walsh directed the Subcommittee's attention to the government's ability to alleviate the suffering and trauma of families with missing children by improving the information available to law enforcement on murder and kidnapping cases.

> I know how frustrated Pierce Brooks is, trying to get this system going, and I beseech you here, we are talking about less than a $1 million a year to fund the whole system, to get it going, and because of the huge amount of murders in this country, serial murders, and the frustration of police chiefs, coroners, detectives that I have experienced, I beseech you to carry it further.[30]

Missing Children's Assistance Act of 1984

In the wake of these Senate hearings on child kidnap and murder cases and sustained media attention, the issue of missing children began to pick up steam. The TV docudrama about Adam Walsh had been aired, dozens of magazine and newspaper articles had been published on missing children, and there were many more ideas, on a grander scale, about how to change federal and state legislation to provide assistance to missing children and their families.

At the federal level, the most comprehensive of these bills was Senate Bill 2014, which was introduced in October 1983 by Senators Arlen Specter, Paula Hawkins, and twenty-two others. The bill was much more sweeping than the 1982 legislation (which was limited to changes in the NCIC system). A series of hearings (five in all) were held in the beginning of 1984 to address the proposed bill.

Again, the hearings included personal testimony by parents whose children had disappeared. The testimony at these hearings encompassed a wide variety of cases that constituted the general category of missing children. For example, in her testimony, Senator Paula Hawkins focused on the extremely serious cases—small children who are kidnapped by strangers and killed. Interestingly, the testimony of many other witnesses before the Subcommittee on Juvenile Justice did not dwell on such severe cases; rather, they described cases that were statistically more common and less violent.

Much of the testimony, focused on parental abduction, not abduction by strangers. Jean Humphrey of Sallisaw, Oklahoma, relayed to the Subcommittee how her ex-spouse had abducted her child. Gloria Yerkovich, who founded Child Find, Inc., also testified at length about her experience with parental abduction. Even Mitch McConnell, chairperson of the Kentucky Task Force on Exploited and Missing Children, devoted most of his testimony to parental abduction cases. The testimony given by other witnesses pertained to runaways. Senator Jeremiah Denton (D-Ala.) specifically directed the hearing away from just young children kidnapped by strangers. As he said, "Usually the term 'missing child' implies that a child has been kidnapped, however, it is my belief that this term should include those children who roam the streets: the runaways and castaways. These children often lead similar life-styles and face similar circumstances to those who have been abducted."[31]

By 1984, many senators were joining the missing children

bandwagon. They became part of the missing children hearing record in a variety of ways: they gave direct testimony, submitted written statements to the Committee, and introduced citizens from their home state as witnesses. For instance, both senators from Oklahoma, David Boren and Don Nickles, introduced Pearla Peterson of Oklahoma City, whose thirteen-year-old daughter disappeared from a carnival.

In their testimony, many senators recounted the terrible tragedy of missing children, and often parroted the figures that had been given by others two years earlier. Senator Jeremiah Denton of Alabama submitted a prepared statement in which he said that "as many as fifty-thousand young Americans are reported as having been abducted by strangers."[32]

Senator Strom Thurmond (R-S.C.) probably summed up the feelings of most senators with the prepared statement he submitted to the hearings.

> These hearings are intended to examine both the legislation and the problem. Too many Americans are saddened each year with stories of child murder and abduction only to dismiss the news by saying, "that could never happen here" or "my child would never talk to strangers." The story of Adam Walsh and the Atlanta tragedies serve as vivid reminders that it can happen anywhere to anyone.
>
> It is not my intention to scare the people; rather the purpose of this hearing is to make them aware of the problem. Adults and children alike must be educated. Everyone must be taught ways of protecting our children. We must lessen the likelihood of future tragedies.[33]

The Provisions of the Act

Once again, Senator Hawkins was successful in getting the bill she had drafted with the help of other senators and missing children lobbyists enacted. The legislation, called the Missing Children's Assistance Act of 1984, was incorporated into the Juvenile Justice and Delinquency Prevention Act of 1974. Included in the preamble to the new law were several congressional findings pertaining to the types of missing children cases encompassed in the act:

> The Congress hereby finds that—
>
> (1) each year thousands of children are abducted or removed from the control of a parent having legal custody without such parent's consent, under circumstances which immediately place them in grave danger;
> (2) many of these children are never reunited with their families;
> (3) often there are no clues to the whereabouts of these children;
> (4) many missing children are at great risk of both physical harm and sexual exploitation;
> (5) in many cases, parents and local law enforcement officials have neither the resources nor the expertise to mount expanded search efforts;
> (6) abducted children are frequently moved from one locality to another, requiring the cooperation and coordination of local, state, and federal law enforcement efforts;
> (7) on frequent occasions, law enforcement authorities quickly exhaust all leads in missing children cases, and require assistance from distant communities where a child may be located; and
> (8) federal assistance is urgently needed to coordinate and assist in this interstate problem.[34]

The new law defined a missing child in the following terms:

> (1) . . . "missing child" means any individual less than eighteen years of age whose whereabouts are unknown to such individual's legal custodian if—
> (A) the circumstances surrounding such individual's disappearance indicate that such individual may possibly have been removed by another from the control of such individual's legal custodian without such custodian's consent; or
> (B) the circumstances of the case strongly indicate that such individual is likely to be abused or sexually exploited. . . .[35]

Subsection A in the above definition was general enough to encompass both stranger and parental abductions. But subsection B is curious, and appears to have created more, rather than less, confusion as to how many of the one million children who run away each year would be considered missing and what circumstances would qualify a case as involving abuse or sexual exploitation. Would a sixteen-year-old boy who had run away five previous times (and come back unharmed each time) be considered a missing child under this definition if he ran away again?

The overall intent of the law was to coordinate federal, state, and local activities, and specifically to "make such arrangements as may be necessary and appropriate to facilitate effective coordination among all federally funded programs relating to missing children (including the preparation of an annual comprehensive plan for facilitating such coordination)."[36]

The new law had a wide variety of provisions; its more important and novel provisions—mandating research projects, establishing the National Center for Missing and Exploited Children, and establishing the United States Attorney General's Advisory Board on Missing Children—are described below.

Research and Programs. The act authorized the administrator of the Office of Juvenile Justice and Delinquency Prevention (OJJDP) to "make grants and enter into contracts with public agencies or nonprofit private organizations . . . for research, demonstration projects, or services programs" regarding all aspects of the missing children problem.[37] Not surprisingly, several of the research projects dealt directly with the issues debated during the congressional hearings. For example, among the first of the research projects undertaken pursuant to this legislation was the National Incidence Studies of Missing, Abducted, Runaway, and Thrownaway Children (NISMART), discussed in detail in chapter 2.

Due to the criticisms levied by John Walsh, Senator Hawkins, and other spokespersons against law enforcement's handling of missing children cases, a study began under the auspices of OJJDP to examine this issue in great detail. In 1986, a research project entitled National Study of Law Enforcement Policies and Practices Regarding Missing Children and Homeless Youth was undertaken jointly by the URSA Institute of San Francisco and Research Triangle Institute of North Carolina. Some of the findings of this study will be provided in subsequent chapters.

Other OJJDP-sponsored research examined the effects (particularly the psychological consequences) of abduction on the abducted children and their families, and how social services and other governmental agencies handle runaways. The problem of parental abduction, in particular, has continued to receive attention from federal lawmakers; in 1988 Congress specifically ordered OJJDP to undertake a study on "the obstacles that prevent or impede individuals who have legal custody of children from recovering such children from parents who have removed such children from such individuals in violation of law."[38] The results of this study are to be presented to Congress no later than 1991.

The Office of Juvenile Justice and Delinquency Prevention also had the authority to award grants or contracts to various organizations engaged in the prevention and recovery of missing children. In 1987, OJJDP awarded almost $600,000 to nine organizations that provided services to help locate missing children or to assist their families. The OJJDP also distributed $25,000 grants to several agencies; the recipients of these funds included New York City's Children in Crisis International, which operates the Missing in Manhattan Program; Phoenix's Hide and Seek Foundation, for its parental abduction program; Boston's Adam Walsh Resource Center, to teach children how to protect themselves from sexual abuse and kidnapping; the Tucson, Arizona, Family Crisis Service, for crisis intervention and family counseling; Identi-Find-A-Child in Albuquerque, for its Safety Smart Program; Michigan's Saginaw County Youth Protection Council, to expand its program to find one hundred missing local children; and Minneapolis's Missing Children Minnesota, for a clearinghouse to locate missing children.

National Center for Missing and Exploited Children. One of the most well-known programs created by the 1984 Missing Children's Assistance Act has been the National Center for Missing and Exploited Children. The National Center has several missions to fulfill. first, it functions as a centralized communication system for information on missing children. As mandated by the act, the Center operates a "national 24-hour toll-free telephone line by which individuals may report information regarding the location of any missing child. . . ."[39] But the communications system of the National Center handles more than reports. Operators accept sightings of missing children, and have direct conversations with runaways in need of help. National Center staff help reunite missing children with their families and give runaways the names and locations of shelters or other safe places to stay. Police officers from throughout the country call in to the National Center to provide information about cases, or to request assistance in a case. Any leads or sightings are forwarded to the appropriate local law enforcement agency, or to the FBI if that agency has been called in.

Next, the National Center provides technical assistance to a wide variety of agencies or organizations. Specifically, it offers technical assistance to local law enforcement agencies concerning the investigation of missing children cases. It advises local detectives about how to follow leads, how to use federal resources, and specific investigative techniques. The National Center operates a training program for law enforcement. Seminars and conferences are frequently given. National Center staff have organized at least four national conferences. In addition, the National Center offers training through local and regional courses. It also provides legal and technical assistance to individuals and agencies. For example, National Center personnel make the necessary contacts and obtain the legal documents required to search for children abducted by their parents and taken out of the country. On occassion, legal staff testify before Congress and take part in court cases involving missing children.

The National Center also publishes and distributes numerous manuals and brochures. These range in scope from the more technical training materials, such as the *Investigator's Guide to Missing Children* for local police detectives, to *Just in Case . . . You Need a Babysitter,* to educate parents about crime prevention measures. Center staff mail these publications to individuals and agencies on request.

Finally, the National Center must, by statute, ". . . coordinate public and private programs which locate, recover, or reunite missing children with their legal custodians."[40] Part of this coordination involves other federal agencies. For example, National Center staff work with the Office of Citizens Consular Services of the U.S. Department of State on international parental abduction cases, and with the U.S. Postal Service and the U.S. Customs Service regarding child pornography and the exploitation of children. The National Center's coordination activities include nonprofit organizations that help missing children or their families. The National Center's Nonprofit Organization Liaison Committee, for example, exchanges information with local community programs, as well as provides them with technical assistance.

Advisory Board on Missing Children. The 1984 Act also created the United States Attorney General's Advisory Board on Missing Children to formulate recommendations for future policymaking. The Advisory Board, chaired by Donna Owens, mayor of Toledo, Ohio, was composed of nine members, most of whom were professionals with backgrounds in law enforcement or medicine. Only one of the members was a parent of a missing child—Julie Patz, mother of Etan Patz.

After collecting data and holding hearings, the Advisory Board concluded its work in March 1986 with the submission of a report to Congress. The report was entitled *America's Missing & Exploited Children: Their Safety and Their Future.*

Conclusions

The awareness of the problem of missing children, christened as such by the media and dedicated lobbyists in the early 1980s, resulted in substantial political action. Some of the individuals urging legislative change were parents whose children had been kidnapped by strangers. But many of those testifying before Congress were concerned about runaways and the victims of parental abduction.

Although these three categories of missing children cases are legally, if not conceptually, distinct, spokespersons for each joined forces to lobby on behalf of missing children in general. Together, they proved to be a powerful lobby. Who could argue against wanting to prevent and recover missing children? The national cause of missing children became attractive to legislators who could join the bandwagon to help unfortunate kids at no cost to their political careers; in fact, for a few up-and-coming junior politicians, giving support to such a cause was a way to further their careers.

Two main pieces of legislation at the federal level resulted from the political campaign on missing children. The first, the Missing Children Act of 1982, was of minimal significance. The idea behind this law was to establish a national computer system for missing children. But such a system had already existed at the federal level since 1975.

The second law, the Missing Children's Assistance Act of 1984, is more difficult to evaluate. Some might argue that the law helped to expand our knowledge of the problem of missing children. No doubt it has. And it may have helped to reunite some children with their families. But it has had minimal impact on the numbers of children reported missing each year.

5

Kidnapping
A Parent's Worst Nightmare

KIDNAPPING extends back thousands of years in western civilization. For example, in ancient Babylonia about 2000 B.C., the Code of Hammurabi referred to the theft of persons for enslavement or for other purposes as being a capital offense. Kidnapping was also mentioned in ancient Hittite law and in the writings of Homer. According to these sources, the abduction of persons and taking them to another country as slaves was a common practice in ancient times.

The Bible also mentions kidnapping. In Exodus under a general section on the Law Concerning Violence, it states "He that shall steal a man, and sell him, being convicted of the guilt, shall be put to death" (Exod. 21:16). The "and sell him" exemplifies the notion of abduction for the purposes of slavery or enforced labor. A modern translation of that same biblical passage uses the word kidnap: "Whoever kidnaps a person . . . ."[1] Another passage in the Bible states, "If someone is caught kidnaping another Israelite, enslaving or selling the Israelite, then that kidnaper shall die" (Deut. 24:7). Indeed selling individuals or groups of persons into slavery is a theme in the history of kidnapping law—that is, until relatively recently. The victims of kidnapping in earlier times were rarely children; kidnapping typically involved the taking of adults, usually men.

History of Kidnapping

The contemporary American definition of kidnapping has roots in both Roman law and English common law. What follows is a brief history of kidnapping and the related offenses of abduction and false imprisonment.

Roman Law

Kidnapping in Roman law was called *plagium.* Although the etymology of the word is uncertain, it appears to come from the Latin *plaga,* meaning wound, injury, or misfortune. The Roman law of kidnapping dates back to about 200 B.C. with a codification called the Fabian Laws, and specifically the Fabian law of kidnappers (*lex Fabia de plagiariis*). Most scholars assume that the act of kidnapping existed well before 200 B.C. and the Fabian Laws, because it was customary among Romans to formalize legal provisions only after years of practical experience. The kidnapping provisions in Roman law underwent many revisions. One of the final versions appeared in the Justinian Code about A.D. 530. In between these two codes, a steady series of enactments against kidnapping emerged in Roman society.

The victims of kidnapping belonged to every category or social class. Historical records reveal cases involving the kidnapping of slaves, and of free persons (of small children, adults, both males and females), and of individuals as well as entire groups of persons. Formal organizations of kidnappers existed—Roman historians refer to "confederates" of kidnapping, and it appears that there were such criminal organizations in Rome. There is also evidence of an organization for the kidnappings of children. These abducted children, like adults, were usually slaves stolen from one master and sold to another.

Kidnapping appears to have been practiced for a variety of motives. In some cases, the act of kidnapping was done for revenge. In others—when slave girls were taken—it was "for the sake of lust." In still others, in fact in many of the documented cases, it was for profit. Although kidnapping for ransom was not uncommon, the majority of kidnap cases involved the taking of someone else's slave and selling the kidnapped person as a slave to another owner. The children of slaves were also kidnapped and sold into slavery. Kidnapping and selling a "free person" (including a child) into slavery occurred occasionally, but not nearly as commonly. In addition, it was a legal wrong for a person to talk a slave into running away from his master.

The Roman law of kidnapping was related to Roman social and family structure. The Roman family existed in a kind of hierarchy; the head of the family was the father, the so-called *paterfamilias.* Every one else in the family was subordinated to the father, but in different degrees. For example, wives were subjected to fewer controls than children, but basically the wife and child were considered the property of the husband. Roman society was also divided into free people and slaves. Naturally, slaves were considered the property of the *paterfamilias* as well.

Under early Roman law, the distinction between a crime (*crimen*) and a civil wrong (tort) was not clear for many forms of behavior. For example, a theft (*furtum*) was considered both a tort and a crime, depending on the circumstances. Kidnapping was either a crime or a tort, depending on the status of the person taken. Initially, the kidnapping of anyone other than the head of the household was handled as a civil matter, not as a crime. The act was considered to be a theft of property—that is the theft of the property of the *paterfamilias.* Kidnapping also constituted the civil wrong of undue appropriation of power—the power that the head of the household exercised over his wife, children, and slaves.

Only the kidnapping of the *paterfamilias* was deemed a true crime, on the theory that this was a truly free person, and the abduction and false imprisonment of a free person was considered a "rape of liberty." As Roman society developed, the status of wives and children—but not slaves—was elevated. In later Roman law, when wives or children were kidnapped, the act was considered a crime instead of a tort, on the theory that their abduction was a violation of *their* liberty rights.

Roman legal penalties for kidnapping also evolved over time. Criminal sanctions were originally relatively mild—normally a fine, although scholars have not been able to determine the precise amount of the fine. When kidnapping began to be viewed as a serious legal wrong—the violation of liberty rather than simple theft—the penalties also increased. Some form of physical punishment was provided for in later Roman law—either as a period of "working in the mines" or banishment and forfeiture of half the offender's property. The most serious cases were subject to the most onerous penalties—such as "exposition to the wild beasts" or crucifixion.

English Common Law

The early law of England—referred to as English common law—was the law beginning around A.D. 1000 that evolved through judicial decisions. These court decisions defined the various acts that came to constitute the law of crimes—for example, homicide, robbery, burglary, rape, and theft. These court decisions also developed the law on the crime of kidnapping. Kidnapping was a relatively rare crime in old England, and it had a special and narrow meaning that was consistent with the theme of enforced labor or slavery. Kidnapping originally meant the forcible abduction or stealing away of a man, woman, or child from his own country and sending him to another. Kidnapping according to early common law was a misdemeanor, not a felony.

The specific use of the term *kidnapping* emerged in English common law toward the end of the seventeenth century. Legal scholars trace the first cases found in the English courts to the early 1680s. The crime was specifically used at that time, pursuant to its narrow meaning, against the taking of another person out of the country. Piracy was a serious problem then—particularly pirates taking people for enforced labor to the American colonies. This practice died a sudden death in England as colonial independence approached the 1770s. Thereafter, the crime of kidnapping, as defined in English law, was rare indeed. Crimes that we consider to be kidnapping in today's meaning were prosecuted under other offenses, such as false imprisonment and abduction. It was not until 1937 that the English courts declared that removal from the country was not a necessary element of the crime of kidnapping in England. This was about one hundred years after the American courts came to the same conclusion.

The famous legal historian William Blackstone chronicled the development of the common law in his *Commentaries on the Law of England,* which he wrote between 1765 and 1769. According to

Blackstone, kidnapping was derived from the Old Testament, quoted previously, and also from the Roman crime of *plagium*. Blackstone stated, "This is unquestionably a very heinous crime, as it robs the king of his subjects, banishes a man from his country, and may in its consequences be productive of the most cruel and disagreeable hardships . . . ."[2] Blackstone also reported that the law of kidnapping in England was "principally intended against pirates."[3] Thus, much of the early law of kidnapping had to do with abducting individuals to work on a ship, for enslavement, or a taking to another country as a laborer. This relationship between kidnapping and piracy in English common law was found in the late Roman law: Julius Ceaser's abduction was considered an act of piracy rather than kidnapping.

The English common law definition of kidnapping was limited to the taking of persons out of the country, and it did not address the acts of detaining or abducting a person *within* the country. However, the common law also developed other crimes that covered these acts. The two crimes related to kidnapping—false imprisonment and abduction—concerned the takings or detention of persons within the borders of the country.

False imprisonment meant, generally, the unlawful restraint of a person's liberty. It was a common crime that applied originally to a governmental agent falsely imprisoning someone—often for political reasons. This meaning stems from as far back as 1215 with the signing of the Magna Carta by King John. In addition, false imprisonment meant the unlawful detention or restriction of one person's liberty and movement by any other citizen. Kidnapping was generally viewed as "the most aggravated form of false imprisonment"; it was an unlawful detention aggravated by carrying the imprisoned person to another country.

The crime of abduction meant the taking away of a woman or a child for some improper purpose. Abduction was not a common law crime. Rather it was made a crime through a parliamentary act passed in England a few years before Columbus discovered America. This act, which made abduction a felony, became the forerunner of all present abduction statutes. The early abduction statute was intended primarily to protect young heiresses from designing fortune hunters, although its wording was not so limited. The introduction to the law stated that an abducted woman was often "thereafter married to or defiled by the mis-doer."[4] Although sexual misdeeds were not made an element of the original crime of abduction, such behavior or motivation was included in American abduction statutes.

In old England, these two crimes—false imprisonment and abduction—were more likely to be used in those instances handled as kidnapping under today's law—detaining or restricting a person's liberty or stealing away a person for some immoral or improper purpose. As we shall see, when all of these crimes were imported to America, they evolved with changing social conditions. The legal meaning of kidnapping changed drastically; it became more inclusive and incorporated the elements of both false imprisonment and abduction.

Kidnapping in Literature

Kidnapping is an act that arouses deep emotions—not only in those people directly affected, but also in those who experience it vicariously and empathize with the victims. It is not surprising, then, that kidnapping has been used to arouse the emotions in various dramatic forms, from the opera to novels to short stories.

Adults are the victims in some of the literature (and other art forms) with a kidnapping theme. One example is Mozart's 1782 opera, *The Abduction from the Seraglio.* The opera, set in sixteenth century Turkey, tells the story of a Spanish nobleman, Belmonte, who comes to rescue his betrothed, Constanze. Constanze had been captured by pirates and held captive. In Voltaire's *Candide* (1759), the protagonist is forcibly abducted, placed in irons, and taken to the King's army regiment; there he is put through endless drills and nearly beaten to death. Victoria Holt, the prolific and popular novelist, published a romantic-suspense novel, *The Captive,* in 1989 with a kidnapping theme. The story revolves around a woman who finds herself shipwrecked on the African coast. She is saved from the raging seas by the ship's "handsome, mysterious deckhand." But then they are both abducted by pirates and she is sold to a Turkish Pasha. The story shares some interesting parallels with the Mozart opera.

Although historically children have been less likely to be kidnapped than adults, a disproportionate amount of the literature portrays children as the victims of kidnapping. *Oliver Twist,* Charles Dickens' 1837 novel, relates the story of an orphan boy, Oliver, who faces constant maltreatment as a child—first in a workhouse and then by Sowerberry, an undertaker to whom Oliver had been apprenticed. Oliver runs away to London and falls in with Fagin, a master criminal, who teaches Oliver the tricks of the trade. In one episode, Oliver is framed on a pickpocketing caper. His innocence is soon discovered, and he is taken home by the crime victim, Mr. Brownlow. Fagin is unhappy that Oliver is free; he knows too much about the exploits of Fagin's gang. Two of Fagin's associates then kidnap Oliver and Fagin holds him captive. Eventually, Oliver frees himself, is adopted by Mr. Brownlow, and with his new father, settles down into a new life in a peaceful village.

One of the classics of English literature is *Kidnapped* by the Scottish author Robert Louis Stevenson. *Kidnapped,* published in 1886, is set in Scotland in 1751 when highland clans were banding together to battle the English and put Bonnie Prince Charlie, the Scottish prince, on the British throne. In this setting, a sixteen-year-old boy named David Balfour leaves home looking for adventure. But the real world is filled with danger; he can't trust anyone, even his relatives. David runs into his sea-going uncle, Ebenezer, and although David thinks his uncle will help him, Ebenezer aids in the boy's abduction and sells him into slavery aboard a ship. David's words could just as well have been spoken today:

> With the clear perception of my plight, there fell upon me the blackness of despair, a horror of remorse of my own folly, and a passion of anger at my uncle, that once more bereft me of my senses.[5]

Luckily, David is befriended by Alan Breck Stewart, a rebel supporter of the Scottish prince. Alan helps David escape his captors, and the two travel across the Scottish moors to freedom.

The kidnapping/piracy theme is found in Richard Hughes's *High Wind in Jamaica,* published in 1929. Five children of an English family, the Bas-Thorntons, live in Jamaica, and they have two friends who are well-to-do Creoles, the Fernandez children. After an earthquake and hurricane hit the island, the children begin a journey to England on a ship. But the ship is captured by pirates and the children are kidnapped. The children in *High*

Wind in Jamaica free themselves and capture their abductors. In the end, the pirates are tried and executed in England. This story was made into a feature film in 1965 that starred Anthony Quinn. *Kidnapped* and *High Wind in Jamaica* are also of interest because piracy and abduction outside of the country most closely follow the original definition of kidnapping.

Interestingly, one of the most famous examples of kidnapping in literature is O. Henry's short story, *The Ransom of Red Chief.* Two small-time swindlers are traveling through the flatlands of Alabama near the town of Summit. The crooks have $600 between them, but they need $2,000 to pull off their next swindle in Illinois. They decide that the easiest way to pick up some quick money is to kidnap a child and ask for ransom. They hatch a plan to snatch the only child of Ebenezer Dorset, a prominent citizen in Summit. The two crooks abduct the freckle-faced boy of ten from in front of his house and take him to a cave two miles out of town. But the boy doesn't mind his captivity. In fact, he loves to play "Indian" and calls himself Red Chief, although his name is Johnny. The boy has such a good time playing Indian that he doesn't want to go home. He tells his captors that he hates school and his home town is too boring—he is having more fun as a "victim."

From the beginning of the abduction, the boy makes the lives of both crooks miserable. He keeps them up all night; then he tries to scalp one of the kidnappers with the knife used to cut the bacon. After that episode, the kidnappers are afraid to fall asleep at night and take turns guarding the boy. A few days after abducting the boy, one of the kidnappers goes into town to see if the kidnapping and ransom note have had their intended effect. The kidnapper expects to see search parties frantically looking for the boy. What he finds is a town at peace. The citizens are happy the boy is gone. Originally, the kidnappers had sent a ransom note to the boy's parents asking for $1,500. In response, instead of money, they receive a note from the father saying that if the kidnappers bring Johnny back and *pay* the parents $250, the parents would take him off of their hands! Anxious to get rid of the boy—who turns out to be a pain in the neck instead of a way to easy money—the kidnappers oblige and leave town.

Numerous examples of child kidnapping stories have more

recently emerged, mainly in the mystery genre. The 1959 novel by American mystery writer Ed McBain (Evan Hunter), *King's Ransom,* is a good example. McBain's book was the basis of a famous 1963 Japanese movie, *High and Low,* directed by Akria Kurosawa and starring Toshiro Mifune. The story focuses on an incident in the life of an executive in a shoe company. He is having financial trouble with his board of directors and is planning a coup, whereby he will gain control of the stock and the company. He mortgages his home and belongings to get enough money to make the initial payment. He then receives word that his small son has been kidnapped and the ransom for his return is about the same amount the father had just raised for his business deal. Faced with the dilemma of ruining his professional career or rescuing his son, the father quickly realizes his son's return is the more important of the two. However, before the father delivers the ransom money, his son returns home. A mistake was made—the kidnapper had taken the boy's playmate, who is the son of the father's chauffeur. Now the industrialist faced a new dilemma: is the chauffeur's son worth as much as his own son? He wrestles with this moral issue and finally resolves to pay the ransom for the return of his chauffeur's son. But the industrialist is spared the sacrifice—the police catch the kidnapper and the boy is safely returned.

While some of the stories of kidnapped children are largely written for the adult reader, the theme of kidnapping is popular in literature for children as well. Margery Sharp, for example, published *The Rescuers* in 1959. In this story, which was later adapted for the Disney animated movie of the same name in 1977, Miss Bianca, Bernard, and Nils, three mice, go on an adventure to rescue a Norwegian poet from the Dungeon of the Black Castle. (This is clearly a case of false imprisonment.) In the Disney studio's twenty-ninth animated movie, *The Rescuers Down Under,* Bianca and Bernard return in 1990, on a mission for the Rescue Aid Society to travel to "the land down under." There, they must save a boy named Cody who has been kidnapped by an evil poacher. The book version of this movie was released in 1990.

The kidnapping theme is also found in books for the pre-teen book market. James Duffy published *Missing* in 1988. The story is about a fifth grader, Kate Prescott, who fails to come home from school one afternoon. Because she has run away from home twice before and returned safely each time, nobody, including the police, thinks she is in danger. But her sister, Sandy, does. Sandy and a retired police officer put together clues on Kate's disappearance and eventually learn that Kate has in fact been kidnapped.

These literary examples suggest that society's fascination with the perpetrators and victims of kidnapping has a long history. Kidnapping is an emotional topic. It touches basic anxieties we all have about losing loved ones to unknown or unseen evils. For parents in particular, kidnappings of children evoke anxieties about being able to protect those who are dependent and vulnerable from harm and suffering. In modern culture, which values rationalism, individualism, and scientific explanations of phenomena, kidnapping may bring to the fore the fact that these values do not equip us to deal with—and may even lead to heightened levels of—fear about the harms that befall us that we do not "deserve," we cannot foresee, and we cannot control. This fear is reflected in the way contemporary popular literature deals with the theme of kidnapping. It is painted as a terrifying experience, often with a tragic and brutal ending. Kidnapping in classical literature, on the other hand, tends to be romanticized—as an adventure or a mystery.

The Transformation of the Common Law in America

The English law of crimes, imported to the new world with the colonists, included kidnapping, false imprisonment, and abduction. The states followed the narrow common law definition of kidnapping until the early 1800s. For example, an early Illinois statute defined kidnapping as "the forcible abduction or stealing away of a man, woman or child from his or her own country, and sending or taking him or her to another."[6] An early New York statute held that kidnapping included procuring the intoxication of a sailor as a means of getting him aboard a ship without his consent and then taking him to the ship in that condition. This "Shanghaiing" implied a kidnapping for enforced labor or slavery—and particularly taking a person outside the country. And an early Maine statute defined kidnapping as the transportation of the victim "out of this state . . . to parts beyond the sea."[7] The Maine Supreme Court ruled in one case that to constitute kidnapping, the carrying or transporting must be to a foreign port, not merely to another state. Also consistent with common law, kidnapping was a misdemeanor in colonial times, and it remained a misdemeanor for a century or more in some states after the American revolution.

In the mid- and late 1800s, state courts expanded the scope of the crime of kidnapping to include the taking of a person against his or her will from one state to another. In the 1837 case of *State v. Rollins,* the Supreme Court of New Hampshire was the first court to hold that a kidnapping did not require the taking of the victim out of the country. In a 1907 North Carolina case, a man was charged with and convicted of kidnapping a boy after he took the boy to another state. The defendant appealed the conviction, contending that he should not have been convicted of kidnapping, because kidnapping was then defined by North Carolina law as taking the victim out of the country. The North Carolina Supreme Court disagreed with this logic and held that a more reasonable definition would include the taking of a victim out of the state, but not necessarily out of the country.

With the change in its legal definition to include a greater variety of circumstances, kidnapping became more common at the beginning of this century. With the advent of the automobile and a modern transportation system, criminals could kidnap and move their victims swiftly and thereby avoid detection. The importance of the automobile became clear in the late 1920s and early 1930s, when the United States witnessed a wave of adult kidnappings associated with the rise of organized crime and racketeering. At that time, Al Capone and other notorious members of the underworld made huge profits through the illicit trafficking of liquor; they maintained their empire and enforced their demands through extortion, and backed up their threats with the kidnapping and shooting of those people who did not cooperate.

Gradually, the definition of kidnapping came to require less and less movement—or "asportation"—of the victim. The definition of kidnapping expanded to any asportation outside the county limits. It was then extended to any movement of the victim *vithin* the county. Eventually, as we shall see, some states now require no movement of the victim to constitute a kidnapping. Some jurisdictions recognize what has been termed *standstill kidnapping*—no movement of the victim occurs but the victim's liberty is restrained.

The biggest change in the laws on kidnapping occurred after the 1932 Lindbergh kidnapping. (This case also had a major effect on federal law.) As one authority stated, "The much publicized kidnapping for ransom of the Charles Lindbergh baby and other kidnappings during the 1930s led many states to expand the definition of kidnapping to include kidnap for ransom and to provide heavier penalties, including capital punishment in some circumstances."[8] Thus, many states after the 1930s retained their original "simple kidnapping" statutes, which included asportation or confinement within the state, and enacted new statutes for "aggravated kidnapping" to include kidnap for ransom.

One interesting sidelight of early American law and its evolution from English common law concerns the development of the legal rule that permits offenders to be tried for murder if they commit a felony—such as rape, robbery, burglary—that results in the death of the victim. The "felony murder rule" holds that if a death is the direct result of another felony, the person who committed the felony could be found guilty of first degree murder, even if he did not actually commit the killing. Under this approach, the prosecution need not prove that the defendant intended to kill the victim—a requirement the state otherwise has to meet in murder prosecutions; rather, the prosecutor need only prove that the defendant committed some felony and this act led to the victim's death.

Interestingly, kidnapping maintained the status of a misdemeanor in the American legal system long after the revolution. For example, the New Jersey statutes listed kidnapping as a misdemeanor as late as the 1930s when the Lindbergh baby was kidnapped and eventually found dead. The authorities did not catch the man they believed to have committed the kidnapping, Bruno Hauptman, until a few years later. The evidence against Hauptman on the Lindbergh baby's abduction seemed fairly compelling, but the evidence that he had actually killed baby Charles was less clear. Although Hauptman would have readily been found guilty of kidnapping, the punishment for this crime was relatively minor: a year or less in jail. Because of the tragic proportions of the Lindbergh case and the harm and suffering brought to the victim and the family, the prosecutor wanted Hauptman to be found guilty of an offense that carried a more severe penalty. So the prosecution built the case for Hauptman's conviction and execution around the felony murder rule.

The felony that the prosecution wanted to get Hauptman on was burglary. At common law, burglary was breaking and entering of a residence at night with the intent to commit a felony therein. Hauptman had entered into the Lindbergh residence at night with the intent to commit a crime. Unfortunately for the prosecution, the crime Hauptman intended to commit—kidnapping—was only a misdemeanor, not a felony, at the time, so the felony murder rule would not apply. To pursue the case under the felony murder rule, the prosecutor then had to establish Hauptman had committed some other crime during the burglary that was a felony. He therefore contended that Hauptman had actually intended to steal the clothing the baby was wearing when he broke into the house—and this theft of the clothing was a felony! The jurors bought the prosecutor's theory, found Hauptman guilty of homicide under the felony murder rule, and he was sentenced to death.

Kidnapping, Abduction, and Children

Many states also began to include in their kidnapping statutes those acts that were formerly covered under the crime of abduction—specifically those offenses related to the abduction of children. The early abduction statutes were designed to protect females from being victims of immoral or exploitative behavior—specifically to shield them from being forced into marriage, prostitution, illicit sexual intercourse, concubinage, or other acts that would cause their "defilement." Some of the abduction statutes prohibited the unlawful taking or detaining of any woman, but other statutes limited the crime to unmarried females, or to an unmarried female under some specified age. A few statutes permitted prosecution for abduction only if the victim was a "chaste" female.

Abduction was a crime that was charged by the prosecution up through the 1930s in cases involving the taking of persons for sexual exploitation. Around the turn of the century, the abduction of young women or older teenage girls for purposes of prostitution became a growing social problem. By the 1910s, young women could be caught in what was then termed *white slavery*. This crime entailed the abduction of young women or teenage girls—usually immigrants or naive country girls who had just arrived in the big city—and their introduction into prostitution. Investigations of this crime industry, which had begun in the 1890s, eventually resulted in several startling reports, such as the *Vice Trust* report by the New York district attorney. One of these reports, the *Rockefeller White Slavery* report claimed that fifty thousand girls disappear yearly as victims of organized crime. The fifty thousand figure will not go away!

These revelations caused a sensation in their day, because sex was rarely explicitly referred to in the media. The allegations immediately inspired lurid headlines in the newspapers, and became the basis for plots of novels and several Broadway plays, such as "The House of Bondage," "The Lure," and "Damaged Goods." White slavery also became the subject of one of the first feature films, *Traffic of Souls,* released in 1913. The story centers on a wealthy young society woman who is duped into prostitution by con men posing as members of the International Purity and Reform League. The woman's sister along with her police officer boyfriend work together to find the woman and bring the crooks to justice.

Many later abduction statutes expanded the laws on abduction to encompass any child victim, male or female. Without the gender-restriction, the distinction between the traditional scope of the crime of abduction and the crime of kidnapping was blurred. Morever, to the extent kidnapping statutes have incorporated the unlawful takings of adults and children of both sexes, the abduction statutes have generally fallen into disuse.

Although kidnapping and abduction are separate crimes in most states under current law, they are not mutually exclusive. The penal codes in some states, in fact, use the words *abduct* or *abduction* to set forth the meaning of kidnapping. It appears that the difference between the two crimes—to the extent there are any differences—is the person considered to be the victim of the crime. Generally speaking, abduction is considered an unlawful interference with a family relationship. Thus, the parents of the abducted person are the victims of abduction. Kidnapping, by contrast, is considered a violation of personal liberty. The person taken is thus the victim no matter what his or her age.

Modern State Statutes

Every state in the country now has a kidnapping statute of some sort. Most states divide the crime into simple kidnapping and aggravated kidnapping (or first and second degree kidnapping). Generally speaking, simple kidnapping is the seizure and transportation or detention of a person, without any other harm done. Aggravated kidnapping is the taking of a person for the purpose of ransom, robbery, or reward, or when injury is done to the victim.

One typical example of a kidnapping statute is found in the Connecticut Codes:

> (a) A person is guilty of kidnapping in the first degree when he abducts another person and when: (1) His intent is to compel a third person to pay or deliver money or property as ransom, or to engage in other particular conduct or to refrain from engaging in particular conduct; or (2) he restrains the person abducted with intent to (A) inflict physical injury upon him or violate or abuse him sexually; or (B) accomplish or advance the commission of a felony; or (C) terrorize him or a third person; or (D) interfere with the performance of a government function.[9]

Under Connecticut law, "A person is guilty of kidnapping in the second degree when he abducts another person."[10]

Other states specifically mention children in their kidnapping laws. One example is the Idaho statute, which defines kidnapping as:

> Every person who willfully:
>
> 1. Seizes, confines, inveigles or kidnaps another, with intent to cause him, without authority of law, to be secretly confined

or imprisoned within this state, or to be sent out of this state, or in any way held to service or kept or detained against his will; or,

2. Leads, takes, entices away or detains a child under the age of sixteen (16) years, with intent to keep or conceal it from its custodial parent, guardian, or other person having lawful care or control thereof, or with intent to steal any article upon the person of the child; or,
3. Abducts, entices or by force or fraud unlawfully takes or carries away another at or from a place without the state, or procures, advises, aids or abets such an abduction, enticing, taking or carrying away, and afterwards sends, brings, has or keeps such person, or causes him to be kept or secreted within this state; or
4. Seizes, confines, inveigles, leads, takes, entices away or kidnaps another against his will to extort money, property or any other thing of value or obtain money, property or reward or any other thing of value for the return or disposition of such person is guilty of kidnapping.[11]

Both of these statutes, which are typical of most in the United States, encompass a wide range of behaviors. Courts have had to interpret their applicability under a variety of factual circumstances, and have developed rules to resolve such legal issues as the amount of movement of the victim, the consent of the victim, multiple crimes, and bodily harm to the victim.

Elements of the Crime

The modern crime of kidnapping is extremely broad and often confusing, and has departed from its legal origins in many ways.

As a basic element of the crime of kidnapping, most state statutes require some sort of taking of a victim—such as a seizure or confinement. This terminology implies the perpetrator has some form of physical control over the victim; it also suggests a greater interference with the person's liberty than a simple assault. But the extent of the interference required in order to constitute a kidnapping is not always apparent. One clear circumstance of kidnapping is when an individual has been seized by force.

As noted earlier, beginning in the early 1900s, the circumstances encompassed by kidnapping statutes were greatly expanded. Calfornia is but one of many states that revised its kidnapping laws. The taking of a person by force was eliminated from the definition of the offense. However, the language of the 1933 amendment to California's kidnapping statute included various other methods by which a person might be placed under the control of another: "Every person who seizes, confines, inveigles, entices, decoys, abducts, conceals, kidnaps, or carries away any individual by any means whatsoever. . . ."[12] However, some of the terminology used in the statute, such as *inveigle*, was given no clear or precise meaning.

The traditional meaning of kidnapping implied an element of secrecy—the whereabouts of the victim was unknown. Consistent with this notion, some statutes, like Idaho's described previously, also listed the element of secretly detaining the victim in the definition of the crime. But this definition was inadequate for a hostage situation, in which the authorities know exactly where the victim is. To encompass this situation, most states eliminated the secrecy requirement to permit a charge of kidnapping when the crime involves the taking or the possession of hostages.

Kidnapping statutes also contained a word or phrase dealing with the fradulent or forcible restraint of a person with the intent to demand some concession or other valuable thing—such as a ransom—for the victim's release. In practice, many courts broadly interpreted this notion, and extended it beyond the traditional notions of monetary ransom. For example, in a Connecticut case, the defendant kidnapped a six-year-old girl for sexual gratification. This purpose was considered a demand for a concession from the victim, and so it was treated as falling within the meaning of the law. The court stated, "Restraint for sexual gratification has been considered within the purview of kidnapping statutes."[13]

Force, Consent, and Children

In general, there can be no kidnapping if the person taken freely consents to the taking, provided that he or she is capable of giving consent and there is no fraud. But under what circumstances should a victim's consent—particularly a child's—be nullified because it was obtained through trickery, immaturity, or ignorance?

In a few states, it is the consent of the parent, not the child, that is required. In Georgia, for example, it was considered kidnap even if the child gave consent, if the taking was against the will of the parent (or guardian). Under this approach, kidnapping has been viewed as a violation of the parents' custody rights—not as a violation of the liberty rights of the child.

Another approach taken by most states has been to view children as being incapable of giving a valid consent. (Likewise, the consent of an idiot is no defense to kidnapping.) A number of court cases in different jurisdictions have been decided according to this principle. One example is a 1972 Connecticut case in which the defendant lured a six-year-old girl into his car and sexually assaulted her. He claimed that he did not "force" her, that she consented, and that she had ample opportunity to escape, and therefore it could not be a kidnapping in the legal sense of the term. The state supreme court disagreed, stating, "We need not dwell further on this argument because, as a matter of law, the victim, a child of tender years, could not consent to being taken by the defendant."[14]

The age at which a child is considered old enough to give consent continues to be disputed by the courts. There are no hard and fast rules, and it depends on the jurisdiction and the circumstances of the case. Generally speaking, in most states a child under the age of ten years is regarded as being incapable of giving a valid consent. However, for older juveniles, the law has been less clear. There has been a trend to recognize consent as a defense to takings involving teenage victims. Leading the trend is a 1946 U.S. Supreme Court case.

This case involved the conviction of three members of a fundamentalist cult of the Mormon faith for kidnapping. The cult sanctioned plural or "celestial" marriages. In August 1940, the key defendant, who was then sixty-eight years old and a widower, hired a young housekeeper, who was nearly fifteen years of age (but had a mental age of seven) to work at his home in Santaquin, Utah. The girl's employment was approved by her parents.

The defendant taught the girl that celestial marriage was in conformity with the true principles of the original Mormon church. As a result of these teachings, the girl converted to the cult's beliefs and entered into a celestial marriage with the man on

December 19, 1940. The girl became pregnant soon thereafter, and the pregnancy was discovered by her parents on July 24, 1941. The parents informed the juvenile authorities of the state of Utah, and they took the girl into custody as a delinquent on August 4, 1941, making her a ward of the court.

On August 10, 1941, the girl, accompanied by a juvenile probation officer, went to a motion picture in Provo, Utah. The probation officer left the theater but instructed the girl to remain until he returned. On her own, the girl left the theater and walked around the streets of Provo. There, the girl met two married daughters of her celestial husband, and they gave her enough money to travel from Provo to Salt Lake City. In Salt Lake City, the girl went to the home of two other male members of the cult, and they, along with the girl's celestial husband, convinced her to obey "the law of God rather than the law of man . . . ."[15] They convinced the girl that she should go with the three men to Mexico to be legally married to her celestial husband, and then remain in hiding until she reached the age of majority under Utah law. Then they could return to the United States to live in Utah. The girl agreed to the plan.

On October 6, 1941, the three men drove the girl from Salt Lake City to Juarez, Mexico; there she went through a civil ceremony of marriage on October 14, 1941. She and her husband then settled in Short Creek, Arizona. The two lived in Arizona under assumed names until they were discovered by the federal authorities over two years later, on December 9, 1943. While in Short Creek, the girl gave birth to two children by her husband. The transportation of the girl to Mexico and then to Arizona was without the consent of her parents or the juvenile authorities in Utah.

Once apprehended, the three men were charged under the Federal Kidnapping Act. The act provided, in part, that it was unlawful to inveigle or decoy a victim across state lines to be "held for ransom or reward or otherwise."[16] The three men were tried in the United States District Court where they were found guilty. They then appealed the conviction all the way to the U.S. Supreme Court. In 1946, the Supreme Court overturned the convictions, holding that what the men had done did not fall within the prohibitions of the Federal Kidnapping Act. The rationale for the

Court's decision was largely based on its handling of the issue of the victim's consent.

> The act of holding a kidnaped person for a proscribed purpose necessarily implies an unlawful physical or mental restraint for an appreciable period against the person's will and with a willful intent so to confine the victim. . . . [However,] there is no competent or substantial proof that the girl was of such an age or mentality as necessarily to preclude her from understanding the doctrine of celestial marriage and from exercising her own free will, thereby making the will of her parents or the juvenile court authorities the important factor. At the time of the alleged inveiglement in August, 1941, she was fifteen years and eight months of age and the alleged holding occurred thereafter. There is no legal warrant for concluding that such age is ipso facto proof of mental incapacity in view of the general rule that incapacity is to be presumed only where a child is under the age of 14.[17]

More recent cases have followed the same principle. One 1983 case involved what the U.S. Court of Appeal called a "transcontinental copulation spree."[18] A seventeen-year-old female high school dropout was forced into a car one night in Tampa, Florida. The offender was supposed to abduct a specific girl named Carol for his boss. It became clear not long thereafter that the abductor had taken the wrong girl. Realizing his mistake, the abductor explained the situation to the girl and was willing to release her. But she, in essence, chose not to leave. They spent the night in the car, and the girl voluntarily engaged in sexual relations with the man. The following day, they drove to two other parts of Florida. During the course of their travels, the girl shared in driving the car.

The man and the girl eventually decided to go to California. At the stops en route, the two acted like a couple: they held hands on the beach, sat next to each other in eating establishments, and shared in the driving to reach their destination. All through their travels, the girl had many opportunities to leave or ask for help. She never did. Eventually the two made it to California, where the man was arrested. He was put on trial for violating the Federal Kidnapping Act—specifically for abducting a person across state lines for ransom, reward, or other purpose. The man was found guilty and appealed the conviction. The U.S. Court of Appeal reversed the conviction, on the grounds that the "victim" consented to the transportation to California.

> We cannot escape noticing that walking hand in hand in the presence of others, riding piggyback in a public place, declining to take advantage of any number of golden opportunities to ask for help or escape, including not a word in the presence of a policeman, as evidenced by her own testimony, simply cannot pass muster in the reasonable mind that an individual is being detained and transported against his or her will.[19]

Amount of Movement

As mentioned, the original meaning of kidnapping as a legal term required movement (asportation) out of the country after the seizure of the victim. Subsequent modifications of the movement requirement permitted movement within the county in which the seizure occurred. However, the amount of movement has been left largely unspecified. Generally the courts have held that any movement was sufficient to justify a kidnapping—for instance, a matter of feet, or from one room to another within the same residence. The famous California case of Caryl Chessman involved such circumstances. Chessman abducted a young woman and transported her a few feet to a car where he sexually assaulted her. He was prosecuted for several counts of robbery, rape, and kidnapping. Under California law at this time, the crime of kidnapping carried the death penalty. The defense objected to the charge of kidnapping in this instance, and argued that the facts could only support a conviction for robbery and rape. The California Supreme Court discounted the objection, declaring "It is not a matter of how much distance, it is the fact of the movement."[20]

Some states loosened the requirements of kidnapping to apply to situations that involved detention or confinement, without any movement. This has led to what some scholars have called a *standstill kidnapping*. In those jurisdictions that require no movement, there appears to be no difference between the crime of kidnapping and false imprisonment.

A recent example of kidnapping without movement involved teens as both the victim and perpetrator. (It also shows that teenagers can perpetrate kidnappings as well as be victims of the crime.) In September 1990, a seventeen-year-old boy from Cumming, Georgia, entered a local school armed with weapons. There, he held fifty-three students hostage. The armed teen did not compel the students to move in or away from the school. He released hostages throughout the day, until he only had nine left. At that point, the teen demanded a school bus and $3,000. Shortly after he made the demand, the youth became dizzy and surrendered to the police. No one was injured during the five-hour ordeal. However, the teen was charged with fifty-three counts of kidnapping, one for each of the fifty-three students he had held hostage. Authorities also filed nine counts of kidnapping for ransom against the teen because he demanded $3,000 when he had nine students left.

This case also illustrates one of the points made in chapter 2 about the relationship between kidnapping and missing children. There we noted a kidnapped child is not necessarily a missing child. The school hostage case is a classic example. If the crime statistics for this city were examined at the end of the year, they might have indicated that there were fifty-three incidents of kidnap—that is, fifty-three children kidnapped at the same time in a hostage situation. But none of the children would be considered missing. Everyone was in school right where they were supposed to be. This distinction between missing children and kidnapped children is illustrated again in our later discussion of kidnappings involving bodily harm.

In 1923, a famous legal scholar, Joel Bishop, stated, "The terms 'kidnapping' and 'false imprisonment' do not differ greatly in signification, yet they are not so far identical as to justify the treating the two offenses as one."[21] This no longer appears to be the case. With the extension of the definition of kidnapping to constitute the offender's mere control over the person's liberty or movement, there is not much difference between the two crimes. The crime of kidnapping is often charged by the prosecution as a means to tack on additional penalties, when really there is no separate incident.

Kidnapping and Other Crimes

An issue closely related to the movement of the victim pertains to the charging of kidnapping as a separate and distinct crime when the victim is moved during the commission of another crime—for example, robbery or sexual assault. The courts have had to decide whether it is simply a robbery if a victim is moved a few feet in the course of being robbed or whether movement of any amount gives rise to the crime of kidnapping as well.

Generally, the states have followed one of two legal theories to deal with this issue. The first legal theory—the incidental rule—holds, in essence, that confinement or removal that is merely incidental to the commission of another crime is insufficient to constitute a kidnapping. Thus, there is only the original crime—for example, robbery or sexual assault.

Conversely, the second legal doctrine—the any movement rule—states, in essence, that any movement is sufficient to establish the independent act of kidnapping. A 1983 case decided by the Florida Supreme Court illustrates this doctrine. The defendant first entered a business office and assaulted a female receptionist who was alone at the time. After dragging the woman from the front of the office to the rear, the offender raped her. The offender then fled to a nearby neighborhood and broke into a house. There he had a fight with another woman during which she was rendered almost unconscious. The offender carried this woman from her kitchen to the bedroom where he sexually assaulted her as well.

At his trial, the man was convicted of one count of first degree burglary, two counts of sexual assault, and two counts of kidnapping. He appealed the kidnapping convictions, contending that they did not constitute a separate offense and were merely "incidental" to the sexual assaults; that is, he moved the victims only a matter of a few feet in order to accomplish another crime (sexual assault), for which he was convicted. Both the Florida Third District Court of Appeal and the Florida Supreme Court upheld the separate convictions of kidnapping, saying that the movement, though slight, had significance independent of the sexual assaults.

Thus, the any movement rule has been yet another doctrine that has greatly expanded the meaning and usage of the kidnapping laws. As modern legal analysis shows, the acts committed in these cases are a far cry from the act of kidnapping contemplated at common law.[22]

Bodily Harm

Some state statutes have taken serious bodily injury to the victim into account in their kidnapping laws by creating different degrees of the crime—simple or aggravated kidnapping—or by imposing more severe penalties. What constitutes serious bodily injury has varied somewhat by state, but Montana's approach is typical. Specifically, the Montana Criminal Code states, in relevant part, that serious bodily injury is injury that "creates a substantial risk of death" or "which causes serious permanent disfigurement or protracted loss or impairment of the function or process of any bodily member or organ."[23] Montana state law provides for a harsher sentence for a conviction of kidnapping if the victim suffered serious bodily injury. Under the Montana kidnapping statutes, a person can be found guilty of aggravated kidnapping, and be subject to a sentence of up to one hundred years in prison, unless the defendant "has voluntarily released the victim alive, in a safe place not suffering from serious bodily injury."[24]

The 1984 *State v. Goodwin* case illustrates how the appellate court has interpreted Montana's definition of serious bodily injury. The offender, a middle-aged male, abducted and took a seven-year-old girl to a secluded place in the country. He took off her clothing and tied her to the seat of his truck with rope. He then assaulted her, physically and sexually, and threatened to kill her if she told anybody what happened. He then took the victim back to town and released her about five blocks from her home. She and her parents reported the crime to the police and then she had a physical examination. The examination revealed a severe laceration in the vaginal area. Surgery was needed to repair the laceration and prevent infection.

The prosecution charged Goodwin with sexual assault and aggravated kidnapping (as opposed to simple kidnapping). From the evidence, it was clear that the defendant committed the sexual assault and that he kidnapped the victim. The question was whether the kidnap was aggravated or simple. The defendant did release the victim alive, and in a safe place. If the injury was not serious bodily injury, he could be convicted only of simple kidnapping. If the injury was serious bodily injury, he could be convicted of aggravated kidnapping, which carried the longer prison term.

The jury heard all of the evidence, including testimony from medical doctors about the nature of the injury. The jury found the defendant guilty of the sexual assault and aggravated kidnapping. The defendant then appealed the conviction of aggravated kidnapping on the theory that the injury sustained by the victim did not constitute serious bodily injury because there was no substantial risk of death because there was no infection and there was no serious permanent disfigurement.

The Montana Supreme Court disagreed with the defendant's contentions and affirmed the conviction of aggravated kidnapping. The court held that there was a substantial risk of death because the laceration suffered by the victim was near the perineal membrane, so the abdominal cavity could have been exposed to bacteria normally present in the vaginal and rectal areas. And although there was no infection, the court held there was a substantial risk of death if the victim had not received appropriate medical treatment. With respect to the defendant's contention that there was no permanent disfigurement or protracted loss of function to the victim's bodily organs, the court disagreed. Even though a subsequent examination of the victim revealed no problems with the functioning of the urinary tract or rectum, the court found the girl had suffered permanent disfigurement in two senses: first, the injury resulted in a scar in the vaginal and perineal area, and second, a portion of the victim's hymen was ruptured.[25]

Like the earlier example of the student hostages, this case illustrates a distinction that needs to be made between kidnapped and missing children and serves as a reminder that children reported as missing are often not the victims of kidnap, and children who have been kidnapped are often not missing. In the *Goodwin* case, the victim was not missing in the normal sense of the term. She was kidnapped and assaulted, and brought home after a relatively short period. There was no search for her, no missing persons report was made. Such circumstances constituted the bulk of child kidnapping cases reported by the National Center for Missing and Exploited Children study cited in chapter 2, which found that the vast majority of kidnap victims were released almost immediately by their abductors. Thus, it would be erroneous to infer that the total number of child kidnapping cases was directly related to reports of missing children.

Federal Kidnapping Laws

There is a basic division of labor between the federal government and the states in the American legal system that has given rise to the development of a dual system of laws. Under this division, matters determined to be state issues are not subject to the oversight or resolution by the federal courts or Congress. For many years, kidnapping was regarded as a matter to be governed by state law only. Traditionally the crime of kidnapping was prohibited by state law; local and state authorities were responsible for investigating and prosecuting violations of the kidnapping statutes. As a result of this division of authority, there was relatively little involvement of the federal government in kidnapping cases in the early years of the country.

However, kidnapping was the subject of federal laws related to slavery. After the Civil War, Congress enacted a statute that made it a felony to bring into this country "any person inveigled or forcibly kidnapped in any other country" in order to hold that person here "in confinement or to any involuntary service."[26] This law, like early Hebrew, Roman, and English laws, related to enforced slavery or labor. In one interesting case, the federal courts found the federal kidnapping statute applied in the case of a boy who was brought to this country from Italy to become a street beggar or street musician for the profit of the person controlling him, in spite of the fact that the boy had consented to the arrangement.

Several notorious child kidnap cases occurred in the United States in the late 1800s and early 1900s. Among these was the case of Charles Brewster Ross, the four-year-old son of a well-known and respected citizen, who was kidnapped on July 1, 1874, from the Germantown suburb of Philadelphia. The parents received a total of twenty-three notes demanding a ransom of $20,000. The case became a cause célèbre, but the boy was never found. Another was the case of Edward Dudahy, son of a wealthy packer, who was kidnapped on December 18, 1900, in front of his Omaha home. The kidnapper threatened to blind the boy with acid unless the parents paid $25,000 in ransom. The boy was eventually freed. The case of Alexis Stockburger, an eleven-year-old student at the Cathedral Academy in Albany, New York, was more disturbing. The Stockburger child was kidnapped in May 1919 and never heard from again. The Marion Parker case had a particularly tragic ending. Marion was the twelve-year-old daughter of a rich Los Angeles banker. She was kidnapped on December 5, 1927. The kidnapper demanded $1,500 in ransom. The family put up the money but the girl was killed.

While the public was alarmed when these and other child kidnapping cases occurred, it was not until the Lindbergh tragedy in 1932 that this alarm was translated into demands for *federal* action to investigate or prosecute the crime of kidnapping.

The Lindbergh Law

By the end of the 1920s and beginning of the 1930s, crime was booming in the United States. As two authorities put it, "The millennium for criminals had arrived."[27] All types of racketeering—illegal liquor trade, highjacking, extortion, and gambling—were thriving. Kidnapping for ransom, or as it was then called, *the snatch racket,* was on the list.

According to reports from the chiefs of police of 501 cities, 279 kidnappings took place in 1931. These included both adults and children, but the breakdown between the two was not known. One scholar at the time noted a weakness in the collection of crime data that still exists today: "The Uniform Crime Reports do not compile kidnappings."[28]

The problem with handling kidnap as a state crime was that the states by themselves could not cope with investigating or prosecuting offenders who crossed state lines. It was not that neighboring states were uncooperative. It was a matter of efficiency, or inefficiency. By the time local cooperation was secured in another state, the trail of the kidnapper was often cold, and the investigation hit roadblocks.

Just before the Lindbergh case, pressure on Congress had begun to mount to change federal law so that U.S. agents could become involved in those kidnapping cases in which the perpetrator took the victim across state lines. Such intervention by the federal government was permissible because the commerce clause of the federal constitution authorized the Congress to regulate matters of interstate commerce. Such regulation was presumed to encompass the interstate transportation of kidnap victims.

Curiously, citizens of St. Louis, Missouri, led the movement for a federal law against kidnapping. In the 1920s and early 1930s, St. Louis had numerous kidnappings (mainly of adults). It was a border city on the Illinois state line so kidnappers were often able to elude apprehension by Missouri law enforcement officials by crossing the state line. In 1931, members of the St. Louis Chamber of Commerce, the mayor, chief of police, and other officials organized a committee to lobby for passage of federal kidnapping legisation. The committee persuaded one of Missouri's senators, Republican Roscoe Patterson, and one of the state's representatives, Democrat Charles Cochran, to introduce such legislation into their respective houses in Congress in December 1931.

The bills probably would have died in committee because of lack of widespread support for the expansion of federal authority over the states if it had not been for the kidnapping of the Lindbergh baby on March 2, 1932. Stirred by the enormous media attention about this case, the public instantly demanded that Congress "do something." Action on the bills was delayed, however, because the baby was not found right away. Authorities feared that if a harsh new federal kidnapping law were passed while the Lindbergh baby was still held captive, the kidnappers would be more likely to kill him. While the Lindbergh family's misfortune became the catalyst for passage of a new federal kidnapping statute, it also constituted an impediment to Congressional actions. Some lawmakers were reluctant to enact legislation drafted in the heat of anger over the Lindbergh baby and the desire for vengeance because it was likely to call for draconian measures.

Once the baby was found dead, Congressional leaders resumed their efforts to draft a federal kidnapping statute. The Senate and House versions of the proposed legislation differed somewhat, and prompted considerable debate. Most of the debate concerned the extension of federal authority over the states. Many legislators wanted the new law, because it would assist local police and lead to more effective enforcement of state law. Other legislators were afraid of what they considered a usurpation of states' rights. They felt it would be dangerous to have the federal government extend its authority. They feared such legislation would open the door to federal encroachment in a variety of areas—specifically a federal takeover of local law enforcement prerogatives.

Related to this concern were questions about the actual mechanics of the law. Some legislators wanted to give the FBI the authority to enter the case and take whatever law enforcement procedures were necessary to recover the victim and catch the kidnapper. However, those legislators who worried about the usurpation of state authority wanted federal agents to deputize local officers as federal officers during the course of the investigation. These deputized local officers would then have special powers to cross state lines to carry out their investigation.

Federal lawmakers also debated what penalty would be appropriate for the new federal offense. The House bill proposed the death penalty, but the Senate version chose life imprisonment as the maximum penalty. At first it appeared as if the differences between the two sides were too great for the passage of the law. Even the attorney general at the time was opposed to the new law on two grounds: the increased expense that would be associated with federal enforcement, and state resentment toward the federal government.

But because members of Congress continued to feel pressure from their constituents to enact some form of a federal kidnapping law, they drafted a compromise bill that was passed in both houses. In June 1932, President Hoover signed the bill, known as the Lindbergh law, and federal jurisdiction over interstate kidnapping became the law of the land. Conviction under the new statute carried a sentence of life imprisonment.

Soon after the new law went into effect, problems with its enforcement began to emerge. One problem with the original law, as written, was that it made parental abduction subject to federal law. This was objectionable to many legislators, particularly because few states at that time considered parental abduction a crime. It was felt that the federal kidnapping law should not cover such domestic matters, and that the force of the federal government should not be involved in family cases—that it was never the intent of the original legislation to apply to such cases.

A second problem pertained to the sentence. In the original bill, the House version provided for the death penalty, which was dropped in the final bill as a concession to those advocating a lesser penalty. By 1934, the death penalty was once again being pushed.

The third issue related to the problem of acquiring information about the kidnapper's whereabouts and when the movement of the victim across state lines occurred. The Lindbergh bill only regulated the *interstate transportation* of a kidnap victim. Thus, if the kidnapper kept the victim within the state, it would not be a federal crime, only a state one. The problem was that if the victim of a kidnapping disappeared, it was often impossible for state law enforcement authorities to know if the kidnapper crossed a state line, and if federal agents had the authority to provide assistance. Unless the kidnapper sent a ransom letter from a different state or was spotted in a different state, the FBI would never know when to enter the case.

In 1934, Congress passed three amendments to the Lindbergh law to address these problems. Federal lawmakers specifically excluded the prosecution of parents for the abduction of their own children. This exclusion has remained in effect to the present time. After extensive debate on the death penalty, members of Congress agreed to permit it, but only in some cases. The compromise they reached was to consider the death penalty as a vehicle to help save the lives of victims. The new amendment prohibited the death penalty if the victim was released unharmed, but authorized the death penalty if the victim was harmed. This strategy was seen as an inducement to kidnappers to return their victims safely instead of killing them, lest they should testify. And finally, to help state authorities determine when the interstate travel occurred, Congress created a presumption that the kidnapper transported the victim across state lines after a certain period of time had lapsed after the initial taking. Having decided to take this approach, members of Congress still had to decide how long the FBI should wait before the presumption that the kidnapper had crossed the state line could take effect. They eventually agreed to set the cut-off at seven days. This seven-day presumptive period was subsequently shortened to twenty-four hours.

When these amendments were finalized and passed in the House of Representatives, they met little opposition in the Senate. President Roosevelt signed them into law on May 18, 1934.

Current Federal Law

Since 1934, the Federal Kidnapping Law has been modified several times. Most of the more recent modifications relate to the kidnapping of political figures or hostage situations.

The current federal kidnapping law reads in relevant part:

> (a) Whoever unlawfully seizes, confines, inveigles, decoys, kidnaps, abducts, or carries away and holds for ransom or reward or otherwise any person, except in the case of a minor by the parent thereof, when—
>
> (1) the person is willfully transported in interstate or foreign commerce;
>
> (2) any such act against the person is done within the special maritime and territorial jurisdiction of the United States;
>
> (3) any such act against the person is done within the special aircraft jurisdiction of the United States . . . ;
>
> (4) the person is a foreign official, an internationally protected person, or an official guest as those terms are defined in section 1116(b) of this title; or
>
> (5) the person is among those officers and employees designated in section 1114 of this title and any such act against the person is done while the person is engaged in, or on account of, the performance of official duties,
>
> shall be punished by imprisonment for any term of years or for life.
>
> (b) The failure to release the victim within twenty-four hours after he shall have been unlawfully seized, confined, inveigled, decoyed, kidnaped, abducted, or carried away shall create a rebuttable presumption that such person has been transported in interstate or foreign commerce.[29]

Conclusion

The crime of kidnapping was initially treated in English and early American law as a crime with quite specific and limited application: the transportation of an individual out of the country for purposes of enslavement or ransom. In large part that was because other crimes—false imprisonment and abduction—dealt with the illegal movement of individuals or the restraint of their freedom under other circumstances. Initially, these three crimes were relatively distinct. Now the legal definition of kidnapping has expanded to encompass unlawful acts that were previously defined as other crimes, or had no criminal status.

Historically, as well as according to modern crime reports, most kidnapping cases concerned the unlawful taking of adults. For example, most of the cases involving the crossing of state lines during the 1920s and 1930s had adult victims. Yet, sensationalism about and widespread attention to the few cases involving children led to significant changes in the legal definition of kidnapping. It was the Lindbergh baby kidnapping that aroused public indignation and brought pressure on Congress to make the most significant change in federal kidnapping law in American history.

With the perceived rash of child kidnappings in the 1980s, there have been further changes in federal and state law, mainly state law. While these changes have not modified the substance of the law, they have increased the penalties. Kidnappers who take children as their victims now face much harsher sentences.

Finally, kidnapping as a theme in literature has brought greater social consciousness to the crime. This literature—along with the popular media, such as TV, movies, magazines, and newspapers—has helped to heighten society's fear of children being taken as victims of kidnapping. This perception exists despite the fact that adults, rather than minors, are more likely to be the victims of this crime, and small children, in particular, are rarely kidnapped and harmed.

6

Parental Abduction
Keeping It in the Family

IN the last chapter we saw that although the kidnapping of children by strangers is a very serious, sometimes deadly, crime, it is an uncommon event. Much more common, and often traumatic, is the abduction of children by their own parents. The numbers of children who are victims of parental abduction are just beginning to be documented. The most comprehensive study to date—the National Incidence Studies of Missing, Abducted, Runaway, and Thrownaway Children—estimates there were as many as 354,100 children in 1988 taken or detained by their parents in violation of a custody agreement or court order; nearly half of these cases involved efforts to conceal the child and to permanently deprive the other parent access to him or her.[1] Experts testifying before Congress have estimated that twenty-five thousand to one hundred thousand children are abducted by their parents each year.[2] Researchers in California concluded that in 1986 in just that state, over three thousand children were abducted by their parents.[3]

These figures vary widely and suggest our knowledge of parental abduction continues to be limited. However, existing information about divorce and custody conflicts in this county gives us some estimates of the numbers of children at risk for child snatching. The risk has increased markedly in the last twenty years. In 1970, there were 708,000 divorces in this country involving 615,960 children. By 1983, those figures had increased to 1,158,000 divorces involving 1,091,000 children. More recent statistics show divorce and custody conflicts in the 1980s and

1990s are on the upswing. According to a 1986 U.S. Department of Commerce report, nearly one in every two marriages currently ends in divorce; and more than 60 percent of these divorces include couples with minor children. In 1979, sociologists found between 8 and 17 percent of divorcing couples were involved in custody disputes; they projected that figure would rise to 33 percent by 1990.[4]

Custody Issues in Historical Context

The increasing numbers of children abducted by parents and the current societal attitudes toward parental abduction are unprecedented. As Representative John "Jimmy" Duncan (R-Tenn.) noted during Congressional hearings on the issue:

> . . . [T]aking a child across a state line in violation of a court custody decree has recently risen to high social visibility. It, like domestic violence, has been with us for many years, but because of changing social mores and regulations, has only recently come to national attention.[5]

The Father's Unquestioned Authority as Guardian

Until recently, the legal rules for determining custody rights have been gender based—either the father or the mother was presumed to possess the right of guardianship. Under the Roman Empire, the doctrine of *patriae potestas* gave the father absolute authority over his children, who in the eyes of the law were treated simply as his property or chattel. This absolute authority meant that fathers had the lawful right to sell their children into slavery or to have them put to death. However, beginning in the fourth century, some limits were placed on the father's ability to do what he wished with his children. In A.D. 315, Emperor Constantine outlawed infanticide, and in A.D. 321, the emperor prohibited fathers from selling their children as slaves. Emperor Justinian later ordered the parental rights of fathers be terminated if they left their children to die.

Under English common law, fathers also enjoyed near absolute rights over their children. Feudal law did not recognize wives or mothers as "legal persons." According to Blackstone's *Commentaries,* the role of a woman entitled her to "respect but not to authority."[6] Fathers were seen as the "natural" guardian of their children, and they controlled their educational and religious training. In turn, fathers also bore the responsibility for the care and support of their children. As late as 1836, the law permitted the father to exercise authority over a child as he would other property. This authority included the prerogative to terminate its life. Fathers had a right to the services of their children as well, and could sue another who "seduced" a daughter or "enticed" a son to leave home.

There were some exceptions to the rule of paternal custody, for example, where the father's "fitness" as a guardian was called into question. One notable case in English legal history was that of the poet Percy Bysshe Shelly. Shelly lost custody of his children after his wife committed suicide. Historians suggest that Shelly lost his paternal rights because the court disapproved of his religious beliefs and his "profligate conduct"—he had taken up with another woman while his wife had been pregnant with their second child. In another early English case concerning a father who brought an action to obtain custody of his daughter, the court held that generally a father had a natural right to his children. But because the father in this instance was bankrupt, had not contributed to the support of his children, and had engaged in "improper conduct," the court ruled that he lost his right to custody.

Legal scholars have referred to England as a "divorceless society" until the 1850s. Prior to that time, marital claims were handled by the ecclesiastic courts, the courts of the church. Custody disputes were rare because the court's rule on guardianship was clearly stated: fathers had a near absolute right to custody. However, Parliament began to enact legislation in the 1800s that weakened paternal authority and began to give a place in the law for the custody rights of mothers. The passage of Lord Talfourd's Act of 1839 brought about a drastic change in the English civil laws governing child custody. The act gave the English courts the authority to award custody of children under seven years of age to the mother. In 1873, the mother's right of custody was extended to encompass children up to the age of sixteen. This gender-based presumption of custody was removed from English law in 1886 when Parliament passed the Guardianship of Infants Act. Under this act, each parent had an equal right to be considered as the appropriate guardian of the children from the marriage.

The Importation of English Custody Law to America

The English common law of divorce and custody was imported to the American colonies, and the father's right to custody was presumed. Even as English statutory law changed to equalize the custody rights of mothers in the late 1800s, American courts continued to view the father as the natural guardian. Legal historians suggest that this presumption fit with the economic necessities of rural and agrarian America in the 1700s and 1800s. Fathers were entitled to the services of their children; the economics of apprenticing children out to craftsmen, tradespeople, and businesspeople, and the requirements of a family farm made children economically valuable to their fathers. In turn, fathers were responsible for providing for their children's care and education.

In the few cases in which mothers were awarded custody, they were not given an award for child support, because it was assumed the children would themselves produce an income. On some occasions, judges made the custody determination based on which parent was at fault for the divorce; whether mother or father, the "innocent" party was given custody of the children.

While feudal notions of children as paternal property continued to influence American custody law, new conceptions of the nature and status of children as well as parental responsiblities for child care emerged in the 1980s. One notion, voiced by none other than Thomas Jefferson, was that children were separate entities independent from their parents. He believed parents should have charge of their children insofar as they acted on their children's behalf and in their best interests. Another notion was the changing ideal of proper parental care; rearing children with love and nurturance was deemed more conducive to their proper development than giving them stern discipline and guidance. While fathers were traditionally looked to as the dispensers of discipline, mothers were considered to possess the "natural" capacity to be affectionate and nurturing.

During the 1800s, American courts occasionally departed from the paternal preference and justified their decisions based on one or both of these ideas. For example, a Rhode Island court decision in 1878 gave custody of a four-year-old daughter to the mother, even though the father was deemed to be a fit parent. The court had determined the child's welfare would be best served if she were within the mother's care. A Maryland case had a similar outcome. While the court acknowledged that the father was "the sole and legal guardian of all infant children," and "no court could take them from him and give them to his wife," it nonetheless went on to say it could not

> snatch helpless, puling infancy from the bosom of an affectionate mother and place it in the course hands of the father. The mother is the softest nurse of infancy and with her [the child] will be left in opposition to this general right of the father.[7]

The Shift toward Maternal Custody Rights

These court decisions granting custody of young children to mothers laid the foundation for two legal doctrines that became popular in the United States in the 1900s—the "tender years doctrine" and the related "doctrine of the child's best interest." The tender years doctrine gave preference for guardianship to the mother, based on the belief that a mother's love, affection, and care of a young child were essential to the welfare of the child. While the best interests doctrine appeared neutral, making both mother and father equally eligible for guardianship, the emerging social ideal of motherhood cast the mother in the position, by definition, of being better able than the father to attend to a child's needs.

By the early 1900s, courts had begun to award custody of children to mothers on a more regular basis. Historians suggest this shift in bias was due once again to economic and social changes. The industrial revolution changed the nature of work and brought about a sharp separation between the work world and the home. Men and fathers labored in factories and businesses away from the home, women and mothers remained at home to run the household and care for children. At the same time, child labor laws limited the economic usefulness of children and discouraged their employment outside the home or away from family-owned business. In addition, the advent of public education extended the period during which children were unavailable for work and instead remained dependents. Their free time outside of school hours was given to recreation; mothers were expected to supervise the leisure activities of their children.

In addition, by the turn of the century a new cadre of professionals—child welfare professionals and child psychologists— were influencing how society viewed children and parenting. Based on their training and research on child development, these new professionals encouraged judges, teachers, and parents to view children as vulnerable and malleable. In order to develop properly and to proceed through the various stages of physical and psychological maturation, children needed "tender loving care" from the earliest days of their infancy. Such care could be provided best by mothers, who were by the nature of their gender, presumed to be nurturers and caretakers. Furthermore, mothers were expected to remain in the home full-time, and were therefore available to provide supervision, care, and nurturance. Fathers were presumed to be working outside of the home so their time for child and home care was much more limited.

The Legal Status of Parental Abduction

In the United States, historically, conflicts over child custody and custodial rights were within the province of the civil courts; with the advent of specialized courts after the turn of the century, these conflicts came within the domain of family or domestic relations courts. Several states had criminal laws prohibiting child stealing, but these statutes were applied to the taking or detaining of a child by a stranger, or a person unrelated to the child. For example, a 1860 Pennsylvania law stated that a person was guilty of child stealing if he or she "maliciously, either by force or fraud, carried away any child with the intent to deprive its parent or parents, or with an intent to steal any article of apparel on the child."[8] The law specifically excepted the father of an illegitimate child or the father with a right to possession of the child from being prosecuted under this criminal statute. However, court records indicate that there were cases in which fathers had been tried and convicted of child stealing by the local criminal courts, only to have such convictions later overturned by the higher courts.

For example, in a 1889 child stealing case against a father, the local prosecutor argued that the child stealing statute was applicable to parents, and that an aim of the law "was the prevention of quarrels and breaches of the peace over possession of the children." The Pennsylvania Supreme Court disagreed and declared that, in the absence of any breach of the peace, "a father who takes and withholds his child from the wife and mother . . . does not thereby become a kidnapper." The court construed the child stealing statute to protect parental and other lawful custody of children against "the greed and malice of the kidnapper"; thus, the statute was not designed to "prohibit one parent from asserting a claim to the possession of his or her child against the will, and to the exclusion, of the other."[9]

Changing Family Structure and Gender Roles

The preference for awarding mothers custody and fathers visitation according to statute and judicial practice continued into the 1950s and 1960s. By the 1960s, some states began to amend their custody laws to give both parents equal eligibility for custody. Judges were expected to decide each case based on what was in the child's best interest, given the particular circumstances presented. However, most custody awards continued to be made to mothers. Custody awards were often accompanied by child support and alimony payments for which fathers were made liable. While before the turn of the century, children were seen as economic boons to the parent who was granted guardianship, by the 1900s children were treated as dependents who, because of the lengthening period of formal schooling, would not be wage earners until they were in their late teens.

The law generally looked to fathers for child support and alimony because they were wage earners, and mothers were housewives. However, such support did not assure mothers and children that they could continue to live at the level of their predivorce life-style. After divorce, women were expected to remain in the home as full-time mothers and homemakers. Social norms of childrearing and motherhood stigmatized women who were employed outside the home, even if their changed economic circumstances necessitated such employment.

Beginning in the 1960s, major changes in family patterns and roles brought into question many of the assumptions and practices that had guided child custody decisions. The number of divorces began to increase as did the number of disputes over custody handled by the family courts. Couples found the legal process for obtaining dissolutions archaic and cumbersome. The traditional grounds for obtaining a divorce and the protracted legal process did not relate to the circumstances of modern couples. Many states adopted no fault-divorce laws to replace those that had permitted divorce only on the grounds of adultery, abandonment, or cruelty. With liberalized divorce laws and the availability of a more accessible legal process for terminating unhappy or mistaken marriages, divorce became an option for larger numbers of couples than in the past.

At the same time increasing numbers of couples were turning to divorce to deal with their marital problems, changing husband/father and wife/mother roles were transforming the traditional conception of the middle class American family. These changes made real family life far removed from the idealized portrayals depicted in popular TV shows of the 1950s, such as "Leave It to Beaver" and "Father Knows Best."

Economic pressures moved many mothers to take on a part-time or full-time job to make ends meet in the family budget, or to provide greater material comforts for the family. Moreover, it became socially acceptable for women who had families also to have careers outside of the home. With the women's liberation movement in the 1970s, women were encouraged to see opportunities for personal development, fulfillment, and status in the corporate world. The movement also encouraged women to consider themselves equals with men in the workplace; they were equally capable of competing with men for positions, responsibility, power, and income. Women began to return to school for more advanced training to compete with men for jobs, or entered the job market directly in fields traditionally restricted to men.

And for many divorced women who were single parents, full-time work out of the home became a necessity rather than a choice or an opportunity for personal advancement.

As women spent more time away from the family's homemaking activities, men came under pressure to take up the slack. Child care and home care became their responsibilities as well. Many men began to see opportunities for personal fulfillment in the home and in spending time developing close and nurturing relations with their children.

These changes had profound effects on family life for children. As mothers increased their time away from their children working at full-time jobs, more children—preschool and school-age—were spending longer hours under the care of others or unsupervised at home. For some families, the breaking down of traditional gender roles and expectations meant children saw less of their mothers but more of their fathers. For others, it meant children saw less of both parents. And for still others, it meant the family itself dissolved.

Problems with the Laws on Child Custody

By the mid-1970s, it became apparent to many parents involved in divorce and custody actions that the laws were not keeping pace with the demands of family life or the changing family structure. The family court's approach to dealing with custody conflicts seemed to cause more problems for children and parents than it solved. These problems cropped up because of the nature of the legal process for deciding custody matters and the options open to parents and judges.

Theoretically, custody orders were fashioned to serve the needs of the child. A custody order was basically a blueprint laid out by the family court judge for parents to follow to meet the child's needs and interests. The custody order set forth the child's rights to have access to and support from one or both parents under specified terms. It was not meant to confer parental rights to or in children. But parents and lawyers viewed custody awards as if they created such parental rights. They often approached custody of a child or children as if it were a matter of personal right or claim. For many parents, disputes over custody became disputes about power and control over what was left of the marriage. If one parent was angry at or resentful toward the other, he or she often disputed custody with the intent to diminish or limit the other parent's power. These power struggles had much more to do with getting back at the other party for marital infidelities and disappointments than with what custody arrangement would promote the child's welfare and happiness. Parents made use of the family courts to engage in open and bitter struggling over custody. Unfortunately, their use of the courts to vent their personal conflicts undermined the ability of the family courts to stabilize the family situation and to shield children—who became the objects of these conflicts—from being adversely affected by such parental discord. While family court judges tried to reassure children that the parent's divorce was not their fault, and their parents would love them and continue to care for them, the dynamics of the legal battle and the animosities the parents exhibited over the question of child care gave children a very different message.

Moreover, the adversarial, winner-take-all style of litigating child custody fostered the attitude that what was being decided concerned parental rights rather than the child's welfare. In court, lawyers represented the interests and needs of the client who hired them—the mother or father. They were advocates of the parent-client's needs and interests. Lawyers addressed the matter of the child's needs and interests only by suggesting they were synonymous with their client's needs and interests. The court became a legal battleground where parents fought over these issues; the children were the spoils of the war. Winning the battle meant one parent had possession of the child and virtually total control over the child's life and future; the loser had little contact and no control. There was no middle ground. Rather than ending the power struggle between ex-spouses, custody rulings often fueled animosities and the desire to continue fighting out rights and fault in court.

The judicial preference to award sole custody to mothers did not take into account changing social roles, economic conditions, or ideals of parenting; for example, mothers were spending as much time as fathers out of the home and in the workplace, and fathers were as capable as mothers of nurturing and caring for their children. Yet mothers continued to be awarded sole custody under the assumption they would be more available to their children and would be more responsive to their children's needs.

Parents unhappy with the outcome of a child custody award did have legal recourse; they could return to the same court to complain that the other party was not complying with the existing order, and to petition for a modification of the custody order. They could also petition a family court in a different jurisdiction all together to issue a new order that was unrelated to the initial order. Ironically, this continual access to the family courts was a source of problems as well. It kept the opportunity open for each of the parents to challenge the other's ability to parent; it also kept open the door for parents to use problems over custody of the children as the excuse to continue fighting over conflicts that stemmed from the marriage, rather than the care of the children. Unlike court rulings on other civil matters, custody orders did not have the effect or status of *res judicata*—that is, the matter is final and not subject to further litigation. At a parent's request, a judge could reassess a custody order at any time, and thereafter modify it as often as was warranted. Nor, and more important, was a family court in one jurisdiction bound by the custody orders issued from a family court in a different jurisdiction. If a parent left the home state and brought a petition regarding child custody to a court in a new state, the new court could grant the petition and award sole custody.

The family court derived its open-ended authority to render a custody decision or to modify a previous custody determination at any time from its responsibility to protect and promote a child's best interests. These interests and needs could change as a child matured and as a parent's ability to meet a child's needs changed. To have the court modify an existing custody award, however, the parent had to show changed circumstances and the child's best interest warranted it.

The open-endedness of custody orders and the absence of any mechanism to ensure that orders were enforced out of the jurisdiction from which they originated made child abduction a viable option for parents who were dissatisfied with the custody arrangement. It was easier for a parent to take a child to another state where, having physical possession of the child, he or she was likely to have the petition for sole custody granted. To return to the original court to make a case for changing the custody orders and to have to deal with the other parent in court was more stressful and less predictable.

Angry at the other parent, or frustrated with the legal options, parents resorted to abducting their children as a way of taking control over a situation that was often out of their control. In some cases, this meant that either as a temporary measure to change the grounds for negotiation with the other parent or as a permanent step to deprive the other parent access to the child, the dissatisfied parent moved to another state with the child. Sometimes the fleeing parent provided information to the left-behind parent about the whereabouts of the child; other times parent and child simply disappeared without a trace.

Once in a different state, the fleeing parent could begin a new life by assuming another name for him- or herself and the child; the parent could take precautions to avoid creating a trail that would lead the other parent or the legal authorities to discover the child. Sometimes, the fleeing parent would hire an attorney in the new state and petition a court there for sole custody. Mere physical presence of the parent with the child in the state provided a court with grounds to exercise jurisdiction. In many cases, the new court would award sole custody to the parent without regard to the fact that a custody order had already been issued by another state and this parent had violated it. Although the second court might disapprove of the fleeing parent's conduct, it would often grant full custody to this parent anyway, in order to provide the child with a stable residence. This objective was often not accomplished. The left-behind parent could travel to the new location to contest the new custody order; or he or she simply could resort to using the same tactics as the offending parent—resnatch the child, return to the home state, and regain lawful custody with yet another court order.

The parent with the original court order had few *legal* recourses for dealing with the child's abduction. The left-behind parent could litigate custody in the jurisdiction where the child was taken. However, this parent was often first burdened with having to track down the whereabouts of the fleeing parent. Law enforcement officials often were of no help, so parents often had to resort to hiring a private detective to conduct the search. Such measures were costly and did not always lead to the return of the child. The left-behind parent was often not the favored party in the new court. Judges were reluctant to uproot the child once again, especially if the abducting parent had established ties in the new community.

Thus, for many years the courts seemingly condoned the snatching and resnatching of children by their parents. By their willingness to accept jurisdiction over a parent who violated the custody orders of a court in another state, and to grant that parent's request for custody, the courts, in effect, rewarded parents for taking the law into their own hands. Judges did not have to exercise jurisdiction and could refer the fugitive parent back to the court in the original state to pursue the matter. However, many judges often felt a child's immediate welfare and need for stability required intervention. Many judges also felt they could be better decision makers than their colleagues who made the initial custody determination. Ironically, by offering a haven for the abducting parent, the courts failed to provide a stable and safe environment for the person who was the subject of the custody struggle and in whose behalf the courts were purportedly acting—the child.

The battle that billionaire banker Seward Prosser Mellon and ex-wife Karen Leigh Boyd Mellon waged over the custody of their two daughters illustrates the way in which the courts aided parental abductions. The Mellons were divorced in 1974. A Pennsylvania court awarded custody of the two girls—Catherine, aged seven, and Constance, aged five—to their father. While the girls were visiting their mother in December 1975, she took them to Brooklyn, New York. Once there, the mother obtained an order from a New York court that granted her sole custody of Catherine and Constance. Then in March 1976, Mr. Mellon had his daughters abducted on their way to school and returned to him in Pennsylvania. Mrs. Mellon went to the authorities in New York to obtain help in enforcing her court order and getting the girls returned to her. After an extensive investigation, the Brooklyn District Attorney determined there were no grounds for prosecution because the father had legal custody of the girls according to the original Pennsylvania decree.

The willingness of courts to render new and conflicting

custody orders led to child snatchings between countries as well as between states. In one case, an American serviceman stationed in West Germany had forcibly removed the children from his wife prior to the completion of divorce proceedings in that country. The father took the children to the United States, where he remarried and established residence in West Virginia. In the meantime, the mother was awarded custody of the children by a West German court. She traveled to the United States to regain her children. However, the West Virginia courts did not recognize the foreign court order as determinative, and found that the children had adjusted to their new life in the States; their return to their mother's home would have involved major disruptions and adjustments for the children—different customs, language, schooling, friends, and the like. Moreover, the American courts believed that they should protect the custody interests of an American father who wished to have his children live with him in the United States; thus, the father was accorded legal as well as physical custody of the children, and the mother returned to West Germany with a custody order from her country that had no effect.

In some instances, a parent abducted a child during a pending separation, divorce, or custody action and before a court rendered any official determination of custody. In the absence of a divorce or custody decree awarding custody to a particular parent, state laws recognized each parent to be entitled to custody of the child. Thus, a parent who abducted a child or prevented the other parent from having access to the child was regarded as having lawful possession of the child—regardless of the fact that such "lawful possession" deprived the other parent of also exercising equal and lawful custody. Again, this statement of the law encouraged the left-behind parent to resnatch the child.

Reforms in the Custody Laws to Minimize Parental Abductions

By the late 1960s, lawmakers began to realize that the rules for court intervention in child custody disputes had in fact created havoc in the legal system, and severely limited the courts' ability to deal effectively with these kinds of cases. Indeed, a Florida appelate court judge noted in a child custody case that "child-snatching is one of the evils of custody fights."[10]

The fact that there were many grounds on which courts of different states could assume jurisdiction and reverse a custody award issued by another state contributed to the havoc and ineffectiveness of custody law. Aside from mere physical presence in the state, a court could accept jurisdiction over a custody case under five other conditions: if the child and one or both parents had resided in the state within six months of the custody proceeding; if the child and one parent had a "significant connection" to the state; if an emergency situation existed in which a child's health was at risk; if the child had been abandoned; or if no other state appeared able or willing to exercise jurisdiction. While multiple grounds were intended to allow the courts to intervene in custody matters to respond to the changing needs and welfare interests of a child, in practice they fostered confusion and insecurity in the child's family life. Children who were victims of parental abduction were often hurt rather than helped by the ability of the courts to intervene at any time.

To clarify the authority and effect of custody orders and to eliminate so many different grounds for jurisdiction, the National Conference of Commissioners on Uniform State Law drafted the Uniform Child Custody Jurisdiction Act (UCCJA). The act, completed in 1968, was a model for state legislation on child custody. It contained a specific set of criteria for courts to follow when determining jurisdiction. Under the terms of the UCCJA, a state court could assume jurisdiction over a case under three circumstances: if (1) the state was the child's home state (defined as the place of residence for the child and one parent at least six months prior to the request for court action); (2) the child and one parent had significant connections in the state—that is, their ties were equal to or stronger than those with another state; or (3) emergency intervention was required to protect the child from physical harm.

Once a state court assumed jurisdiction in accordance with the standards of the UCCJA, its custody order was to be recognized by all other states that had adopted the UCCJA. The act also prohibited a court from accepting jurisdiction over a case if the parent who was filing for an initial custody order or a modifation had abducted the child in order to litigate custody.

Drafters of the model UCCJA hoped the new standards for jurisdiction would help judges know when they should exercise jurisdiction over a custody matter. They also wanted to close the legal loopholes that permitted parents dissatisfied with a custody order from taking their child to another state to obtain a more favorable determination. By eliminating such options, the drafters hoped to eliminate conflicting court orders and to increase compliance with lawful custody orders. They thought these conditions would lead to greater stability in a child's home environment and family relations.

Lawmakers of each state were free to adopt the language of the model code, or adopt some version of it. Moreover, adoption of the UCCJA, in any form, was optional; states could choose whether to incorporate it into their state codes.

North Dakota was the first state to adopt the UCCJA in 1969. By 1978, nearly half the states in the country had passed legislation to incorporate the act into their state laws on custody. Thus, the opportunities for "legal" parental abduction were minimized, but they still existed for several years while other states failed to restrict the grounds for allowing family courts to accept jurisdiction over custody suits. It was not until 1983 when Massachusetts passed the UCCJA that all states had some version of the act included in their state statutes.

New Laws Governing the Custody Process

Many lawmakers hoped that the UCCJA legislation would address the defects in child custody law that permitted parents to abduct their children with impunity. (Indeed the defects in custody law had rewarded parents for taking the law into their own hands.) Under pressure from parents, family lawyers, and child welfare professionals, some lawmakers went further and enacted laws to change the rules judges followed in making custody determinations. These laws increased parental input in custody decision making, and permitted parents to have joint physical and legal custody of their children. These measures were intended to minimize the antagonisms and frustrations between parents that often led one parent to resort to child stealing.

As one such measure, new legislation in some states mandated that couples filing for divorce use mediation to resolve their disputes over custody prior to their appearance in family court. The goal of such legislation was to provide parents the opportunity, with the help of a professional mediator, to air their grievances and fashion a custody plan that was satisfactory to each parent. The plan would then be presented to the family court judge for approval.

The other measure adopted by state legislators gave family court judges the option to award joint physical and legal custody of a child to each parent. This legal reform reflected the new approach to parenting being advocated by child psychologists and family counselors in the 1970s—that is, that children needed to have access to and ongoing relationships with both parents for their proper social and psychological development. In 1980, California became the first state to enact a joint custody statute. Currently, joint custody is available in more than thirty-five states, either as a statutory option or presumption. It is the custody arrangement favored by statute in Florida, Idaho, Kansas, Louisiana, and Montana.

The new laws providing for mediation and joint custody have had mixed results. Researchers who have studied mediated custody have found this approach more often resulted in custody orders that reflected the needs and interests of both parents. In turn, parents were more willing to abide by the terms of such orders, and, when problems arose, were more willing to return to the appropriate court to work out a new solution. However, sometimes when parents were unable to come to an agreement on the terms of custody, the mediator imposed a solution, or the judge decided the matter. Not surprisingly, in these cases, the process of mediation often failed to produce a custody arrangement both parents were truly satisfied with.

Studies of parents who were awarded joint custody have found the rate of custody relitigation between parents sharing custody was lower than between parents when one of the parties had sole custody. Joint custody was found to work best in families in which the parents were willing to cooperate around the needs and upbringing of their children and avoided engaging in conflicts that stemmed from their former marital relations. In those cases in which joint custody was forced against the wishes of one parent, however, researchers found the relitigation rate was similar to that of parents dealing with sole custody awards.

The Criminalization of Parental Abduction

While some sought to deter parental abduction through reforms in the custody laws, others pressured legislators to deter this behavior by making it a crime. Left-behind parents became vocal lobbyists; they made their plight known to their representatives in Congress and their state legislatures. They urged the laws be changed to recognize that parental child stealing was a serious problem that should be dealt with by the criminal justice system. They encouraged lawmakers to see children and left-behind parents as victims who suffered significant psychological, and sometimes, physical harm.

One case—a particularly tragic story of a father's deceit in hiding an infant daughter from her mother—started in California in 1976. The left-behind mother, Georgia Hilgeman, eventually coped with her baby's abduction by starting a support group for other parents. Out of this group grew one of the largest and most well-known nonprofit missing children's organizations in the United States—Vanished Children's Alliance.

Ms. Hilgeman's baby daughter was visiting her father, Juan Rios, when he reported to the police that his daughter had disappeared. The child was thirteen months old at the time. In meetings with the press after the baby's disappearance, the father speculated on what might have happened—the baby had somehow "wandered away and fallen into a ditch where construction workers might have inadvertently covered her over with dirt and cement," or she had been "stolen to be sold through a Black Market Baby Ring."[11] The father later gave Ms. Hilgeman a ransom note for the baby, which he said he had received at his place of work. The local police department, fearing a stranger had kidnapped the baby, or worse, initially assigned two homicide detectives full-time to the case. The father then refused to cooperate with the mother and the police in searching for their child. He claimed the mother had turned the police against him.

After three months, the detectives were reassigned to other cases and the police department's interest in the case fell off. Ms. Hilgeman continued searching for the child and made several inquiries with the father's friends and relatives as to the baby's possible whereabouts in this country, and in Mexico where the father had family. On one trip to Mexico, the mother received a threat; if she continued to look for her daughter, the child of the friend the mother was staying with would be harmed. After spending thousands of dollars over a four and one-half year period, taking seven trips to Mexico and several trips to cities in the United States to follow up reports of sightings, Georgia Hilgeman found her daughter in Mexico. She had been secreted there by her father with the help of his relatives.

Relaying thousands of similar cases, lawyers and their clients urged lawmakers to see parental abduction as an act of selfishness, spite, or ignorance that caused great harm, rather than an act motivated out of a parent's love and concern for a child. They asked legislators to recognize child stealing as something society had a responsibility to prohibit and condemn. As one New York attorney testifying at a legislative hearing put it, "child snatching is a crime by any reasonable test of what constitutes criminality."[12]

As further evidence of the harm abducting parents caused, left-behind parents who had regained possession of their children gave testimony on the long-lasting traumatic effects of abductions on their children. They spoke of dramatic changes in their children's personalities. Once independent and outgoing, or affectionate and friendly, their children had become withdrawn and afraid of strangers and new situations. Parents told stories of sons and daughters having recurring nightmares of their abduction. These children needed constant reassurances from the left-behind parents that a kidnapping would not recur.

Parents also complained to lawmakers that they were left to their own devices to track down the abductor or to get their child returned. Many left-behind parents spent thousands of dollars—often their life savings—or gave up their jobs in order to search for their children full-time. They knew that if they did not actively and continuosly look for their child, no one else would—and certainly not the police. Desperate, naive, and vulnerable, many such parents hired private investigators (P.I.s) to follow leads to locate their abducted child. Indeed, the growing numbers of children missing as victims of parental abductions brought a boon to the private investigations industry. Because law enforcement officials did not get involved in these cases, P.I.s had a virtual monopoly over them and could charge exorbitant fees for their services. Their services often included reabducting the child. One P.I. interviewed by the press reported he had personally resnatched one thousand children in his thirteen-year career and had recieved fees for these snatchings that ranged from $1,000 to $10,000. Unfortunately, instead of paying for services that resulted in the recovery of their children, many parents were victimized by the very people they hired to help them.

Georgia Hilgeman was just one of many parents swindled by unscrupulous private investigators. In her case, she was exploited by a P.I. who had, ironically, been recommended by a police department. A year after Ms. Hilgeman's baby was reported missing, she hired a private investigator to search for her daughter. Not long after the mother hired him, the P.I. called her and told her he a good lead on her daughter's whereabouts and needed $4,000 to pursue it. Ms. Hilgeman paid him the money. She received another call from him some time later; he said he had located the daughter and needed $6,000 more. He arranged to meet the mother at the closest airport; there she would hand him the money and he would get on a place to bring her daughter back. Once at the airport, however, Ms. Hilgeman was stopped by two law enforcement officials. They had learned from an informant that the P.I. had planned to get information about the Hilgeman baby by kidnapping the father and threatening to beat him up and break his kneecaps.

At the airport, the police arrested both the P.I. and Ms. Hilgeman. Ms. Hilgeman was charged with solicitation and conspiracy to commit kidnap, murder, and assault. Insult added to injury! The mother endured the indignity and trauma of a criminal trial for a scam plotted by the P.I. she had hired. She was acquitted by the jury on all counts; the P.I., on the other hand, was convicted and sentenced to prison. In the meantime, the police, who suspected the father, Juan Rios, of having perpetrated the abduction, left Mr. Rios alone and did nothing to locate the still-missing daughter.

Eventually, testimony from victim parents, legal professionals, missing children's organizations, and child psychologists led to the enactment of a number of state statutes making parental abduction a criminal offense, either as a misdemeanor or a felony. States such as Georgia, South Dakota, Virginia, and Massachusetts made the seriousness of the offense dependent on whether the abducted child was taken out of the state; if the child was taken across state boundaries, the crime was deemed to be a felony; if the child was kept within the state, the crime was designated a misdemeanor. (The majority of states now classify parental abduction as a felony, regardless of where the child has been taken to or detained.)

In their new laws, different states used somewhat different terminology for the crime; some referred to is as parental abduction, others as custodial interference, child abduction, or child kidnapping. Some states specifically made it a criminal offense for one parent to interfere with the custody rights of the other parent or to deprive a parent of access to the child. A few states made the taking or concealing of a child, in the absence of any custody order at all and without consent of the other parent, a separate offense from the taking, detaining, or concealing of a child in violation of a custody order.

The new state statutes also varied in the penalties they assigned to the crime of parental abduction. In those states treating it as a misdemeanor, the offense could result in up to a year jail time, probation, a fine, or some combination thereof. In those states giving the crime felony status, one act of parental abduction could result in a prison term of a year or longer, in addition to the sanctions applicable to misdemeanors. Initially, state legislatures were reluctant to impose severe penalties that involved extended prison time. But with continued lobbying by individual parents and missing children organizations, lawmakers in some states were persuaded to increase the sanctions for this offense. In California, for example, the penalty was increased from a one-year prison term to up to seven years.

Problems with the New Criminal Laws

Making parental abduction a crime helped to bring greater recognition to the harmfulness of this behavior. It also committed greater government resources to investigating parental abductions and sanctioning parents who committed this offense.

By criminalizing parental abduction, state legislators increased the lawful resources available to left-behind parents to search for their children and the absconding parent. When they reported to the authorities that their child was missing as a victim of a parental abduction, parents were in effect reporting a crime had been committed. Police personnel were bound to treat such a report as they would any other crime involving an identifiable victim and a perpetrator. They could invoke the same investigative and communications resources available to solve crimes and to prosecute offenders. For example, police and highway patrol officers could issue "be on the look-out" alerts to fellow officers throughout the county or the state who might come in contact with the abducting parent and missing child. Prosecutors could issue warrants for the arrest of the abducting parent in the state where the abduction occurred. By registering the warrant with the NCIC and a national teletyping system, prosecutors and law enforcement officers could also receive the assistance of criminal justice system personnel in other states where the parent might have traveled to or be residing in. Once the abducting parent was located in another state, the attorney general of the state where the arrest warrant had been issued could seek extradition of the offending parent for prosecution in the original state. Authorities of the other state were expected to honor requests for extradition even if parental abduction was not a crime in their state.

In those states where parental abduction was made a felony and a prosecutor had issued a felony warrant for the parent's arrest, state officials could request the assistance of the FBI to locate the offending parent as well. In addition, in conjunction with the state's warrant, an attorney with the U.S. Department of Justice could issue an Unlawful Flight to Avoid Prosecution—UFAP—warrant. This warrant authorized federal investigators to participate in the search for the abducting parent. Once they located the absconding parent, FBI officers were to notify the authorities of the searching state who would then bring the parent back to the original state to face prosecution.

Unfortunately, the criminalization of parental abduction had less of an impact on deterring and resolving these cases than supporters of the new criminal parental abduction statutes had hoped. In many locales victim parents and their attorneys found that help from state and federal law enforcement was not forthcoming. In spite of the change in the laws, police departments and prosecutors continued to treat parental abductions and violations of custody orders as domestic problems, not crimes. They told complaining parents there was "nothing they could do," that, "it was a matter for the family courts to handle," that they should "go back to their attorney to get a change in the custody order," and "hire a private detective" to search for the child.

In other areas, law enforcement officers and prosecutors did take action. They issued a warrant for the offending parent's arrest and committed investigative resources to locating the absconding parent and the missing child. But once the parent was returned to the proper jurisdiction and agreed to go back to family court to work out the custody problems, prosecutors dropped the case. They felt that the ultimate goal of getting the parent and child back to the proper forum for settling their dispute—the family or domestic relations courts—was better served this way.

Aggressive prosecutors who stayed with the case and brought it to trial were often discouraged by the way judges and juries decided the outcome. Judges tended to impose very light sentences, if they imposed any at all, because—compared with the other offenders they saw—abducting parents were relatively nondangerous; the community's welfare did not require their imprisonment. Surprisingly, juries often acquitted the parent on trial because they were moved by the reasons she or he gave for taking or detaining the child: concern for the child's well-being, concern the other parent was not taking proper care of the child, or frustration in dealing with the other parent who was uncooperative or hostile. When information about ongoing conflicts between both parents came out during the trial, jurors sometimes sympathized more with the absconding parent than with the left-behind parent, or believed that both parties had created the situation that led to the abduction and the abducting parent should not be singled out for punishment. When considering whether to proceed with a case, prosecutors often took into account how a jury would react to the defendant and the victim parent; if he or she thought the left-behind parent would not elicit the sympathy of a jury, the case would be dropped.

Other problems with enforcing the new criminal laws

emerged as well. In many instances, federal officials refused to cooperate with state and local officials to use the resources of the FBI for locating the fugitive parent. To the extent the U.S. Department of Justice did permit FBI involvement, it was limited to those cases in which the abducted child was known to be in physical danger. Even in those circumstances, FBI agents could only help *locate* the parent; they could not take possession of the fugitive parent and the abducted child and return them to the home state.

In response to complaints by parents and state criminal justice personnel, federal officials justified their virtual noninvolvement in parental abduction investigations on two grounds. First and foremost, when Congress passed the Lindbergh kidnapping law, it had exempted parental abduction from the scope of the act. Federal officials interpreted this as a very clear statement of federal policy—parental child stealing was not to be treated as a crime subject to prosecution through the use of federal resources. Secondly, Department of Justice personnel insisted that even when parental abduction was a felony according to state law, it was a local, domestic issue. They believed—based on federal and state law as well as historical practice—the federal government was not supposed to involve itself in domestic matters; such matters were within the exclusive domain of state authorities.

Federal Action to Deal with Parental Abduction

In addition to pushing for state criminal laws against parental abduction, missing children organizations and parents lobbied Congress to get the federal government to recognize such abductions as crimes as well. As early as 1973, Representative Charles Bennett (D-Fla.) drafted the first version of a bill making parental abduction a federal crime. Initially, Bennett's proposal did not receive much support from other federal legislators. However, he persisted in circulating bills among members of Congress, and eventually succeeded in gaining the attention of his colleagues. Senator Malcom Wallop (R-Wy.) joined Representative Bennett as an active spokesperson in Washington, D.C., for victims of parental abduction. Beginning in 1975, Senator Wallop introduced into the Senate various versions of a bill to make parental abduction a federal misdemeanor. The bill was amended several times as members of Congress began to debate the problem of interstate child snatchings and appropriate measures to address the problem.

The 1979 version of Senator Wallop's bill represented his efforts to create a comprehensive federal law to redress the loopholes and confusion created by existing civil and criminal laws relating to child custody. It was co-sponsored by sixty other legislators. The Senate held two hearings on the bill. These hearings were presided over by the members of the Judiciary Committee's subcommittee on Criminal Justice and the Labor and Human Relations Committee's subcommittee on Child and Human Development.

The vast majority of parents, attorneys, and state officials who testified at these hearings were in favor of the Wallop bill. They informed Senate committee members that many abducted children were still missing because the parents had been unable to gain help from federal and state officials to recover them. Parents and lawyers also told committee members that while some abducted children had been returned, their home life was in limbo because the parents were still dealing with conflicting orders for custody issued by different state courts. Prosecutors and law enforcement personnel told committee members of their frustrations in trying to obtain the cooperation of the FBI and law enforcement personnel in other states who refused to lend the assistance that was needed to track down fugitive parents and abducted children. These witnesses urged Congress to enact the Wallop bill. In addition, several groups sent letters of endorsement for the Wallop bill to their representatives in Congress. These groups included the American Bar Association, the New York State Council of Churches, Children's Rights Inc., Parents against Child Stealing, and Male Parents for Equal Rights.

Legislators themselves testified at the Senate hearings on the need for a federal statute on parental abduction. For example, senator Alan Cranston (D-Calif.) referred to the enormous social costs of the problem of parental child snatching, and reminded his colleagues that "thousands of parents and thousands of innocent children are subject to emotional and psychological damaging ordeals" because of this behavior. Senator Cranston urged his colleagues to see parental abduction as a "serious form of child abuse."[13] As author of the bill, Senator Wallop pointed to the responsibility of Congress to "establish a national policy against child snatching and . . . fair adjudication of custody and visitation rights where both fathers and mothers are treated equally."[14] He believed it was up to Congress to provide a leadership role on this issue.

However, representatives testifying before the Senate Committee from the Department of Justice and the Federal Parent Locator Service (FPLS) did not support the Wallop bill in its entirety. They strongly opposed the sections that dealt with the federal government's involvement in parental abduction case investigations or prosecution. They specifically objected to the language that would make parental abduction a federal crime and that would mandate federal agencies use their resources for locating absconding parents.

Federal officials from both agencies complained that the new provisions would unduly burden their agencies and make them less effective in handling criminal matters and parental searches already with their domain. Department of Justice personnel voiced the opinion that parental abductions involved domestic conflicts that belonged in the civil courts of the states, not criminal matters warranting attention by the FBI.

Supporters of the Wallop bill severely criticized the position taken by the Department of Justice and the FPLS. They were angered by the hypocrisy of the Carter administration's professed concern for human rights. While President Carter was pushing for the release of Americans kidnapped and taken hostage in Iran, he was refusing to make federal resources available to rescue kidnapped children within the United States. Disappointed with Carter's lack of support for his bill, Senator Wallop himself commented, "Apparently it is the administration's position to pay lip service and clutch its heart strings and appear noble on the childsnatching problem and then do nothing."[15]

An amended version of Wallop's 1979 bill was eventually enacted by Congress and signed into law by President Carter on January 28, 1980. The bill was called the Parental Kidnapping Prevention Act (PKPA) of 1980. It contained several key provisions. Two provisions addressed jurisdictional authority of state courts over custody matters and the binding effect of custody orders. To rectify some of the confusion caused by the UCCJA, the act set forth criteria for determining jurisdiction that was applicable to all states: first, the child's home state was presumed to exercise original jurisdiction over any custody matter involving the child; second, the court of the home state was presumed to exercise continuing jurisdiction as long as the child resided in the state or had ties with the state; and third, the courts of other states were mandated to recognize this authority.

In addition, one of the provisions of the PKPA made the Full Faith and Credit Clause of the Constitution applicable to the custody orders of a state court when they were issued in conformance with the jurisdictional requirements of the act. The court exercising lawful jurisdiction over a custody matter continued to enjoy the flexibility to modify orders at any time, as warranted by a change in the needs or circumstances of the child. However, by being brought within the scope of the Full Faith and Credit clause, these orders attained the same legal status and binding effect as if they were final court orders. Courts in other jurisdictions were expected to recognize these orders as binding; they were to refuse to accept jurisdiction over any custody matter that had been previously decided by a court in another state.

A third provision of the act made the resources of the FPLS available to help victim parents locate an abducting parent through searches of federal records, such as income tax, military, and personnel records maintained by the Social Security Administration, the Veterans Administration, the Internal Revenue Services, the Department of Defense, the Department of Transportation, and the National Personnel Records Center of the General Service Administration. These records often contained address information on the fugitive parent.

Originally, the FPLS had been created to assist federal and state welfare departments in locating parents who had defaulted on their child support payments. The federal law that had created the FPLS also required each state to establish its own state level parent locator service to access state income tax, personnel, and motor vehicle records for address information on parents who had failed to make court-ordered child support payments. In 1976 California was the first jurisdiction to expand the activities of its state parent locator service to assist in the location of parents who had abducted their children.

Two provisions of the PKPA concerned the criminal status of parental abduction. Under pressure from the administration, drafters of the 1979 Wallop bill dropped the language making parental abduction a federal misdemeanor. In lieu of creating a new crime of parental abduction, Congress extended the Federal Fugitive Felon Act to apply to absconding parents who took a child out of a state in which parental abduction was a felony offense. The Federal Fugitive Felon Act declared that individuals who traveled to another state to avoid prosecution from a crime that was a felony in the jurisdiction from which they fled committed a federal crime as well. Thus, in an indirect way, Congress made interstate parental abduction a federal crime to the extent it occurred in jurisdictions where parental abduction was a state felony.

In addition, Department of Justice officials promised Congress they would make the investigative resources of the FBI available to state prosecutors and law enforcement agencies pursuing parental abduction cases across state lines. The Department of Justice argued that this promise eliminated the need to make parental abduction a separate and distinct crime in order to involve federal law enforcement agents in interstate cases. Specifically, the Department of Justice agreed to issue Unlawful Flight to Avoid Prosecution (UFAP) warrants and to have federal records be made available to search for the absconding parent.

A final provision of the PKPA required Department of Justice officials to provide Congress with periodic reports on interstate parental abductions and on the federal government's response to requests for assistance.

Impact of the PKPA

Unfortunately, even with the change in federal law, it soon became clear that the Department of Justice's reluctance to support the spirit and the letter of the act did not die down with the change in administration or the passage of the PKPA. Senator Wallop and other sponsors of the bill continued to receive complaints from their constituents about the FBI's refusal to provide the promised assistance. In 1981, the House of Representatives held hearings on the implementation of the PKPA. Members of Congress were disturbed to learn of the restrictive criteria—to involve the FBI only in parental abduction cases in which the child was being abused or neglected—still being used by the Department of Justice. The Department of Justice's administrative guidelines for dealing with these cases ensured, in effect, that very few parental abduction cases received the federal government's attention or help. The Department of Justice's own report to Congress attested to its dismal record in investigating parental abduction cases and in issuing UFAP warrants to track down the offending parent. In one three-month period the Department of Justice had issued only six warrants under the authority of the Federal Fugitive Felon Act from a total of twenty-four complaints that met the statutory requirements for federal action. In that same time period, the FBI had received fifty-six reports that they did not act on because "there was no probable cause to believe the abducting parent had fled interstate to avoid prosecution."[16]

As a result of complaints from parents and state officials, several legislators personally wrote to U.S. Attorney General William French Smith, head of the Department of Justice, to inform him that the department's policies and procedures were in direct violation of the provisions of the PKPA. The failure of the PKPA to stimulate the response intended by the drafters of the bill prompted some legislators to consider resurrecting the proposal to make parental abduction a federal crime. Since that time, a few representatives and senators have introduced bills to revitalize interest in passing such legislature, but to date, none of these efforts has succeeded.

While passage of the PKPA did not bring about immediate changes in the way law enforcement officers in the federal government dealt with interstate parental abduction cases, interestingly, it did spawn a number of changes in state laws. A few states that previously had no criminal statutes against this type of abduction enacted new legislation making parental abduction a crime. Other states upgraded the degree of the crime of parental abduction from a misdemeanor to a felony. Still others increased the length of the prison term applicable to the felony of parental abduction. A few states passed laws mandating that local enforcement officials had to investigate reports of parental abduction.

Current Status of Parental Abduction

The problem of parental abduction remains much in the public eye. It is an issue that continues to receive a great deal of media attention. It is a popular subject of made-for-TV movies, special news programs, and fiction writing. For example, the famous body builder-turned actor—Arnold Schwarzenegger—recently starred in the crime/comedy movie, *Kindergarten Cop,* as an undercover cop on assignment to find a mother who had secreted herself and her son from a gangster ex-husband. In her book *Fine Things* (now in its second printing), popular fiction writer Danielle Steele tells the story of a small girl's abduction by her money-hungry father.

Victim parents continue to appear on TV talk shows and true-life crime drama shows. In November 1990, the crime show "Unsolved Mysteries" featured the case of a father whose two sons were still missing after having been abducted as small children by their mother in 1981. The program interviewed the father who resided in California as well as the law enforcement officials who had been pursuing the case. The day after the show aired, authorities received a tip that the mother and children were living in Albuquerque, New Mexico. With law enforcement officers from California, the father flew to New Mexico where he was reunited with his boys after spending nine years searching for them; the mother was taken into custody by the local authorities for extradition to California. Interestingly, this father was among the early members of the support group formed by Georgia Hilgeman that led to the founding of Vanished Children Alliance in California. He was the last parent of the original group to have his abducted children found and returned.

In recent years, politicians have furthered their political careers by bringing attention to the plight of children abducted by their parents and the frantic parents who are left behind. Indeed, lawmakers such as U.S. Senator Paula Hawkins (R-Fla.), State Controller Gray Davis (D-Calif.), U.S. Senator Arlen Specter (R-Penn.), U.S. Senator Paul Simon (D-Ill.), U.S. Representative Charles Bennett (D-Fla.), and U.S. Senator Birch Bayh (D-Ind.) generally have made a lot of political hay from the issue of missing children. In some areas, their concern has brought visible results: improved laws, preventive education programs, state and national registries, clearinghouses, and hotlines. Higher levels of law enforcement resources have been committed to investigating parental abduction cases and recovering abducted and runaway children.

Generally speaking, in the past twenty years, the American public has become much more sensitized to the problem of parental abduction. More Americans are personally affected by the trauma of divorce and custody battles each year. Unfortunately many are experiencing the problem of getting custody orders enforced or amended firsthand; many others know close friends or relatives who have encountered such problems. The official policies of federal and state governments recognize that the taking of a child by a parent without the consent of the other parent or in violation of a custody order is a serious matter that should be handled by law enforcement officers and the criminal courts.

Yet, ingrained attitudes are slow to change. In many areas law enforcement officials—prosecutors, police personnel, sheriffs—and court officials—judges of the criminal courts as well as the family courts—continue to view parental abductions as a nonserious, domestic problem. When a parent reports a child has been abducted by the other parent or has not been returned after a visitation, many police officers and prosecutors still refuse to take action.

Conclusion

Of those children who are abducted, the vast majority are victimized by a parent rather than a stranger. Until recently, these snatchings were treated as domestic problems. To the extent any authority took notice of them, they were treated as matters for the family or juvenile courts and not the criminal courts. For many years, it was the confusion and chaos of family and child custody laws that created the problem of parental abduction. The open-ended authority of courts in every state to assume jurisdiction over a custody matter meant that parents could disregard the custody orders of one court and shop for a judge in another jurisdiction who would render more agreeable terms. Moreover, because law enforcement officials viewed parental abduction as matters for the civil courts, parents could often take their children into another state with impunity, even when they violated the lawful orders of a family court. Police, sheriffs, and prosecutors, moreover, refused to assist left-behind parents or lawful custodians in tracking down the absconding parent and recovering the missing child, because such behavior did not constitute a crime warranting intervention by the criminal authorities.

The legal status of parental abduction changed as state and federal governments recognized the seriousness of this behavior and the harm it caused children as well as left-behind parents. In making parental abduction a criminal matter, lawmakers conveyed this message and gave left-behind parents resources to locate and recover their children. In the most egregious cases involving interstate child snatching and threats of harm to the child, law enforcement officials have been willing to use the resources of the criminal justice system to apprehend the fugitive parent and to return the victim child. But in cases of less serious magnitude—noncompliance with the visitation or custody schedule ordered by the court, or a short-term taking or detention of a child—law enforcement officials continue to be reluctant to offer the powers of the criminal law as a resource to left-behind parents.

The criminal statutes and the civil law address the extreme consequences of family discord and conflict—bad marriages and family relations that end in divorce or require some legal determination, and child snatchings that put the child in danger or are planned to permanently deprive one parent of ever seeing the child again. Ultimately, however, the criminal laws and even the civil laws on child custody are awkward devices for dealing with the issues that give rise to custody conflicts and parental abductions in the first place. These issues stem from failed relationships and failed efforts by parents to create satisfying or healthy lives for themselves and their children. The law is not a resource for helping parents improve their problem-solving skills; nor is it a resource for helping parents build their self-esteem or realize their personal or family goals. Other social and economic interventions must be relied on as more appropriate measures for addressing these issues.

7

Runaways

Tragedies on the Installment Plan

RUNAWAYS are by far the most common type of missing children. Because their numbers are so large, individual cases throughout the country vary enormously—ranging from the disgruntled teenager who leaves home for a couple of hours to the youth who has been living on the streets for months (or years) and is assaulted and killed.

In American culture and literature, running away from home has been treated in the light of an adventure undertaken by bold-spirited and courageous youngsters. It is an act surrounded by a mythology with happy or humorous endings. Mark Twain's story of *Huckleberry Finn* is part of this mythology. The book is about a rite of passage, and coming-of-age in America. Huck runs away from home in Missouri in the 1840s and has a variety of adventures with Jim, a runaway slave. Huck's experiences teach him about life; running away seems like part of the natural process of maturation.

For many, however, the runaway experience can be more like Oliver Twist's, who fled from home because of maltreatment, then fell into the hands of Fagin and other undesirable people. But *Oliver Twist* had a happy ending. The lives of most runaways do not. In the worst case scenario, the runaway dies—either a violent death or a lingering death from AIDS contracted while engaging in prostitution. More typically, the runaway simply goes back home to a dysfunctional family in which he or she may be subjected to physical or mental abuse or neglect.

Runaways in Historical Context

People frequently assume that the runaway phenomenon began recently in American history—for example, in the 1960s with the wanderlust of the hippie movement or in the 1970s with the liberalization of laws that gave juveniles greater freedoms. Although there is some truth to the assertion that the number of runaways increased during this time, it is a gross misconception to conclude that running away from home is a recent social development. When viewed in historical terms, running away is part of the fabric of American society, and, over the past few centuries, it has ebbed and flowed with changing social and economic conditions. As one scholar put it, "Historically, we are a nation of runaways, a nation settled by people who, fleeing oppressive social, economic, and religious conditions, were attracted by the freedom and opportunity America offered."[1]

In colonial times, runaway children were quite prevalent. Historical accounts abound of juveniles who ran away from home and from the hard economic and social conditions in England. They came to the new world in search of freedom and prosperity. The lore of running away focuses on the adventure and excitement of going to new and unknown places. But the larger reality was the dire poverty that existed for many families in England, Ireland, and other parts of Europe that induced families—as well as youths on their own—to leave home and seek a brighter future.

Juveniles ran to port cities where they made arrangements to go to the American colonies. These arrangements typically involved indenture contracts. Youths received free passage to America in exchange for indenturing themselves to a colonist employer as laborers for a specified number of years. At that time, the English government was not well-equipped to take care of homeless children or "street urchins." The practice of indenturing children to the inhabitants of the colonies met with the government's tacit approval—it relieved the state of having to care for some of the country's unemployable or destitute.

The economic circumstances in the colonies also induced children to leave home. While life was hard and uncertain in England, labor was in great demand in colonial America, both in the north and the south. Moreover, conceptions of child labor differed greatly in those days. Children were viewed as an economic resource, and it was common for children as young as seven or eight to join the labor force. Many of the colonists approved the practice of indenturing runaways and saw juveniles who journeyed to the new world on their own as good labor material.

Children in the colonies also ran away from home. Most communities in colonial America had strict religious mores, and youths escaped the oppressive rules of their closely knit towns by running away. Economic opportunities in other parts of the country welcomed those youths who left home. Boys between the ages of ten and fourteen could find apprenticeships that often lasted until they turned twenty-one years old. Girls were also accepted into apprenticeships until they reached the age of eighteen or until they got married. Thus, colonial runaways differed from modern-day runaways in one important way: they were readily incorporated into the economic structure because of the need for cheap and trainable labor. Many runaways easily found work and were given the opportunity to establish themselves as productive members of their new communities. They became indentured or served as apprentices in a booming economy. Most colonial runaways did not hang around the streets and did not become a burden to the residents of the new town.

It was not only the "common" or impoverished youth who ran away. Many juveniles from well-to-do families left home because of dissatisfaction with family arrangements. Some went on to become prominent American figures. Perhaps the best example can be found in the *Autobiography of Benjamin Franklin.*

Benjamin Franklin's family history dates back generations to the English village of Northamptonshire. Ben's father, Josiah, was the youngest of four brothers. Josiah emigrated to Boston at the age of seventeen to seek greater religious freedom; once established in the new world, Josiah had seventeen children by two wives. His youngest son was Benjamin. Ben received some early schooling, but at age ten he began to help in the family business making candles and soap. Ben hated this work and wanted to go to sea. Josiah, fearing that Ben would run away from home, looked around Boston for alternative work for his son. Finally, because Ben loved reading, Josiah apprenticed him to Ben's older brother,

James, who was a printer. At the age of twelve, Ben signed an indenture contract to work as a printer without pay until the age of twenty-one.

Ben found printing laborious, but he loved words and writing. He spent more and more of his time reading and writing, and cared less and less about the printing trade, particularly as an apprentice. Ben and his brother did not get along, and James beat him on occasion. At age seventeen, Ben decided to run away to New York to start a new life. As he states in his *Autobiography,* "At length, a fresh difference between my brother and me, I took upon me to assert my freedom . . . ."[2] He went to Boston harbor. To get on a ship headed to New York City, he told the captain that he was escaping the family and friends of a young woman whom he had gotten pregnant and did not want to marry.

> I sold some of my books to raise a little money, was taken on board privately, and as we had a fair wind, in three days I found myself in New York, near three hundred miles from home, a boy of but seventeen, without the least recommendation to or knowledge of, any person in the place, and with very little money in my pocket.[3]

Ben was eventually referred to a printer in Philadelphia, and the rest is history! His experience, as we shall see, was vastly different from juveniles who run away to New York City today.

Many colonial runaways who were indentured or apprenticed soon became disillusioned with their lives, which for some were exceedingly hard. Running away from an indenture contract was considered a crime, and there are numerous accounts in the court records of juveniles being punished for running away from their masters and not upholding their contractual obligations.

The Formation of the Juvenile Court

Compared with colonial times, the social and economic conditions in America were substantially different by the end of the 1800s. By then, millions of immigrants had arrived in the new world searching for the "streets of gold." Many of these immigrants were illiterate and lacked job skills for the growing industrial economy. These poor and uneducated newcomers often lived in ghettolike conditions with little hope of escape. Moreover, with the advent of child labor laws, employment opportunities for juveniles were restricted.

In these tougher economic times, children of the streets were not viewed as an economic resource, but instead as vagrants and delinquents. Runaway youths commonly hung around the streets—they were idle and often got into trouble with the law. It appeared to many social observers at the time that such youths, with no education and no job skills, had a bleak future. They would lead unproductive if not antisocial lives and pose profound problems for society in general if left to their own devices.

It is within this context that the "child-saving movement" arose. As part of the more general Progressive ideology that emerged at this time, proponents of this social movement sought to improve conditions for the youths of the country, particularly disadvantaged youths. The reforms resulting from the child-saving movement were many: compulsory education, child labor laws, child abuse prevention, public health programs for children, and, of direct interest to this discussion, the formation of the juvenile court.

An integral part of the child-saving movement was the idea of adolescence as a distinct phase of human development that children passed through in becoming adults. This idea was popularized by the famous American psychologist G. Stanley Hall of Clark University at the turn of this century. Hall asserted that adolescence was a preparatory stage for adulthood. During adolescence, youths underwent the biological, psychological, and cognitive changes required for assuming adult roles and functions. Hall believed that in order to make the successful transition from childhood to adulthood, youths in this adolescent stage needed special attention and protection.

Like Hall, proponents of the child-saving movement believed children and youths were different from adults and should be treated differently. They were immature in their physical development, sense of morality, reasoning powers, and ability to exercise sound judgment. Children and youths needed to undergo a period of formal academic training and supervision to acquire these abilities and attributes. The so-called child savers instituted mandatory school attendance and child labor laws to ensure that children received the requisite training and education for adulthood. And when children and youths engaged in wrongdoing, the child savers insisted they be handled by authorities who understood such acts to be the product of immature minds or improper supervision and training, and not of a conscious decision to do evil. The child savers helped to create courts to handle juvenile cases; these courts were separate from those that tried and punished adults for their wrongdoings.

A separate court for juveniles was justified under the ancient legal doctrine of *parens patriae*—a doctrine that gave government the responsibility to care for dependent individuals. They included mentally ill adults, orphans, and any other children without someone to care for them, or with parents who were unable to provide adequate care. Part of the idea of the juvenile court was to create a court that would have broad authority to oversee the welfare of minors. The juvenile court was given the responsibility to ensure that youths were properly cared for, protected, and educated. And for those youths who did not conform to accepted social standards—such as those who disobeyed their parents, ran away from home, or committed criminal acts—the juvenile court became responsible for bringing about their reform.

The first juvenile court was established in Cook County (Chicago), Illinois, in 1899. Within a few years, the juvenile court movement had spread throughout the United States. The state statutes creating the juvenile court were essentially the same. They granted the court broad jurisdiction over troubled minors—often until they reached eighteen or twenty-one years of age. The juvenile courts had jurisdiction over youths who were orphaned or neglected, who broke the criminal law, as well as those who committed "status" offenses, such as skipping school, running away, and staying out past curfew.

To carry out its protective and reformative mission, the juvenile court had the authority to incarcerate wayward or needy youths in special juvenile correctional facilities. Some of these facilities were small local juvenile camps and "halls"; others were large prisonlike state institutions—referred to as industrial or reform schools. Supporters of the juvenile court believed that locking troubled and criminally involved youths in these facilities was sometimes necessary for their own good—they would be protected from victimization by inept parents or exploitation by unscrupulous adults. And while confined, they would be under the care and supervision of experts in the fields of child development, psychology, and education. Unfortunately, the care given to juveniles in these facilities often fell far short of the high standards envisioned by the child savers. As we shall see, the policy of institutionalizing status offenders with those juveniles who broke criminal laws came back to haunt the juvenile justice system.

Social Pressures and Runaway Behavior

Despite new laws making running away a "crime" for juveniles, not surprisingly, minors continued to run away from home in the early 1900s. In the twentieth century, the first major wave of juvenile runaways occurred during the Great Depression. Because of massive unemployment and poverty—and the dire hardships parents faced in supporting their children after losing their jobs or family businesses—juveniles left home with increasing frequency. Their departure helped relieve the family of financial burdens.

In the 1930s, hundreds of thousands of young people ran away from home. Some rode the rails looking for work; some migrated to northern cities from the farmlands of the south and the midwest; some hitched rides to the west. Employment possibilities were limited for juveniles as well as adults. Homeless juveniles congregated in the business areas of towns where they begged for food or loitered. Merchants and customers often complained to the local police that these youths were creating a nuisance. Eventually, the problem of homeless and vagrant youths became so serious that federal authorities were asked to take action. In response, the federal government created the Federal Transient Service, an agency in existence for a few years in the early 1930s to provide housing, work opportunities, and general supervision to homeless juveniles.

Runaway youths were the subject of a few groundbreaking studies at this time. For example, Thomas Minehan published a book in 1934 entitled *Boy and Girl Tramps of America.* In his study of 1,465 youths, Minehan found that many of the juveniles had a hard family life. In over 50 percent of the cases, both parents were dead, and in another 25 percent, the parents were divorced. A quarter of the subjects also said they suffered from frequent beatings.[4] Similarly, George Outland studied 3,352 boys who came to a California camp set up by the Federal Transient Service. The results of his study were strikingly similar. Over one-third of the youths left home for economic reasons, and over 25 percent because of other family tensions.[5]

Between the early 1930s and the early 1940s, social and economic conditions in America had drastically changed. In the 1930s, youths had been compelled to run away because of a bad economy; with the United States's entrance into World War II, new economic prosperity created opportunities for employment in the early 1940s. As older youths and young men enlisted to help the war effort, there was a great need for women and juveniles to enter the labor market. Child labor laws were relaxed during the 1940s in order to allow younger children to work, or to work longer hours.

Plentiful work was an inducement to many juveniles to leave home, and particularly to migrate to urban centers, where they could also live among themselves in relative freedom. The number of working youths increased substantially during this time. In 1940 there were an estimated 872,000 working boys and girls between the ages of fourteen and eighteen. By 1944, the number rose to as many as three million. And whereas in the 1930s these juvenile runaways were persecuted by the authorities because they were a nuisance, in the 1940s they were largely left alone, provided they were employed and did not otherwise cause trouble.[6]

In sum, running away from home has been an integral part of this country's history. The numbers of runaways have fluctuated as has public reactions to them, depending on social and economic conditions. Yet throughout various periods of seeming tolerance or alarm, society has had, and continues to have, ambivalent feelings about runaways. On the one hand, running away from home has been frowned on; since the advent of the juvenile court, it has been proscribed by the law and subject to adult disapproval. On the other hand, this disapproval has been tempered, often by economic necessities as well as at least tacit approval for a kind of youthful adventurous spirit exalted by the mythology surrounding running away.

Deinstitutionalization of Status Offenders

The laws that created the juvenile courts at the beginning of this century authorized the locking up of runaways in local detention facilities and state-level training schools. In many of these state training school systems, a large percentage of the wards were runaways. For example, a 1973 study of the Indiana Boys' School indicated that 46 percent of the boys had been committed to the facility from the local courts for status offenses—running away, truancy, and incorrigibility.[7] Other studies showed that status offender incarceration rates and the length of their institutional stay often equaled or exceeded those of juveniles who were incarcerated for having committed serious criminal acts including robbery, rape, and homicide.[8]

One example illustrates the lengths to which the states went to control runaways. A fifteen-year-old girl ran away from her home in Winfield, West Virginia, on June 1, 1972. The girl's mother swore out an arrest warrant for the girl two days later. The girl was arrested in Wheeling on June 7 and detained for two days in a secure facility until her mother and stepfather came to pick her up. The three went back to the sheriff's department in their home town, and the family tried to work things out. Mediation failed, so the girl was detained in the juvenile section of the county jail. At a hearing on June 12, the judge ordered the girl held in temporary custody by the Department of Welfare. At another hearing on June 21, the judge gave the girl a choice between returning home and going to the industrial home (a state-level juvenile training school). She chose the industrial home, so the judge committed her there until paroled or discharged. By this time, the girl had been in local detention for twenty-three days. Her commitment to the state institution meant she could be incarcerated for another six years—until she reached the age of majority—if the juvenile authorities determined it would be in her "best interests." All this happened to the girl, not because she committed a crime, but because she could not get along with her mother and stepfather.

This is but one of thousands of cases of juveniles incarcerated for long periods of time only because they had family problems, or were experiencing common adolescent urges to rebel against or separate from their parents. Moreover, this case raises a more general question, perhaps applicable to a large percentage of runaways; if this fifteen-year-old girl would prefer to go to an institution, possibly for up to six years, rather than live with her mother and stepfather, what does this say about the nature and quality of her family life?

By the late 1960s, child advocates began to see a number of problems with the policy of institutionalizing runaways and other status offenders. They focused on two problems in particular. First, there was the matter of legal rights for juveniles. Critics felt it was wrong to deprive these youths of their liberty and to in effect punish them by locking them up with juveniles who engaged in serious criminal conduct when they had committed no true crime—they merely had run away or had trouble getting along with their parents. Moreover, it was simply unfair to incarcerate a status offender for the same (or sometimes longer) period of time as a juvenile delinquent who had been adjudicated for serious crime, such as robbery or rape.

Second, critics were concerned with practical problems of reformation; they believed incarcerating status offenders with delinquent juveniles made such youths more troublesome and antisocial. Specifically, runaways were labeled or stigmatized by incarceration. Those runaways who were incarcerated at a young age, at twelve or thirteen years, and then were confined for several months or years because they had no satisfactory home to go to, were more likely to become institutionalized—that is, they were likely to take on the norms and beliefs of the delinquent kids. Therefore, as a result of being committed to a juvenile correctional school by the juvenile court, runaways and other status offenders would be *more* likely to become delinquent and get into trouble with the law after release than if they had had their problems dealt with outside of an institutional context.

With the growing realization that incarcerating status offenders—including runaways—created more problems than it solved, reformers created a movement at the end of the 1960s to remove these youths from state reform schools, local detention centers, and county camps for delinquents. This movement was referred to as the deinstitutionalization of status offenders (DSO).

Some states adopted the DSO policy at the beginning of the 1970s. Other states resisted. The federal government took the lead in promoting the DSO movement by passing the Juvenile Justice and Delinquency Prevention (JJDP) Act in 1974. In the act, Congress expressed a clear intent to have the states institute measures for handling status offenders that did not involve incarceration. Congress made it the policy of the federal government to discourage the confinement of status offenders and other juveniles who committed nonserious criminal offenses in secure facilities, to prohibit the housing of juveniles with adult offenders, and to prevent the placement of youths charged with criminal offenses with those charged with status offenses.

To encourage the states to adopt these policies, the JJDP Act offered a financial incentive. Those states that revised their laws to prohibit the institutionalization of status offenders could continue to receive federal funding for their juvenile justice systems and could receive additional funds to develop innovative, alternative programs for status offenders. Those states that did not pass DSO laws lost federal funding. To date, all but five states (Hawaii, Nevada, North Dakota, South Dakota, and Wyoming) have complied with the act's DSO policy.

As a result of the DSO movement, local juvenile justice systems cannot detain runaways, or other status offenders, in state institutions, local jails, or secure juvenile facilities. When placed in housing by the police or the juvenile court, status offenders are kept in nonsecure settings—shelters, group homes, or foster care. Without secured entrances and exits, these placements are ones from which youths can easily run away again. In addition, Congress attempted to address the problem of runaway youths in the same legislation by passing the Runaway Youth Act. We discuss this part of the JJDP Act later in this chapter.

Current Laws Regulating Runaways

While current laws in most states prohibit law enforcement and juvenile court authorities from incarcerating status offenders, the juvenile court in the majority of states continues to exercise jurisdiction over juveniles who commit status offenses. The language of many of the state juvenile codes has been changed to reflect the preference for noncoercive, nonstigmatizing interventions. For example, the laws refer to status offenders as children in need of supervision (CHINS), minors in need of supervision (MINS), and persons in need of supervision (PINS).

But what has not changed is the vague and all-encompassing definition of who a status offender is and what status behavior warrants the intervention of the juvenile court. In a few states, the juvenile code specifically refers to running away from home as a status offense. South Dakota law, for example, defines a status offender as "any child who is an habitual truant . . . [or] . . . who has run away from home. . . ."[9] Many states tend to use more general language in their juvenile codes on status offenses. For example, a number of states authorize juvenile courts to take action when a child is "beyond the control of the parent or guardian" or is "incorrigible."[10]

Generally speaking, the appellate courts have held that running away from home is a form of behavior that comes within the meaning of incorrigible or beyond parental control. Many cases are obvious. The child runs away from home, goes to another county or state, and refuses to return home. Other circumstances less clearly fall within the scope of the juvenile court's authority over status offenders. The appellate courts in some states have interpreted the laws broadly to encompass a wide variety of "undesirable" behaviors. For example, a lie to a parent about where the youth was going has been deemed to create sufficient grounds to bring the youth before the juvenile court, as one California case clearly illustrates.

In this case, a fourteen-year-old boy left home after receiving his mother's permission to spend the weekend with friends at Stinson Beach (near San Francisco), about forty miles from the youth's home. However, when the boy left, he went to San Diego instead. He was apprehended while attempting to cross the border into Mexico. The boy admitted that he had deliberately lied to his mother because he knew she would not have given him permission for the trip to San Diego. On the basis of that incident, he was made a ward of the court as "beyond the control" of his parents. The California State Court of Appeal upheld the order.

Other states have been more restrictive in their use of the

courts to govern runaways. New York is one such state. There, status offenders are called persons in need of supervision, or PINS. The goal of the status offender law is to alleviate the symptoms of family breakdown and to provide rehabilitation to minors who exhibit socially inappropriate behavior, such as running away and truancy. As specified in the New York statute, a PINS is a male or female juvenile who is "... habitually disobedient and beyond the lawful control of parent or otherwise lawful authority. . . ."[11] The requirement that the behavior be habitual meant that one-time runaways would not fall within the scope of the law.

One case from the New York courts illustrates the caution judges have demonstrated in defining the scope of the PINS statute. The case involved an eleven-year-old girl who ran away from her home on September 12, 1977. She went to her maternal grandparents' house on the same street and a short distance from the mother's home. The mother knew where the girl was, but the girl refused to come home, and the grandparents refused to make the girl go home. The eleven-year-old girl already had a thirteen-year-old sister living at the grandparents' house.

The mother filed a petition in the family court that the eleven-year-old was a PINS. Testimony at the hearing showed that the main reason the child did not want to return home was that the conditions in the home "were less than ideal." The mother had several children and little money, and the child stated that she did not receive adequate food. The house was unsanitary; the mother had two dogs and five cats who left "excretions within the house." The mother disciplined the child rather severely with a stick, which left "marks upon the child." And on occasion, the mother used "loud and obscene language." By contrast, the grandparents' house was peaceful and nurturing; the girl felt loved and wanted there. The grandparents could afford the cost of raising the child. The court noted that, except for running away, the girl was a "well-behaved, neat-appearing, polite, and otherwise obedient eleven-year-old child."[12] She also attended school regularly and was liked by her teachers. The court concluded that the act of running away from home, in and of itself, did not warrant labeling the child a PINS and making her a ward of the court.

The movement to deinstitutionalize status offenders swept the country in the 1970s. Except in five states, status offenders have been prohibited by law from being locked up. Instead, runaways and other status offenders are placed in nonsecure facilities that permit them to come and go freely. However, it is a slight overstatement to say that runaways cannot be detained. Most states allow a short period of detention for various reasons. California law provides that runaways who live in California can be held in a police station for up to twelve hours while officers arrange the return of the minor to his or her parents. Runaways from out of the state who come to California can be held in a secure facility for up to three days while their parents are contacted. But these periods of detention frequently give parents insufficient time to retrieve their children. Youths are often either released to a nonsecure facility or simply return to the streets.

Runaways and Missing Children

Officials agree that many thousands of children run away from home each year; what they do not agree on is the exact number. As noted in chapter 2, estimates vary, from four hundred thousand to two million annually. The federal Department of Health and Human Services claims that there are a total of about 1.3 million.[13] The recent study sponsored by the federal government (the so-called incidence studies) concluded there were about 450,700 "broad scope" runaways in 1988.[14] A few estimates exist for individual cities as well. About twenty thousand to forty thousand runaways are in New York City. The United Way Planning Council of Los Angeles estimates that there are about ten thousand runaways in Los Angeles and about three thousand youths on the streets in the Hollywood area at any given time. Many of these estimates are based on police department statistics. However, the police statistics do not encompass all true cases. One study in California showed that only one in six runaways was reported missing by parents. The others may be roaming the streets without being counted.

The profile of the runaway also varies, depending on the source of the data. Some studies show that more girls than boys run away from home, but these are studies conducted in shelters where girls are more likely to go. The general consensus is that there is about an equal number of boys and girls who run away from home each year. The average age of a runaway youth is about fifteen or sixteen, but the range extends from as young as seven or eight years up to age eighteen when the juvenile reaches the age of majority. Many juveniles run away from home more than once. Again, studies disagree on the number, but the proportion of multiple runaways ranges from 25 to 60 percent of the total.

Most runaways are away from home for a relatively short time. While the Health and Human Services study put the *total* number of runaways at 1.3 million, estimates based on the more restrictive definition of staying away from home at least one night are much lower—about seven hundred thousand. These findings indicate several hundred thousand of the runaways (almost half) are back home before bedtime. Of those who remain away overnight, the vast majority return home within two or three days, after they have cooled down from a family fight or have begun to realize that life away from home can be tough. But even if a minority—say 10 percent—of all runaways are gone from home for a long time (or permanently), that still makes at least tens of thousands each year. It is these runaways who cause the greatest concern. They live on the streets, become involved in prostitution, and engage in other behaviors that put them at risk for victimization and serious medical problems.

Curiously, much of the testimony presented to Congress in the early 1980s regarding missing and exploited children related specifically to runaways and not to small children abducted by strangers, like Adam Walsh. Many experts testified about the plight of runaways, including Lucy Biggs, acting commissioner, Administration for Children, Youth and Families, U.S. Department of Health and Human Services; June Bucy, chief executive officer, National Network of Runaway and Youth Services; and Jeremiah Denton, U.S. Senator (D—Ala.).

One of the key spokespersons for runaway and homeless youths in the 1970s and 1980s was Father Bruce Ritter. Father Ritter founded New York City's Covenant House as a shelter for street kids. In a prepared statement for Congress, Father Ritter told how he first became involved with runaways and street youths.

> It may interest you to know that my own initiation to the problem was quite accidental. I am a Franciscan priest who was teaching medieval theology at Manhattan College in 1968. During one of my lectures on the need to become actively involved with the poor, my students challenged me to practice what I preached. With the consent of my superiors, I soon found myself living in New York's East Village, which, then as now, is an extremely poor area frequented by drug addicts, illegal aliens, and homeless children. It was there that around 2:00 A.M. one snowy winter day, I was awakened by six kids, aged fourteen to seventeen, who asked to spend the night on my living room floor. It turned out that they had just been burned out of an abandoned building that was their home by some junkies who wanted them to work as prostitutes—that was after they had run away from a "friendly" couple in Yonkers who made them pay for their room and board by starring in pornographic movies.
>
> Later that day, after twenty-four different telephone calls to public and private child welfare agencies, the best advice I received on how to help these children was to have them arrested. Since it should not be a crime to be homeless and hungry in our country, I decided to care for them myself. In that way was Covenant House born.[15]

Father Ritter provided some of the most dramatic testimony in the hearings regarding missing and exploited children, particularly regarding runaways. He wanted to relate the complexity of the problem, and to point out that these children often had hard lives, even before they ran away. They were often victimized by their parents and other adults. Their treatment was usually a far cry from the ideal of solicitous protection and care suggested by political slogans and rhetoric claiming children to be this country's most precious resource. Father Ritter stated:

> There are no easy solutions. You could throw enormous amounts of money at the problem and nothing really would happen. Things will change in this area when the American people decide to change their attitudes.
>
> Our kids are not the problem. It is we adults who are the problem. We have decided in our society quite clearly that sex is entertaining and that it is OK to pay the entertainers, even when, God help us, they are children. And until this attitude

> gets changed we are going to witness an ever-increasing number of young people involved in and caught up in a life of prostitution, a street life of unbelievable degradation.[16]

Father Ritter talked about the sexual exploitation of young boys, in particular. On the streets, when they became prostitutes they were referred to as *chickens.* The male johns who paid them for sex were *chickenhawks.*

> You know, the two favorite television shows in this country are "General Hospital" and "Dallas." The themes of these shows are adultery, fornication, homosexuality, greed, lust, cruelty—our two favorite shows. You know, the word on the street is, "Johns prefer chickens." . . . I have had conversations with eighteen-year-old prostitutes to the effect that "Bruce, the kids are putting us out of business."[17]

Why Kids Run Away from Home

As with other social problems, experts disagree as to the causes of running away from home. Explanations have varied over the years, first with emphasis on the individual child's psychological problems, and then emphasis on problems within the family.

At the beginning of the century, numerous well-respected psychologists and child welfare professionals tended to believe running from home was a sign of individual psychopathology on the part of the juvenile. For example, Clairette Armstrong saw running away as a psychoneurotic reaction, and she believed that runaways were likely to suffer from mental deficiencies and poor impulse control. Morris Riemer, another expert, concluded that runaways had a severe narcissistic disorder—that is, they only thought of themselves and did not care about the consequences of their acts on people around them. Ames Robey and Frederick Rosenheim suggested that the act of running away was caused by resurgent Oedipal conflicts that could be solved only when the juvenile physically separated from the parent.

More recently, a growing number of scholars have come to view running away as a psychologically *healthy* reaction to a dysfunctional family situation. Children in dysfunctional families are often the victims of physical or sexual abuse, emotional abuse, or simply gross parental neglect.

Interestingly, the stories about runaways found in the literature from a century ago tell us the same thing about the causes of running away as modern social scientific studies. Huck Finn's fictional experience is strikingly similar to the ordeal of many runaways of modern times. Huck had to deal with a father who was a drunkard and physically abusive as well. Huck tells why he ran away:

> But by and by pap got too handy with his hick'ry, and I couldn't stand it. I was all over welts. He got to going away so much, too, and locking me in. Once he locked me in and was gone three days. . . . I was scared. I made up my mind I would fix up some way to leave there.[18]

A similar scenario is found in *The Adventures of Tom Sawyer,* published in 1876. Because he thought "nobody loved him," Tom decided to run away. He encountered another boy, Joe Harper, who had also decided to leave home. The reasons for his wanting to run away are not unlike those social workers hear today.

> His mother had whipped him for drinking some cream which he had never tasted and knew nothing about; it was plain that she had tired of him and wished him to go; if she felt that way, there was nothing for him to do but succumb; he hoped she would be happy, and never regret having driven her poor boy out into the unfeeling world to suffer and die.[19]

Modern studies have shown that runaways are frequently abused or neglected by their parents or guardians. The specific statistics vary somewhat, depending on the sample of children interviewed, but the thrust is always the same—large percentages are seriously victimized by their families and guardians.

For example, a study of 149 runaways, sponsored by the federal Office of Juvenile Justice and Delinquency Prevention, found that 73 percent reported being physically abused. And 43 percent of the sample stated that the physical abuse was the specific reason for running away from home. Over 36 percent of these juveniles reported having had sex against their will, 31 percent had been sexually molested, and 19 percent had been forced to watch pornographic films. In another study, 78 percent of the runaways who had run to a shelter and were interviewed there reported they had been the victims of parental violence in the previous year.[20]

One of the more comprehensive studies of runaways was conducted by the New York City Police Department in 1986. In the study, called Operation Outreach, the researchers interviewed 168 runaway youths who came from outside of New York City. (This sampling procedure probably selected the more serious and hard core runaways. Most runaways, as noted, remain close to home and return on their own in a few days.) The profile of the typical runaway was a fifteen-year-old white female, who had dropped out of school and had very little money. Nineteen percent of the runaways stated that they panhandled as a means of survival. Of the 168 runaways in the sample, about 40 percent became involved in prostitution. And 14 percent of the females had been recruited by a pimp.[21]

Father Bruce Ritter also testified before the Senate Committee on the Judiciary in 1981 about the family life of many runaways. He stated, "Basically, the kids who run away and stay away are children whose families have disintegrated, who really do not want the kids, most of the time."[22]

Even if they are not physically or sexually abused by their parents, some number of children run away because of neglect. Their parents pay them little or no attention and do not provide for their physical or emotional needs. Many parents, particularly those with substance abuse or mental health problems, are not able to address the needs of their children. When they run away from home, children from such families are often seeking love and approval outside the home. They are easily exploited and look to sexual involvement as a poor substitute for parental love and affection.

In sum, mounting and incontrovertible evidence suggests that inadequate or abusive family life prompts most youths to run away. As two experts have said, "The runaway's home life offers an explanation for his inclination to solve his problem outside the home."[23]

Victims on the Streets

Not only are runaways victimized at home, they face victimization when they are away from home, particularly if they become children of the streets. One study showed that by the second week on the streets, 75 percent of the youths had become involved in prostitution, pornography, theft, drugs, or some other exploitative activity.[24]

Operation Outreach, the New York City study mentioned previously, found a substantial degree of victimization of runaway youths. In all, 59 percent of the sample reported victimization on the streets. Among the specific types: 35 percent had been propositioned for prostitution, 10 percent had been robbed, 7 percent had been sexually assaulted, 5 percent had been physically assaulted, and 2 percent had become heavily involved in drug abuse.

There is debate about the extent to which runaways and street youths are involved in prostitution or are exploited sexually in other ways—for example, involved in child pornography. Most of the studies of runaways have involved those youths who have been away from home for a period of time, who are street youths or repeat runaways. These studies reveal that a shockingly high percentage of runaways engage in prostitution or similar forms of exploitation. For example, one expert believes that as many as six hundred thousand children under the age of sixteen are engaged in prostitution in the United States.[25] A report from the U.S. General Accounting Office, by contrast, claims that there are 1.2 million children under sixteen involved in prostitution.[26] And juvenile prostitution appears on the increase. As one expert states, "Child prostitution grew dramatically during the 1960s and 1970s. Contributing to that growth was the enormous number of children who ran away from home during that period."[27]

Another study was conducted of runaway and street youths at the Larkin Street Youth Center in San Francisco, which is the main program serving long-term runaway and homeless youths in that city. Researchers interviewed 892 youths on the streets (through outreach) and 220 who came into the program during 1984. The researchers found that 54 percent of the boys and 22 percent of the girls had been involved in prostitution. The average age of juvenile prostitutes was 16.6 years.[28]

Estimates of the amount of children involved in pornography are also problematic. Experts vary their estimates from the thousands to the tens of thousands. One recent government report stated that "child pornography accounts for a sizable portion of the $2 billion to $4 billion pornography industry."[29] Runaway youths get involved in pornography when they arrive in a city and are without money or resources to survive. They meet street youths or adults who tell them about getting food, shelter, and money at a "crash pad."

Father Ritter's testimony before Congress described the almost inescapable victimization and exploitation runaways face:

> This year we expect twelve thousand to fifteen thousand children to come to our center. Most of them will have been involved in prostitution and pornography. Hundreds of them, literally hundreds, will have been beaten, raped, tortured, and held prisoner. And some of them will be killed. There is not a single public jurisdiction in New York City or New York State that will accept responsibility for a homeless sixteen- or seventeen-year-old boy or girl.
>
> I mean these kids face the cruelest possible dilemma for a kid. One of my boys put it for me very directly. He said, "Bruce, I have two choices. I can either go with a john, a customer, and do what he wants"—his actual phrase was "sell my tail"—"or," he said, "I can rip someone off and go to jail." And he said: "I am afraid to go to jail. I wouldn't make it through my first shower. I can't get a job. I have no skills. I have no place to live."[30]

The personal lives of some juvenile prostitutes became well publicized after a 1988 raid broke up a juvenile prostitution ring in San Francisco. A fifteen-year-old girl called Darlene related how she had run away from home in a rural part of California to escape years of sexual abuse by her stepfather. The irony was that in order to make ends meet on the streets, she turned to the type of activity that she wanted to escape. She "free-lanced" for awhile as a streetwalker, but then got hooked up with a juvenile prostitution ring, a brothel that specialized in runaway girls. She made up to $600 a day at the brothel, before it was closed by the police. She has subsequently returned to her mother to try to work out the family problems.

A few studies have sought to learn in greater depth the motivations and life-styles of juveniles involved in prostitution. Researchers from the URSA Institute of San Francisco conducted a study of boy and girl prostitutes in two locations—the Times Square area of New York City and the Tenderloin area of San Francisco—places where juvenile runaways and prostitutes are known to hang out.

The URSA study found many similarities between the male and female adolescent prostitutes. The majority had backgrounds characterized by broken homes; physical, sexual, and emotional abuse; school failure; and a history of running away and delinquent behavior. Likewise, many young male and female prostitutes engaged in substance abuse. Although some remained involved in prostitution because it appeared exciting and glamorous, most turned to prostitution for economic survival, which then became a way of life.

Despite these similarities, there were some important differences between the male and female adolescent prostitutes. Although many of the male youths were gay-identified, most of females were not. Most males tended to be independent, freelance hustlers, while most females had pimps or operated out of businesses such as massage parlors or escort services. Most of the males involved in hustling were situational hustlers. If the opportunity arose to have paid sex, they took it if they needed the money. However, when they had other sources of money, they did not engage in hustling. Young women prostitutes, on the other hand, tended to become committed to prostitution as a life-style. They viewed it as their job. Adolescent males involved in hustling often formed a close-knit social network marked by mutual support and camaraderie, whereas female prostitutes were isolated from one another and viewed other female prostitutes as competition.

Related to these behavioral differences between girl and boy prostitutes were differences in attitudes and self-image. The research on girl prostitutes suggested they have very negative self-images. These feelings of low self-esteem were the result of early childhood experiences of sexual and physical abuse. For these girls, being stigmatized as promiscuous, runaway, or delinquent reinforced these sentiments. They were given these labels by family and peers, and by the educational and juvenile justice systems. Feelings of negative self-worth prompted these young women to drift into an active involvement in prostitution. Such feelings also made them more vulnerable to the attentions of pimps. Once hooked up to a pimp, the female teen prostitute became involved in a set of behaviors that reinforced her low self-esteem and feelings of self-loathing—addiction to drugs, physical abuse from her pimp, and engaging in degrading sexual acts paid for by male johns. Bad treatment by others reinforced her negative self-image. She believed she was bad and thus deserved what she got. With this type of thinking, young female prostitutes were stuck in a self-perpetuating cycle of low self-esteem, degrading activities to earn a living, and degrading treatment by others. Unable to break the cycle, most female teen prostitutes suffered from bouts of depression and hopelessness.

Many of the same attitudes and feelings existed among boy prostitutes. But there were some differences. More of the boy prostitutes indicated that they found prostitution an exciting life-style. They were more likely to be involved in prostitution for reasons other than economic survival. For example, many said they liked the sociability and adventure, as well as the sex act itself. Nevertheless, many male teen prostitutes also found themselves enmeshed in the destructive aspects of the life-style and addiction to drugs. And, as we shall see, with the AIDS epidemic, prostitution has become a dangerous activity for medical reasons.[31]

Another study conducted by the URSA Institute of San Francisco in conjunction with the Research Triangle Institute of North Carolina (RTI) interviewed 362 runaways in six cities who had returned home. Of the 362, only 4 (or 1.1 percent) admitted to having engaged in prostitution while they were away from home, and none of the 362 respondents said they were involved in pornography.[32] This sample is probably much more representative of the million or so youths who run away each year. It suggests that most runaways are not exploited or do not become involved in illegal activities, mostly because they have not stayed away from home long enough to have to deal with the problems of supporting themselves. Rather, they are children in a family crisis and run to escape the crisis. They return when the crisis is over, without anything happening to them.

But these assumptions should be made with caution. The URSA/RTI study probably underestimated the extent of sexual exploitation among runaways, because of bias in the study sample. The runaways interviewed were the *least* serious cases—most were back home in a matter of a few days. Also, they were probably less likely to admit to illegal acts during the interview because doing so might incriminate them in the eyes of their parents. The true number of runaways who engage in prostitution and pornography is not known—and may never be known. But it is probable that the number is in the tens of thousands each year.

Health Problems of Runaways

Not surprisingly, when juveniles live away from home for long periods, particularly on the streets, risk of all types of health problems increases. Several programs have been established to address the health needs of long-term runaways and street youths. For instance, the San Francisco County Department of Public Health has set up a medical program at three youth-serving agencies.

A model program is the High-Risk Youth Program, which the Children's Hospital of Los Angeles, Division of Adolescent Medicine, and the Los Angeles Free Clinic began in 1982. The mission of the High-Risk Youth Program is to increase access to health services for high-risk young people. Program services focus on the problems runaways encounter: substance abuse, venereal disease, unwanted pregnancy, suicide, and depression.

This program has hosted various medical studies, and has the best data on the medical needs of high-risk youth. The administrator of this program, Gary Yates, and his associates at Childrens Hospital conducted one comprehensive study of runaway youths in 1985. The study compared the health of runaway juveniles with nonrunaways. Seven hundred and sixty-five juveniles who were seen on an outpatient basis at Childrens Hospital in 1985 were included in the study. Of those, 655 were nonrunaways and 110 were runaways. Not surprisingly, the general conclusion of the study was that, when compared with the at-home group, runaways were at greater risk of a wide variety of medical problems and of health-compromising behaviors, including suicide, depression, prostitution, and substance abuse.

Specifically, runaways were more likely to have been diagnosed for pelvic inflammatory disease, hepatitis, uncontrolled asthma, pneumonia, scabies, and trauma (for example, wounds and broken bones). Moreover, runaways were about three times as likely to be depressed, suicidal, or have some other mental health problem. Runaways were also more likely to have drug addiction problems. Almost 35 percent of the runaways admitted to using drugs intravenously, compared with 3.7 percent of the nonrunaways. This has serious implications for AIDS. Runaways also reported a high use of every single drug listed in the study's questionnaire.

The sexual history and behavior of the runaways were markedly different from at-home juveniles. All youths included in the study were asked the age at their first sexual intercourse. Almost 20 percent of the runaways had their first sexual intercourse before the age of ten. (By contrast, 2.1 percent of the nonrunaways had their first sexual intercourse in this age group.) Another 38.2 percent of the runaways had sex for the first time between ten and fourteen years of age. (By contrast, 28.9 percent of the nonrunaways had their first sexual experience between ten and fourteen.) Thus, over 57 percent of the runaways had their first sexual intercourse before their fifteenth birthday.

Other data about the sexual experiences of runaways confirmed findings from earlier studies. Twenty-six percent of the runaways stated that they engaged in "survival sex" (that is, prostitution), compared with 1 percent of the nonrunaways; 21.8 percent of the runaways reported childhood sexual abuse, compared with 5.2 percent of the nonrunaways. And 16.4 percent of the runaways reported childhood physical abuse, compared with 2.1 percent of the nonrunaways.[33]

These findings are disturbing in and of themselves, because they suggest that tragic life events beyond their control prompt youths to run away only to experience additional problems and hardships. One must wonder about how intolerable the home lives of some of these runaways must have been to lead them to put up with the violence and degradation of street life, prostitution, and pornography rather than to return home. But even more ominous is the relationship between the health compromising behaviors of runaways and future health problems—specifically infection with the AIDS virus. The runaways in the Yates study were much more likely to engage in behaviors that put them at risk for AIDS than the at-home juveniles. For example, a higher percentage were self-identified as gay or bisexual, a shocking percentage used intravenous (IV) drugs, and a large percentage engaged in prostitution for economic survival.

Economic pressures put these kids in special jeopardy. Many juvenile prostitutes know that their clients should wear condoms. But because many customers do not like to use condoms, they offer juveniles more money to have unprotected sex. And because many teenage prostitutes are hard up for money, they reluctantly consent.

It is difficult to get reliable and complete AIDS data on runaways, because of privacy and confidentiality laws. But there are emerging data to confirm runaways are at high risk of contracting the disease. Patricia Hersch wrote an article in *Psychology Today* describing the threat of AIDS among juvenile runaways. Ms. Hersch worked with Covenant House staff in New York City. The juveniles she observed and interviewed engaged in behavior—time and again—that placed them at a high risk of contracting the AIDS virus. This was particularly true of the juveniles who engaged in prostitution. But it was also true of those who did not. She found that many homeless juveniles were picked up by adult men who promised to take care of them. The juvenile would then have sexual relations only with that one person, but if that individual carried the AIDS virus and engaged in unprotected sex, that was enough. The medical director of Covenant House claimed to have tested four girls in this situation, and three of them tested positive for the AIDS virus. Given current knowledge about the transmission of the disease, it seems likely that homeless and runaway juveniles will constitute the next wave of the AIDS epidemic.[34]

A specific example of this nightmare was recently uncovered in San Francisco. The San Francisco Police Department arrested a man in 1988 for child molestation. The police searched the man's hotel room and found some disturbing information. The man's diary indicated that he liked sex with male juveniles between the ages five and seventeen. The diary also indicated that he had sexual relations with 139 different boys between 1971 and 1988. Tragically, the police also found documentation that the man had already tested positive for the AIDS virus, but continued having sex with the boys anyway. The police fear that some of the juveniles may have been infected by the man, but they have been unable to locate the victims—some of the boys were runaways; others lived in the area, but were not readily identifiable.

Runaway Youth Act

The plight of runaway and homeless youths—street kids—became public knowledge in the 1970s as their situation became more visible. They were living in open parks or cars, or in abandoned buildings called *squats* (derived from squatter). Social and political pressure began to mount to provide long-term runaways who made their home in the streets with alternative shelter. No longer detainable in secure facilities or state juvenile insitutions, these runaways were viewed increasingly as a social problem as well as a law enforcement problem.

As part of the Juvenile Justice and Delinquency Prevention (JJDP) Act of 1974, Congress passed the Runaway Youth Act. The Runaway Youth Act represented a two-year effort on the part of many politicians to gain federal recognition of the runaway problem. Senator Birch Bayh (D—Ind.), who was the chairman of the Senate Subcommittee to Investigate Juvenile Delinquency, led the effort.

As a preface to the act, Congress reported these findings:

> (1) the number of juveniles who leave and remain away from home without parental permission has increased to alarming proportions, creating a substantial law enforcement problem for the communities inundated, and significantly endangering the young people who are without resources and live on the street;
>
> (2) the exact nature of the problem is not well defined because national statistics on the size and profile of the runaway youth population are not tabulated;
>
> (3) many such young people, because of their age and situation, are urgently in need of temporary shelter and counseling services;
>
> (4) the problem of locating, detaining, and returning runaway children should not be the responsibility of already overburdened police departments and juvenile justice authorities; and

(5) in view of the interstate nature of the problem, it is the responsibility of the federal government to develop accurate reporting of the problem nationally and to develop an effective system of temporary care outside the law enforcement structure.[35]

The Runaway Youth Act was passed by Congress, and signed into law by President Ford in September 1974. Funding to implement the act was initially set at $10 million each year for 1974, 1975, and 1976. In 1977, Congress reauthorized the Runaway Youth Act and raised the level of funding for shelter programs and research to $25 million each year for 1977 through 1979. In 1980, Congress again reauthorized the act, but renamed it the Runaway and Homeless Youth Act. President Carter signed the law on December 8, 1980. Funding remained at $25 million per year. In the mid-1980s, the program received $23 million. This money funded 260 shelters around the country.

The Runaway Youth Act authorized the Department of Health Education and Welfare (now the Department of Health and Human Services) to make grants and provide technical assistance to local jurisdictions and nonprofit organizations "for the purpose of developing local facilities to deal primarily with the immediate needs of runaway youth in a manner which is outside the law enforcement structure and juvenile justice system."[36]

In order to qualify for federal assistance, local agencies were required to meet specified criteria. Each funded program was to:

1. be located in an area frequented or easily reachable by runaways.
2. have a maximum capacity of twenty children and enough staff to provide adequate supervision and treatment.
3. develop adequate plans for contacting the runaways' parents or guardian, and for assuring the safe return of the child, if it was in the best interests of the child.
4. develop an adequate plan for assuring proper relationships with law enforcement agencies.
5. develop an adequate aftercare counseling system.

The basic requirement for runaways who entered a shelter was to tell their parents where they were. Generally, shelters provided each youth with housing for up to thirty days. Although the shelter program was set up to provide youths with food, some medical services, and a bed while away from home, its main objective was to get runaways reunified with their family. But if the family was deemed unfit for reunification, then shelter program staff helped runaways find a permanent placement—for example, foster care, a group home, or approved independent living.

Some city shelters had been established before the Runaway Youth Act. One of the first runaway shelters in the country was originally called Huckleberry's for Runaways. It opened in the Haight-Ashbury district of San Francisco on June 18, 1967, during the heyday of the flower-child and hippie movement. Now called Huckleberry House, the shelter is still going strong, and provides assistance to runaways in San Francisco. Another shelter, the Sanctuary, opened July 1970 in Cambridge, Massachusetts, a couple of blocks from Harvard Square, which has traditionally been frequented by juveniles and runaways.

Some of the shelters that now exist specialize in one type of juvenile client. The problem of juvenile prostitution is so serious in some areas, such as Times Square in New York City and the Hollywood area of Los Angeles, that organizations have been founded just to serve that population. For example, Dr. Lois Lee founded Children of the Night, an organization that gives aid to teenage prostitutes in the Hollywood area. Dr. Lee is a sociologist and anthropologist with extensive experience in social research in an urban environment. Because of the unique focus of her research, she was invited by prostitutes to observe kids on the streets. She was so concerned with what she observed that she started to work with these youths—to find placements and provide other help. Because it was difficult to obtain regular social service agencies to help teen prostitutes, she founded her own organization.

Covenant House, one of the best-known youth shelters, provides basic food, clothing and shelter as well as a range of services to runaways. Father Ritter described the program in his testimony before the Senate: "Located in the heart of Times Square in New York City, we are open twenty-four hours a day to provide anyone under twenty-one years of age with basic food, clothing, and shelter as well as with supportive counseling, medical, legal, casework, educational, and vocational services that are designed to help them make a successful transition into productive adulthood."[37]

By 1977, Covenant House had expanded to ten shelters or group homes in and outside of New York City. In 1987, a Covenant House was opened in New Orleans. In the first year of operation, it served four hundred kids. Since that time it has grown; in 1988 it served one thousand six hundred youths and in 1989, two thousand two hundred. The Covenant House program has also expanded outside the United States. There is one branch in Antigua, Guatemala, and one in Toronto, Canada.

Another youth-serving program is the Seattle Youth and Community Services (SYCS) agency, which began in 1974 as The Shelter. The general mission of the SYCS is to provide quality services to runaway youths and their families and to the homeless and street youths in the Seattle area. Another goal is to help to reunite families. The Shelter is the only walk-in shelter for juveniles in Seattle. It is a short-term crisis facility for youths from eleven to seventeen years of age. Both boys and girls are admitted, and they can remain there up to fourteen days. At The Shelter, youths are offered counseling, academic evaluation, employment and drug counseling, and recreational activities. The individualized needs of the client determine the services given.

In 1982, the creation of the Orion Multi-Service Center expanded The Shelter's connections with other agencies in Seattle. This center is a collaborative effort among Seattle Public Schools, the University of Washington Adolescent Clinic, the Downtown YMCA, Catholic Community Services, and Mt. Baker/Central Seattle Youth Services. The goal of the center is to get runaway and homeless youths off the streets and show them positive alternatives to street life. It serves youths from eleven to twenty-one years of age. In addition to meals and medical counseling and referral, the center provides a learning center where youths can prepare for reentry into public school or to take the GED examination. Youths also receive employment counseling, employment training, and job placement assistance. In addition, the center provides substance abuse counseling and casework to follow and assist youths over time—for continuity of care.

The program expanded again in 1986 to include Threshold, which is the long-range component of SYCS. There was a growing realization that for some youths, reunification with the family was not feasible, or desirable. And because regular shelters permitted stays of only thirty days, there were many youths who needed longer-term services, as well as assistance with the transition to emancipation. The Threshold program was created to fill this void. It offers youths follow-up services after their initial shelter stay and helps homeless kids and runaways who do not wish to return home prepare for emancipation. The Threshold program has received assistance from the federal government, the Washington State Department of Social and Health Services, and the United Way.

Another program for runaways is the Larkin Street Youth Center located in San Francisco. In the early 1980s, the plight of homeless, runaway, and street youths was being publicized around the country, and particularly in San Francisco. In December 1982, Mayor Diane Feinstein of San Francisco established a task force of prominent individuals and agency representatives to develop a plan to aid this population. Funds were sought in 1983, and a federal grant was awarded to a consortium of four San Francisco agencies.

One of the results of this Task Force effort was the formation of the Larkin Street Youth Center in 1984. Like some of the other shelter programs already mentioned, the Larkin Street program provides a wide variety of services to runaway and street youths. The program also included a novel service—street work outreach—which other shelters have since added to their programs. The Larkin Street outreach workers make contact with youths in areas of the city where juvenile prostitution is most prevalent. Center staff offer direct services as well—crisis intervention, intake and referral to other agencies, individual and group counseling, and short-term shelter. The San Francisco Department of Public Health supplements the center's programs with medical services (examinations, lab tests, referral) for this population.

The Larkin Street Youth Center recently received national recognition. The volunteers at Larkin Street Youth Center were named a daily point of light (as part of the thousand points of light notion) by the White House in September 1990. This tribute recognized the center's six years of service, and the seventy volunteers who staffed its counseling and outreach activities.

Funding for the national shelter program network remains relatively strong, because of continued support from Congress. In the 1988 fiscal year, the federal Office of Human Development Services (of the Department of Health and Human Services) allocated about $21.4 million for the maintenance of the shelter program. The allocation for the 1989 fiscal year was increased by $2.8 million to $24.2 million. However, this constituted a drop in the level of funding from the early 1980s, when Congress set aside $25 million to maintain the shelter and research operations instituted under the Runaway and Homeless Youth Act.

About 327 shelters were funded by this program in 1988. The total number is expected to increase by ten or so shelters with the additional money in 1989. Aside from these federally funded shelter programs, there are another 350 or so shelters around the country that rely on funds from other sources.

Although the number of shelters has increased in recent years, the shelter system is still not extensive enough to meet the short-term and long-term needs of runaways. Existing facilities accommodate only about 5 percent of the youths who need shelter. Moreover, the majority of shelters that exist offer only short-term crisis care. Many of the youths who come to these facilities cannot go home or have no home to go to. Others have such serious family problems that even if they went home, they would find it difficult—even unsafe—to remain there.

Most shelters provide runaway youths with counseling to help them through a crisis situation with their families. But the families themselves remain troubled and dysfunctional; all family members need crisis intervention as well as long-term counseling. Unfortunately, the juvenile justice and the social services systems of most counties are not equipped to take such a comprehensive approach. But without attempts to address the larger family problems or to provide families with psychological support once they are reunited, youths will continue to run away.

Conclusion

Although runaways are the least publicized of missing children, in a real sense they are the most pathetic, the most vulnerable and victimized. They are victimized at home by their families through physical and sexual abuse and neglect. They leave home, more often not to experience adventure but to escape from the emotional pain and confusion of living in a troubled family. Those youths who stay away from home for any length of time are further victimized by life on the streets—they exchange sex for food, shelter, clothing, drugs; and they contract sexually transmitted diseases, both treatable and untreatable. The longer youths stay in the street life, the more debased and degraded they feel, and the more entrapped they become in the life. Running away does not solve their problems or ease their unhappiness; sadly, runaways who take to the street find themselves exchanging one set of problems for another.

Runaways are even victimized by the legal and social services systems meant to protect and help them. Housing, medical services, social supports, counseling, drug treatment, remedial education, and job training either are not available at all or are inadequate to meet their needs.

Although stranger kidnappings are serious cases and deserve attention, they constitute a tiny proportion of missing children. What is truly tragic is the way runaways have been ignored in the media coverage and public awareness of missing children. Many runaways face a fate as tragic and undeserved as youths who disappear at the hands of stranger kidnappers. Yet, few notice—or care—if a runaway dies a lingering death from AIDS in a county hospital. Few notice—or care—if a street youth kills herself or himself in a fit of depression while in a psychiatric facility. Few notice—or care—about the thousands on thousands of runaways and homeless youths who suffer from serious medical and psychological problems.

It is time the needs of the runaway population—particularly long-term runaways—are acknowledged and given a high priority on the child welfare agenda. Addressing those needs will take a massive effort that will become more costly, fiscally and socially, the longer it is delayed. In the past, to the extent runaways have been the subject of public policy and social interventions, they have been the objects of extremes—either zealous law enforcement and social control measures, or voluntary crises services and limited-care shelters. Policies that emphasize social supports for the runaway and his or her family would have greater impact and relevance. As one New York Police Department specialist, Joseph Ryan, has stated, "The dilemma faced by our modern Huckleberry Finns calls for a *concerted* effort on the part of social, medical, and legal disciplines responsible for the welfare of our children."[38]

8

Law Enforcement and Missing Children

THE public believes law enforcement agencies should play a critical role in protecting and finding missing children of all types. Yet the police have been subject to criticism for their handling of some missing children cases. The criticism has come largely from parents who have had direct experiences with law enforcement authorities when their children were missing.

Many have given testimony before Congress on the ineffectiveness or lack of interest of the police in locating missing children. For example, at one Senate hearing, Pearla Kinsey Peterson of Oklahoma City related the story of her missing thirteen-year-old daughter. The daughter went to the Oklahoma State Fair with her girlfriend on September 25, 1981. The two were originally supposed to be home at 5:30 P.M., but called to say they had found some work at the fair and would be home at 9:30 instead. When 9:30 passed and the girls did not come home, the parents began to worry. Ms. Peterson soon went to the fair with a friend to look for the girls. She related her frustration with law enforcement officials to Senator Arlen Specter:

> MS. PETERSON: It was approximately 2:30 [the next morning]. I noticed a police car on the grounds. So I approached the policeman, and I told him my problem. I told him we had walked the grounds four or five times, and we were tired and we were scared, and what we did, you know.

His response to me was, "Lady, the only thing I know for you to do is to walk them one more time."

SENATOR SPECTER: And did you do that?

MS. PETERSON: We did this, and still did not see anything. So the friend and I left. . . . We drove up the driveway and I noticed [the other mother's] car, and it was then that we decided to call the police department. We knew something was wrong. In fact, I knew something was wrong at 10:30 when I had not heard from [my daughter]. I just knew something was wrong because she was a very responsible child and did call often.

So [the other mother] went home and notified the police, and I notified the police from mine. There were two officers that arrived at approximately 3:15 to supposedly take a report. . . . After taking notes, and we were actually pleading for help at that time, their response was to chuckle.

SENATOR SPECTER: To chuckle?

MS. PETERSON: Ha, ha, ha, you know, they kind of chuckled at it and said, "I would not worry about it, lady. This happens every year when the fair is in town." He said, "They have probably taken up with the fair, and they will probably show up within the next few days."

And I stressed again that [my daughter] was not the type to run away. She did not take up with the fair, that something was wrong, and he said, "I am sorry. We cannot do anything for twenty-four hours. Wait twenty-four hours, call."

SENATOR SPECTER: Did the policeman say why he had to wait for twenty-four hours before taking any action?

MS. PETERSON: He just said it was standard procedure, that they wait twenty-four hours. So other than waiting twenty-four hours, at approximately 8 A.M., we called the youth bureau at Oklahoma City Police Department. . . . We were told by them that they could actually not do anything, that there was no evidence of foul play, and that it would be against, quote, the little darlings' rights, unquote, for them to do anything.

> SENATOR SPECTER: They said it would be against the rights of your daughter to take any action?
>
> MS. PETERSON: Right, right. After this point we were getting desperate. My husband and I got in our car, drove to her friends, checked with everybody, called everybody she knew. No one had heard anything. So we contacted the FBI.
>
> SENATOR SPECTER: What response did you get from the FBI?
>
> MS. PETERSON: When I told them—I had also called OSBI (Oklahoma State Bureau of Investigation) and was told they could not do anything. . . . (T)hey, too, told me there was no evidence of foul play, and they had actually not been requested by the Oklahoma City Police Department to enter the case. So they could not do anything.
>
> So that is when I called the FBI, and this would have been the third time I was told, "I am sorry. We cannot do anything. There is no evidence of foul play."
>
> At this time I was angry.[1]

Ms. Peterson testified before the Senate in February 1984; she had not seen her daughter for over two years.

This chapter explores how the police respond to reports of missing children. More specifically, it describes the police response to different types of missing children cases, because the police do not handle all cases the same way. The police respond to a stranger kidnap case much differently than a case involving a sixteen-year-old, three-time runaway. Because the missing children problem has been cast as a law enforcement problem, we describe law enforcement procedures in missing children cases in detail. These procedures suggest the everyday realities and capabilities of law enforcement work.

Approximately sixteen thousand law enforcement agencies exist in the United States (mainly police departments) with authority to investigate missing children cases. Of those, only a small number are large departments (1 percent of the law enforcement agencies in the country have three-hundred or more officers). About 90 percent have fewer than fifty police officers.

Because kidnap cases (including parental abductions) occur so infrequently, the vast majority of police departments in the country rarely, if ever, encounter such cases. Even runaway cases are relatively rare for many police departments. It is larger departments that handle the bulk of the missing children cases, and the bulk of these are runaways.

The Initial Call to the Police

Law Enforcement agencies become aware of missing child cases in a variety of ways. The less common forms include patrol units spotting kids they suspect are in need of assistance or are runaways, and encountering youths on the streets who ask for assistance. Sometimes officers become aware of a youth's situation because the youth was either involved in criminal activity or was the victim of a crime. The most common means by which law enforcement becomes involved in such cases is for a person to report a missing child. The initial report can be given in person at the police department, but usually the report is telephoned into the 911 emergency number or the general assistance non-emergency number. Two functions—taking a call and dispatching a police car—are done by the police department's communications center.

Most police departments divide the communication functions between call-takers and dispatchers. Call-takers and dispatchers are typically civilian employees, although some departments use sworn officers as dispatchers. Call-takers (also called operators or communications clerks) are responsible for answering the phones and recording the information necessary to dispatch a car, or, in some instances, to complete a missing persons report. Some departments, usually the smaller ones, use a manual call-recording system, where the call-taker writes down relevant information by hand on an information card and physically passes the card to the dispatcher. Larger jurisdictions generally have the benefit of computer-aided dispatch (CAD). All CAD systems operate essentially the same way. Each call-taker has a computer terminal at his or her station. When a telephone call comes in, the call-taker enters the information into the computer, and when all the necessary data are gathered (some jurisdictions require more information than others before dispatching a patrol unit), the call-taker relays the information via the computer to the dispatcher.

Making a police report can be a frustrating experience for those people who do not speak English, or do not speak it well. In general, communications personnel in most departments accommodate only English-speaking populations. In those cities with large non-English speaking groups, police departments sometimes have bilingual call-takers. But if not, when persons speaking other languages call 911, the call-taker must ask his or her supervisor to locate a translator. Sometimes this happens quickly, other times it does not. Clearly, this procedure may present problems for communities that are registering increases in non-English-speaking populations.

Most cities, even large ones that have multiple precincts or substations, have one centralized communications center for the entire jurisdiction. Police may receive calls for service either over the 911 or the general telephone number at department headquarters. If the reporting party calls directly to his or her neighborhood station, the caller is normally asked to hang up and call the 911 or nonemergency number at central headquarters to report the incident. In some instances, however, the report is taken by precinct personnel. A recent California law, for example, provides that any officer must take a telephonic report if the caller insists. In such cases, once the report is completed, the officer at the substation must then call central communications to have a patrol unit dispatched. In addition, some cities have a policy that all calls relating to juveniles are transferred directly to the juvenile unit (unless the call requires immediate attention, such as kidnapping in progress). This unit records the necessary information and if police personnel determine that the call requires a patrol unit, they enter the necessary information into their computer terminal and relay it to the dispatcher who in turn sends a patrol car.

Some cities have different call-taking procedures, depending on the nature of the case. For example, some cities have the traditional 911 and nonemergency numbers for first-time runaways, but use an additional method for callers who wish to report a repeat runaway. This latter procedure does not involve calls to the central dispatch or notification of the communications section. Such departments have separate units within the police department authorized to take reports of and investigate repeat runaway cases. Parties reporting repeat runaways either can call this separate unit directly or come in to fill out a report in person.

On occasion, the initial report bypasses central communications altogether. Some police agencies *require* the reporting party to come to the department (or the local precinct) to file a report in person. Normally, there is an age-based criterion for this procedure. In a few agencies, for example, persons wanting to report a missing child age twelve and over are instructed by the call-taker to go to their division station to file the report. Exceptions are made, of course, if an older child has been kidnapped or if the reporting party is handicapped and cannot get to the station.

A few departments do not use their communications center to take reports of youths who have run away from local group homes or some type of juvenile delinquency facilities. These agencies have specific arrangements with the various facility staff members on the reporting of runaways. When youths run from their facilities, the counselors write up the missing persons report and either mail it to the police department's juvenile bureau or ask that a patrol unit come pick it up.

Classification of Cases

In most law enforcement agencies, the call-taker makes the initial classification of the child reported as missing—runaway, parental abduction, lost child, and so on. The call-taker determines the case classification based on the information provided by the caller. Officers in the field may subsequently change or modify the initial classification as more information is acquired.

Because a significant number of law enforcement agencies do not have formal written categories of offenses or types of cases, call-takers and dispatchers use their discretion to categorize based on the circumstances of each call. Because few police policy manuals cover this area of communication, departments have developed informal practices that their dispatchers follow. A few departments have only one formal classification code: missing.

Other departments have a classification for first-time runaways. Many jurisdictions have three categories for missing juveniles: runaway, lost child, and kidnap (which is commonly used for both parental and stranger abductions).

Some jurisdictions differentiate missing children based on the age of the child. Several cities, for example, have a formal designation for missing children of "tender age," which means children below some specified age, say, ten. Tender-age cases receive special attention. In other jurisdictions, missing children under the age of twelve are routinely classified as lost child cases; children twelve years and over are considered to be runaway cases. However, classifications based only on the age of the child sometimes present problems in case resolution; children younger than twelve can run away from home and children over twelve can become lost. For example, if a child over twelve were classified as a runaway when indeed he or she was lost (for example, in the woods, down a mine shaft or well, etc.), to the child's detriment, officers would not seriously begin their search for quite some time.

Many departments have an informal category for less serious missing cases. These normally involve cases when a parent calls to report that the child is an hour or two late from school. In this situation, some agencies, for example, use a case category called attempt to locate (ATL). (Other departments use "Be on the look out" [BOLO].) Basically, ATL or BOLO means that the officer patrolling the section of the town where the report originated should keep his or her eyes open for the youth. If the youth is not located within a specified period—say twenty-four hours—the officer then completes the initial report and turns it in to the supervising sergeant. The ATL code is also used in some runaway cases, particularly those involving habitual runaways who are not believed to be in danger. Because no actions are taken during this twenty-four-hour period, the ATL designation could be considered a de facto waiting period.

Few, if any, police departments have a separate classification or code for homeless youths. On the rare occasion that patrol cars are dispatched for such calls, call-takers in some cities assign one of the generic juvenile codes (such as check on health and well being). The dispatcher might also explain to the officer the nature of the call. In other cities the dispatcher simply codes in disturbing the peace. From the dispatcher's point of view, the idea is to get the officer to the scene and let him or her figure out what is going on.

Setting Priorities—Differential Police Response

Response priorities are routinely assigned to each case (although the priority designations are informal in some law enforcement agencies). The system used to set response priorities is generally called differential police response (DPR). Some departments have elaborate and formal DPR systems; other departments' DPR systems are simple and informal. Cases typically receive higher and lower priorities based on their circumstances. However, the nature and level of the number of calls coming into the communciations center at any one time also affects both the time needed to dispatch a patrol car and the car's response time. A first-time runaway, which may normally receive a moderately high priority, for example, could receive a relatively slow dispatch response time if available units are responding to higher priority calls, such as robberies and assaults.

CAD systems can be programmed to assign response priorities automatically based on the case classification entered by the call-taker. For example, some CAD systems automatically assign a code 2 (out of a five-code priority list) for missing children under the age of twelve. However, call-takers usually have the capability (and authority) to override the precoded priority response depending on the specifics of the call. In some departments having CAD systems, the call-taker has the discretion to set the priority level, depending on the circumstances of the case. With or without a CAD system, agencies typically employ differential responses. Some of the smaller jurisdictions, however, do not differentiate among calls because they can generally respond to *all* calls within a reasonably short period of time.

In all departments, call-takers assign a high priority to stranger kidnapping and to very young missing children. The presumption is that children in such cases may be in extreme physical danger. However, almost no type of missing child case receives the highest priority—a response used when an officer's life is in danger. The one exception would be the extremely rare situation in which a child is being dragged into a stranger's car at the time of the call. Routine runaways receive low response priority—assuming that a unit is even sent to the scene. Some agencies, however, make distinctions among runaway cases. In most departments, first-time runaways receive a higher priority than repeat runaways. And in some departments, young runaways receive a higher priority than older runaways.

Dispatching Police Cars

In many jurisdictions, a patrol unit is dispatched to the scene of *every* reported missing child, no matter what the age of the child or what category of case. In habitual (or even routine) runaway cases, it may take an officer minutes or up to a few hours, but eventually he or she will respond to the call. Patrol officers feel extreme frustration at having to respond to habitual runaway calls.

In other departments (either due to the tremendous number of calls for service or because runaway cases receive low departmental priority), a unit is dispatched only if the child is under a certain age. The most common cut-off age is twelve, but in a couple of jurisdictions a unit is sent only if the child is below ten. Even those jurisdictions that have an age criterion for patrol response always send a car if a child of any age has disappeared under mysterious circumstances or foul play is suspected.

A few jurisdictions (in part to reduce departmental overhead) utilize the services of civilians to respond to routine runaway cases. This leaves sworn police officers more available to respond to reports of crime such as burglaries or thefts. Normally, the civilian report-takers work part-time hours. Departments typically have formal criteria for determining when to send either sworn or nonsworn personnel to a call for service. Although dispatchers within these jurisdictions may send a uniformed officer, they prefer to make use of civilian personnel for these kinds of cases. If the civilian report taker suspects foul play, he or she is instructed to request a sworn officer for assistance.

The practice of notifying on-duty units of missing or runaway children depends in large part on the size of the city. Some of the small agencies never broadcast runaway calls unless the child has just run away or there has been a recent sighting of him or her. But some cities, usually the larger ones, always broadcast missing and runaway calls to alert units of the possibility that the juvenile may be in their beat (or area). Other larger cities (with multiple substations) may issue station-wide calls or city-wide all points bulletins (APBs). Region-wide bulletins are used only in unusual circumstances, for example, when there is specific evidence to believe that the child has left the jurisdiction under mysterious circumstances.

The Patrol Response

Getting the Case

When the patrol officer on the beat normally receives a call to action on a missing or runaway child from the communications center, dispatchers have already assigned the case a classification and response priority. What response patrol officers give a case depends in part on the policies the department has set forth, in part on the officers' informal classification of cases, and in part on how busy officers are with other cases. As one patrol sergeant candidly stated, "If a situation arises where I have two or three incidents in program, I am sad to say that a runaway call will have to wait." Top priority is given to those cases in which the child is in immediate danger—stranger kidnappings and lost young children. What is considered a young child, however, varies from officer to officer. Some officers believe that any child under five is young; to some officers, any child under twelve is young. A known runaway rarely, if ever, receives the same priority as a case of a child missing under mysterious circumstances, irrespective of age.

In some jurisdictions, officers may not respond as quickly to a missing or runaway juvenile call because as some officers state, "most missing children are found in the first ten minutes." By the time officers arrive at the home, the mother or father has already found the child. Nevertheless, patrol units respond to all calls for assistance unless the call is canceled by the dispatcher.

Taking a Report

Officers normally take a report of a missing child as soon as they encounter the reporting party. There are a few exceptions to this general rule. If there is impending danger for the child, the officer may defer writing the report. Instead, the officer may begin to search immediately or take whatever action is appropriate. In some cities, no report is written for up to twenty-four hours while the patrol division is attempting to locate a missing child. As mentioned previously, these departments may issue an attempt to locate (ATL). In most cases, ATLs are used for older juveniles or youths who are known to be chronic runaways. This is not a waiting period to respond to the call, but a waiting period to write a formal report. Nevertheless, such a delay can impede the investigation of the case and endanger the child. When police officers do not enter the name of a missing child into the national computer system until after they have completed a report, they delay, or miss out all together, receiving the assistance of authorities in other jurisdictions who may have encountered the juvenile.

Talking to Parents

When patrol officers respond to a call of a missing child, they usually obtain information about the child's disappearance from one or both parents. The interaction occurs when parents are likely to be frantic and need understanding and empathy. Few cities have formal policies dictating how patrol officers should talk to parents of a missing or runaway child. This point of contact determines parents' perceptions of the abilities and responsiveness of the police. Parents of missing children who have been treated poorly or with indifference by the responding patrol officer have vocalized their dissatisfaction to local officials and their representatives in Congress. Bad experiences with these initial interactions cause many of the complaints and criticisms from parents about police handling of missing children cases.

After asking parents for details about the events preceding the child's disappearance and possible leads for locating the child, most officers routinely ask parents (or at least one parent) to stay home. Some officers instruct the parent to stay *off* the telephone, in case the police want to call back with questions. Other officers instruct parents to get *on* the telephone and call all of the youth's friends to help in the investigation. If at least two adults are home, many patrol officers, especially in large cities, will ask one parent to search the neighborhood because he or she is likely to know better than the police where the child might go.

Most patrol officers will ask parents to take a variety of actions: search the house, gather a current photo of the child, start making a list of the child's friends and places where the child might be, call nearby friends. Some officers believe it is important to keep the parents as active as possible to minimize their anxiety.

If a patrol officer is responding to a report of a parentally abducted child or custody violation, the officer will ask the complaining parent for the most recent custody order and for information about the possible whereabouts of the offending parent, including names and addresses of relatives, neighbors, employer, girlfriend or boyfriend, or new spouse. The patrol officer may also suggest the complaining parent contact a family law attorney to file for a change in custody through the civil courts. In those cities where the prosecutor's office has investigative personnel specifically assigned to handle parental abductions cases, the patrol officer may also suggest the parent contact the district attorney's (DA's) office directly for advice on what actions to take. However, in many cities, investigation unit officers rather than patrol officers will suggest these resources, if they are brought up with the parent at all.

Patrol officers do not generally give parents a copy of the incident or missing persons report. In some jurisdictions, the patrol officer gives the parents a receipt of the report that has the report number on it. Parents are told that if they have any questions or new information they should call the specified department telephone number. Parents are also told that a detective will contact them for follow-up investigation.

Actions Taken by Patrol Officers

As noted earlier, the actions taken by patrol officers in the field depend on their on-the-spot assessment of the seriousness of the situation and the need for urgent action. Of primary consideration is the age of the child and the danger that child might be facing. In general, the younger the child the greater the concern exhibited by patrol officers. Most patrol officers operate on the assumption that older children are capable of taking care of themselves, whereas younger ones are more vulnerable to getting into dangerous situations. The time of the day—for example, if the child is missing at night or near dusk—and the location in which the child was last seen—near a body of water, heavy traffic, or a wooded area—may determine the actions taken by the patrol officer. Patrol officers will take a greater variety of actions and act more quickly if the child is missing in a dangerous area or if foul play is suspected (if a child was seen being abducted, etc.). How cooperative and concerned the parents are will also affect the patrol officer's course of action and the thoroughness of his or her inquiries. In addition to these general considerations, the actions taken by patrol officers will also depend on the procedures dictated by state law and departmental orders or policies.

On the initial encounter with the parent (or reporting party), the patrol officer attempts to determine the nature of the case. If the youth appears to be lost, or missing under unusual circumstances, the officer first conducts a search. The nature of the search depends primarily on the age of the missing child and the perceived level of danger. If the child is young (up to eight or ten years of age), the search is likely to be very intensive. It is not unusual for hundreds of officers and volunteers to search for a small lost child. When a child's life is in danger, departments will use every resource at their disposal to effect his or her recovery. For example, departments may call in the canine unit, the mounted patrol, or the helicopter unit—whatever is necessary to prevent injury or death to a vulnerable child.

A November 1990 case from Solano County, California, suggests the kind of all-out attention local police will give to locating a young missing child. A six-year-old girl, who had been playing with her older sisters in the backyard of their rural home, appeared to have wandered off, and was reported missing at 7:20 P.M. Because the girl was so small, it was a cold night, and she was not dressed for cold weather, the authorities were extremely concerned for her well-being. The sheriff's department mounted a massive search that was assisted by scores of volunteers, hound dogs, and the like. The girl was eventually found alive the next day at 5:00 P.M. She was lying in a ditch not too far from her home, with her hands and feet bound. The girl's nineteen-year-old neighbor was linked to her disappearance and was arrested for kidnapping and sexual assault.

Another example comes from Fairfax County, Virginia, where a five-year-old girl disappeared from a Christmas party one evening in December 1989. The county police were so concerned about the child that they called personnel from the U.S. Army to join them in the search. Unfortunately, in spite of the extra assistance, the local authorities were unable to find the girl.

In most cases, search activities consist of searching the home and immediate vicinity (yard and neighborhood) for the child. However, even this practice is inconsistent among police departments. The policies in some departments provide that a search *shall* be conducted in all missing cases in which a patrol car is dispatched. But the intensity of the search can be very low, or even nonexistent, if the missing person is a teenager believed to be able to take care of him or herself. For example, if the teen has been reported as missing in the past, the officer may merely take the report from the parents, drive once around the block, and then terminate the "search." Some departments expect patrol officers to search the neighborhood but not search the child's residence out of the belief that citizens are entitled to their privacy, and that parents can perform a search of their own homes more effectively than the police.

All searches, even small-scale searchers, are normally supervised by the officer's sergeant or the watch commander. In some cities, and under some situations, the patrol officer has the discretion to terminate the search. In one city, for example, the patrol officer is given that discretion when the missing juvenile is twelve years of age or older. Normally, however, only the supervising sergeant or watch commander has the authority to direct or terminate a search.

In a more serious case, such as a lost small child, the supervising sergeant will proceed to the scene of the report and coordinate search activities. A command post may be set up, although its nature can vary significantly. In a very serious case, a command post may be set up in a nearby school or public building. For less serious cases, the "command post" may consist of the front seat of the sergeant's patrol car.

Patrol officers in the field routinely call their supervisors for further instructions regarding any "questionable" cases—that is, if foul play is suspected or if the child is in imminent danger. Usually, the patrol officer's supervisor decides what supplemental actions are to be taken—whether more officers and patrol cars should be dispatched or the investigative unit called in. In some cities the patrol officer is required by policy to notify a specified investigative unit, such as the juvenile bureau or the missing persons unit (if one exists).

When a systematic search is called for, the neighborhood is divided into various sections and patrol officers are assigned to conduct a door-to-door search within each section. Houses are repeatedly contacted by officers until evey residence has been covered. If the child is not found in the first designated search area, the perimeter of the search area is expanded. All activities during the search are documented in a log book to ensure that all areas are searched and that there is no unnecessary duplication of effort.

Talking to Youths on the Street

How patrol officers interact with juveniles on the streets (that is, those that may be runaways) varies substantially. A few cities are quite proactive in their approach. For example, in some cities, patrol officers strictly enforce curfew and truancy laws, particularly in areas where teenagers congregate. This is especially true in those few jurisdictions that still allow the secure detention of status offenders.

In other areas, particularly the larger cities, patrol officers are much less likely to interact with teenagers on the street unless the youth is suspected of being involved in criminal activity. In the absence of criminal activity there is little the patrol officer feels he or she can do or has the resources to do. The officer may stop a youth on the street and ask for identification. Often, the street-wise youth will not have appropriate identification. Even though the officer may believe the youth is lying about his or her identity, without "probable cause," there is no legal basis for taking the individual into custody, and efforts to get truthful information on the teen's situation are often ineffectual.

Even if the officer takes the youth to the police station or to juvenile hall for some status offense (for example, curfew violation), the officer knows that "the kid will be back out on the streets before the paperwork is finished." Thus, there is little point to taking the time to bring a juvenile into custody. Officers learn from experience that apprehending street kids without a criminal charge "is more trouble than it's worth"; they avoid dealing with runaways and simply "turn their heads." Patrol officers consistently use phrases like "extremely frustrating," "banging our heads against the wall," and "shoveling sand against the tide" to describe their experiences in dealing with street youths and the juvenile justice system. Because no lasting effect is likely to come from the apprehension of a runaway or transient youth, patrol officers avoid any intervention unless the juvenile has engaged in criminal activity.

Some patrol officers would like to use detention to hold runaway youths, at least long enough to learn their identities and reunite them with their families. But, as mentioned in the last chapter, a status offender can be detained only for a minimal period in most states—in some jurisdictions, up to three hours of detention is permitted, and in others up to twelve hours for an in-state status offender and up to seventy-two hours for an out-of-state runaway.

In order to detain a youth for a longer period, the officer must find that he or she has violated the criminal law. In arresting a youth on any of the common criminal law violations street youths commit—theft, possession of drugs, prostitution—a patrol officer can have him or her placed in a secure facility until probation personnel or the juvenile court judge has had time to investigate the youth's overall situation, to contact the parents, and to determine if social services or punitive sanctions are warranted. In may cities where serious juvenile crime is a problem, youths arrested on petty offenses are likely to be let loose from detention at the expiration of the maximum legal limit. The youth simply walks out the door and back to the streets.

NCIC Entry

As we noted in chapter 4, the National Crime Information Center (NCIC) is a comprehensive computer system used to help law enforcement officials locate missing persons or property. The property usually consists of stolen cars, guns, or the like; the persons include fugitives from justice (escapees), as well as missing children.

Entering information into the NCIC system is voluntary; the federal government does not force local police departments to use the system. State laws generally govern participation in the NCIC network. Although some state statutes are silent on the matter and leave it to the discretion of local departments, many states do have mandatory entry laws that direct local authorities to register a missing child's name and description with the NCIC system.

Among all of the possible actions taken by law enforcement agencies in missing children cases, entry into NCIC has the widest divergence in practice. However, this divergence is not necessarily related to statutory mandate.

In some departments, an NCIC entry occurs as soon as the patrol officer radios the communications unit that he or she has completed responding to a call of a missing child. In others, the entry is made at the end of the responding patrol officer's shift, after he or she has turned in a written report of the incident to the shift supervisor; this may occur as late as eight hours after the child has been reported missing. In still other departments, entry into NCIC occurs only after the patrol officer's written report has been reviewed by personnel in the investigation unit. In these circumstances, entry may be delayed for up to seventy-two hours after the initial call to the police. And there are some departments that do not make NCIC entries at all, except in the rare instance of a stranger kidnapping or parental abduction when the parent is suspected of leaving the state.

The person responsible for NCIC entry and the organizational mechanics for entry also vary significantly. The most common scenario is as follows. A patrol car is dispatched to the reporting party and a report is taken. Unless the case involves unusual circumstances, the officer turns the report into his or her supervisor at the end of the shift. The supervisor reviews the report and sends it to the records room. Records personnel make a copy that they forward to the appropriate investigative unit; they place the original report into the central case file in the records division. Before the original report is filed, a clerk in the records room makes the NCIC entry. Thus, in the majority of departments that make NCIC entries, the entry is normally completed within several hours after the report is taken—usually after the end of the patrol officer's shift. In a case with unusual circumstances—for example, when foul play is suspected—the officer may leave the beat and bring the report directly to the station for supervisory review and NCIC entry.

In those states with statutory requirements on NCIC entry, most departments comply with the law. As a general rule, the longer the statutory time limit for entry, the greater the compliance with law. That is, for those departments with twenty-four or more hours to enter, agencies are able to register missing children descriptions in accordance with the letter of the law. For those agencies that have a mandate to enter "immediately" or "within four hours," literal compliance is more difficult, often because other, or more serious, criminal matters require immediate attention and take precedence over the immediate registration of missing children into the NCIC.

When the time limit is relatively short—four to eight hours—police personnel may comply with the spirit but not always the letter of the law. When patrol officers responding to a call become involved in an urgent or prolonged search for a missing child and have no back-up, they may not get the missing juvenile report back to the station until the end of their shift or after the requisite time limit has expired.

The patrol officer routinely terminates his or her role in the case when the report is taken, assuming no search is undertaken, and the officer is dispatched to another call for service. If a search is necessary, the officer will stay on the case until the child is found, or until he or she is relieved by another officer. If a child is missing under extenuating circumstances, then another patrol unit is specifically assigned to the search at the end of the shift; this patrol unit relieves the first one, and so on around the clock. If the child is missing and presumed to be in the area, the child's description is given out during officer roll call at the station and officers are alerted to the situation.

Investigation

Organizationally, the investigation of missing children cases can be quite complicated. Most larger cities maintain a separate bureau (usually called the juvenile bureau or unit) or have specialists who handle juvenile-related matters. The size of the unit and its responsibilities are dictated by the size of the jurisdiction, the extent of the missing child or homeless youth problem, and in some cases, local politics. Smaller jurisdictions do not have the need or the resources to have specialized juvenile units; if one exists it usually has a small number of detectives who are assigned to handle all juvenile cases in addition to other responsibilities. Juvenile units may have an officer who specializes in child abuse cases, but it is rare that one officer will specialize only in missing child cases.

The majority of juvenile bureaus have a variety of responsibilities. In addition to their investigative activities on missing youths, these officers frequently are in charge of all missing person reports. Officers in a juvenile bureau are frequently responsible for school/community liaison, child abuse investigations and referrals, gang-related activities, and investigations of crimes perpetrated by juveniles (although some departments assign cases to investigative bureaus based on the type of crime rather than the age of the alleged offender).

In some jurisdictions, the investigation of missing children is conducted by a separate missing persons unit (MPU). MPUs are usually responsible for investigating cases involving both adults and juveniles. These units are often relatively autonomous within the department or are subsumed under another investigative unit, such as the homicide or the juvenile unit. Some MPUs operate more as an information clearinghouse, keeping and providing information to support investigations. In large cities, the identification of corpses is a major function of MPUs.

There is often some overlap of efforts between a juvenile bureau and a MPU. A department's juvenile bureau may be given responsibility for runaways and parental abductions while the MPU is responsible for unknown missing cases—that is, juveniles missing under unusual or mysterious circumstances. Because the line between unknown missing and runaway cases often cannot be firmly drawn, there may be a coordinated investigation for these cases.

In addition to a juvenile bureau or a missing persons unit, some departments use a separate investigative unit to handle the most serious type of missing child case—the stranger kidnapping. In some departments, for instance, stranger kidnappings are investigated by the homicide unit, in others by the robbery unit, and in still others by the crimes against persons (CAP) unit. Stranger kidnapping cases are placed in specialized units because the crime is considered so serious, and departments want to make sure these cases receive a commensurate level of investigation. Parental abduction cases may also be handled by a specialized unit—for example, a unit assigned to handle rape and assault cases.

Getting the Case and Setting Priorities

Typically, follow-up investigations by detectives begin a day or two after the report is taken. The report completed by the patrol officer is forwarded to the appropriate investigative unit for follow-up. However, in cases involving extenuating circumstances (that is, suspected foul play or a small child in danger), an investigator may become involved in the initial investigation with the patrol officer. However, in most situations, investigators will not begin their investigation until patrol officers have finished their activities.

The majority of the departments do not have specific written policies outlining investigative priorities. Investigative priority and intensity, therefore, are dependent on the experience of the investigator and his or her "gut feelings." In many departments there are some informal standards that determine investigative priority. With or without written policies on the subject, case priority is based primarily on the immediate well-being of the child.

By far, kidnapping by a stranger draws the most immediate and highest investigative priority, although such cases are extremely rare. When these offenses are committed, usually at least three separate police units are involved in the preliminary investigation: the patrol division, the juvenile (or missing persons) unit, and some specialized investigative unit that investigates crimes against the person. If a missing child case is classified as a kidnapping for investigative follow-up, the case often is turned over to a specialized investigative unit. In stranger abductions, juvenile units are usually not the lead investigative unit, although they often remain involved in the case.

Investigative priorities attached to parental abductions have the most degree of variance among the missing child case types. A few jurisdictions vigorously pursue some of these cases, but most would prefer that another agency handle them. Some law enforcement agencies simply do not handle most types of parental abduction cases in their jurisdictions. Instead, these cases are referred to the county district attorney's office, which conducts its own investigation.

Many jurisdictions, however, have two levels of investigative response for parental abductions. For "typical" parental abductions (where the authorities feel that the offending parent will not harm the child), detectives do not conduct intense investigations. Because these cases often involve domestic disputes in which the legal status of the parties is ambiguous and case "facts" are unclear, police are discouraged from taking vigorous action. However, at the minimum, investigators will try to contact the parent with the child to ascertain that the youngster is safe. When the offending parent has provided the complaining parent with information on his or her and the child's whereabouts, and the parent responds cooperatively to police contacts, the investigator may be able to resolve the problem without further police intervention. That is to say, the offending parent agrees to give the other parent access to the child, and both parties agree to bring their custody or visitation conflict to the local family court for resolution.

Many investigators who deal with reports of custody violations or child abductions say that a large number of cases involve minor disputes, the majority of which can be handled informally by talking to both parties and getting them to deal with the problem through proper legal channels—going to family court to obtain a lawful custody order, returning to court to obtain a custody modification, getting the family court judge to specify in clear and detailed terms the custody and visitation schedule, and so forth. When custody orders exist and clearly state the conditions of guardianship and visitation, investigators are often able to get the child in the custody of the appropriate parent and resolve the matter without further action, merely by warning the offending parent in a telephone call that criminal proceedings will ensue if he or she persists.

If there is evidence of child abuse in the past on the part of the abductor or the child is taken or detained out of state, investigators take the case more seriously. They will bring the situation to the attention of the prosecutor and if the prosecutor issues a warrant, they will pursue both the recovery of the child and the parent's arrest. Sometimes in the course of talking to one or both parents, the investigator discovers that the parents possess conflicting custody orders or they have violated the court order out of concern for the child's safety; they believe the other parent had or would abuse or neglect the child. Under these circumstances, once the investigator locates the child, he or she may have the youngster placed in a neutral and safe setting—usually in the care of the children's protective services—until the criminal and family courts are able to sort out the facts to determine what laws have been broken and what custody arrangement will best serve the child's welfare.

Most law enforcement agencies consider unknown missing cases to be those instances when a person is missing under unusual, mysterious, or extenuating circumstances, or when there is insufficient evidence to classify the case as a runaway or an abduction. These cases (along with stranger abductions) are usually assigned a high priority, evoke genuine concern from patrol and investigative divisions, and receive rigorous investigations. These cases are given high investigative priority because of the potential physical danger the children face.

How investigators respond to runaway cases depends in large part on the circumstances of the case, and on the juvenile's age. Most agencies place a higher priority on first-time runaways. All departments tend to give the older, repeat (or chronic) runaway the lowest priority. This is especially true if the youth has repeatedly run away from some sort of group home, shelter, or facility. In such cases, often nothing at all is done by the investigative unit. Investigators simply wait until the youth returns voluntarily or is picked up by patrol, possibly on a criminal charge.

In general, police agencies assign almost all runaway cases lower priority than any other type of missing juvenile case. Primarily, runaway cases are viewed as nuisances to the investigator. Even if the youths are found and reunited with their families, they will continue to have personal and family problems and are likely to run away again. Police know that if nothing is done about the youth's problems at home or at school, the conditions which originally motivated him or her to leave home will continue. Officers know they cannot solve the youth's problems or turn an unhappy, dysfunctional family into one that handles its problems appropriately. They are frustrated by the limitations of the criminal and juvenile justice systems, and by the unavailability of nonlegal interventions to help the runaway.

Actions Taken

The number and types of actions investigators *can* take are indeed quite large. The total number they *do* take is much smaller. For runaways and even unknown missing cases, much of the work, at least the important preliminary work, is completed by patrol. By the time the case reaches the investigator, the number of possible actions is more limited.

Generally speaking, most of the investigator's follow-up activities are performed over the telephone rather than in the field primarily due to limited resources. Because most juvenile bureaus are swamped with other types of cases (for example, child abuse and crimes committed *by* juveniles), they do not have sufficient personnel to go out in the field, except for the most important cases.

Initially, all cases receive the same telephone inquiries. The detective assigned to the case contacts the reporting party, usually the parent, to determine if the child returned home, if there has been contact with the child, or if the parent has any additional ideas as to the child's location. The investigator may then contact the child's friends, relatives, schools, social workers, hospitals, shelters, or any other person who may have knowledge of the child. In parental abduction cases, if the investigator is unable to reach the offending parent directly, he or she will attempt to contact relatives, a girlfriend or boyfriend, or other friends.

Part of the process of finding a missing youth, one might assume, would involve going to where juveniles hang out. Unfortunately, few jurisdictions have enough investigators to do this on a daily basis. Therefore, much of this task falls on patrol officers, who, as mentioned in the previous chapter, are generally reluctant to pursue this activity.

Depending on the seriousness of the case, many investigative units issue a teletype to all of the precincts in the city once they have received the report from patrol. Many police departments also routinely issue teletypes to neighboring jurisdictions. This measure is taken on the chance that an officer in the neighboring jurisdiction would somehow run across the youth. However, in some locales, investigators rarely issue teletypes outside the jurisdiction. Officers in these jurisdictions believe such teletypes are generally of little use. They know, based on their own experience and workload, that they do not have the resources to act on the teletypes sent to them. In large cities, officers also have a hard time responding to out-of-jurisdiction reports because of the inadequacy of the child's description. Police frequently get teletypes that say something like, "Be on the alert for so-and-so kid, a white male, age sixteen, brown hair and brown eyes, 150 pounds and 5'7" tall, last seen wearing jeans and a t-shirt." How many kids are there in a large city who fit that descripton? The chances of finding him seem like one in a million.

Assuming that a missing child is not found during an intensive search of the area or that no new leads are found, investigators may, at their discretion, release the child's description to the media. In smaller communities, this action often leads to a successful and quick resolution of the case. Missing children organizations and neighborhood residents may assist the police in disseminating the missing child's picture and physical description by posting flyers in the area where he or she was last seen, as well as in nearby towns.

As noted earlier, patrol officers generally dislike responding to runaway calls, particularly repeat runaways. Investigators are no different. There are few rewards to locating a runaway teenager, particularly a chronic runaway with serious personal and family problems. Because the youth cannot be detained in most states, he or she is likely to be back on the streets before the parents can be reunited with the youth. Even when the family is reunited, the officer believes, based on experience, that the youth may run away again. It appears to the investigator to be a vicious cycle, and little can be done to solve the family's problems. In some cases officers may believe a youth should not be returned home because of conditions there. This can also be a disincentive to vigorous investigation.

The investigation of parental abduction cases involves a different set of issues, actions, and problems. Because of the ambiguities of criminal statutes on this crime and the traditional hands-off attitude law enforcement agencies have had toward crimes associated with domestic conflict (including spousal abuse), investigative personnel either give parental abduction and custody violation cases cursory treatment, or try to refer them to another agency. Some municipal police departments claim the sheriff's department of their county or borough has jurisdiction over these cases. In California, parental abductions and custody violations are, by statute, to be investigated by the local district attorney. Local law enforcement agencies in the state encourage their county DA to take such cases. But even with this clear statement of responsibility, only some California county DA offices have staff who will investigate parental abduction cases and take other follow-up action once a patrol officer has written a report. In many states and counties, no law enforcement agency—police, sheriff, or prosecutor—wants to assume responsibility for these cases and consequently little effort is exerted to investigate them or resolve them.

As noted in chapter 6, some state parental abduction statutes distinguish the degree of the crime—misdemeanor or felony—based on the nature of the taking or detention. If the abducting parent does not leave the state or endanger the child, the abduction is only a misdemeanor or not a crime at all. If the offender crosses the state line, he or she may be charged with a felony. The status of the offense will often determine what level of effort the investigator puts into the case. He or she is more lax in follow-up when the situation involves a nonabusive parent or an intrastate or intracounty taking, and the state criminal code has itself labeled the violation as nonserious.

Parental abduction statutes are often vague on the question of the offending parent's intent in taking or detaining the child, thus inviting police investigators who are already reticent to deal with these cases to use their discretion to avoid pursuing the case. Most parental abduction statutes are also unclear on how much time needs to have elapsed before an overdue return of a child from a visit or an overdue delivery of a child for a visitation constitutes a violation of a court order or the crime of parental abduction. These ambiguities make it harder for investigators to know what cases should be pursued and what cases are, in actuality, prosecutable.

Confusion over the applicability of the state criminal laws on parental abductions and interference with custody is confounded by confusion in the civil law on child custody orders. In spite of the restrictions created by model legislation to establish one state as having jurisdiction to determine or amend a child's custody, courts in different jurisdictions (and even in different counties within the same state) do issue conflicting orders that result in giving each parent full custody. It is far from clear what state's orders should supersede; faced with this situation, the investigator may merely note the problems in a report that is passed on to the prosecutor, or he or she places the child in temporary custody until the civil courts decide between themselves which state will exercise ultimate jurisdiction. Resolution of this matter, in turn, affects the investigator's assessment of what, if any, laws have been violated and if a criminal investigation should proceed.

When police investigators do take on the investigation of parental abduction cases, their first tasks are to determine if the child is safe and if the parent who has possession of the child has broken any laws. The investigator will obtain the facts of the situation either by talking with the complaining parent in person or on the telephone. If a copy of the most recent custody order has not already been filed with the patrol officer's report, the investigator will ask the complaining parent for a copy. The investigator will also talk to the offending parent, if possible, as well and to relatives, neighbors, or friends who can verify the child's location and well-being. The officer will ask the offending parent to explain his or her side of the story, the basis for the actions taken, and what he or she plans to do about the situation. If the matter involves a conflict over different versions of a custody order, the investigator will ask the offending parent for a copy of his or her version.

In the less serious or troublesome cases, by the time an investigator contacts the offending parent, the crises may have passed. The child may have been returned or the parents have hired lawyers and the investigator is able to verify that the couple is going through the proper legal channels to deal with the custody problem. When the abducting parent has not yet thought through what to do next, the investigator may be able to convince the parent to return the child and submit the conflict to the family court. If the parent agrees, the formal investigation may be concluded at this point. Or, the investigative unit may keep the case open pending a follow-up call from the parties stating either that the problems have been renewed, or the matter has been adjudicated by the family court.

Given the vagueness of many parental abduction statutes, investigators are not always readily able to determine if a criminal statute has been broken. They view erroneously removing a child from his or her lawful guardian as a serious mistake that should be avoided if possible. Many investigators would rather err on the side of permitting the child to remain with a parent who in fact does not have lawful authority. However, there are some who are willing to remove the child from the parent if there is any doubt as to lawful custody. They will place the youngster with child protective services pending a court's determination of the facts.

Custody orders themselves are often written in vague or general terms—for example, giving one parent "reasonable visitation," or assigning parents "alternating holidays" with the child. When a parent shows the investigator the custody order, it may not be obvious to him or her what "reasonable" requires or permits, especially when the parents have conflicting ideas about the time span a holiday encompasses or the specific hours at which a visit should begin or end. Unfamiliar with the couple's past practices or verbal agreements, the investigator is not in a position to pass judgment on which parent is in the right and, therefore, which parent is having his or her custody rights violated. If the child is otherwise safe and being properly cared for, the investigator often does nothing to try to change the situation. Rather, he or she passes the case information on to the prosecutor, or merely advises the parents to return to family court to have a judge write an order specifying the terms of the custody arrangement and visitation schedule in greater detail.

When the investigator is not able to get the parents either to comply with an existing custody order on their own or to agree to take their custody problems to family court, the officer may run criminal history checks on both parents. This measure is taken to determine if either parent has had trouble with the authorities in the past, has a record of violent behavior, or has failed to follow-through on legal responsibilities—such as appearing for court dates, paying fines, complying with probation supervision, and so forth. Investigators also use this information to size up both the complaining parent and the offending parent. They use this information to assess the likelihood of cooperation from each parent, the volatility of the child's situation, and the seriousness of the violation.

Aside from the routine nature of the investigation, local law enforcement agencies are hard-pressed to resolve these cases or to bring together the kind of evidence the DA requires for successful prosecution. Moreover, the cases are often difficult to pursue, particularly if the abductor leaves the state. Local law enforcement officials in the home state must rely on police departments in the other state, and those departments are already overburdened with cases. In the situation of the out-of-state abduction, the complaining parent has the greatest need for law enforcement assistance because this parent does not have the leads or the resources to locate or return the child him- or herself. Yet, it is also these cases that investigators find most exasperating and unrewarding, and have the greatest reluctance to do much about.

Even when police investigators take a parental abduction case seriously, investigate it to the fullest, and provide the DA with solid evidence to support a criminal prosecution, the prosecutor's office may be slow to move on it, or refuse altogether to file a complaint. Based on the facts of the case, the DA may decide that the child is better off with the absconding parent or relative than the "lawful" guardian. For example, in one California county, the juvenile investigator in the local police department presented a case to the DA of a mother whose children had been abducted by the grandmother; the grandmother had no intention of ever returning the kids. The police had learned that the mother, a single parent, was pregnant with a third child and had two little ones at home; she also had a substance abuse problem and was on welfare. The grandmother lived in New Jersey and was aware that the daughter had been using drugs. She originally had asked to have the children for a visit for the summer. Initially the mother refused to let them go, but when the grandmother promised to return the children in August, the mother relented. However, once the grandmother had the children with her in New Jersey, she told the mother she was going to keep them; she told the investigating officer she never intended to return them.

Although, as the investigator put it, the complaining parent was not the "ideal" mother, he had felt the evidence was strong: the grandmother had clearly deprived the mother of lawful custody of her children and by doing so had violated the state's criminal statute against custodial interference. Once the DA received the case, however, he refused to file a complaint or pursue extradition of the grandmother, because he felt the children were "better off" where they were.

Many prosecutors say they do not like to deal with parental abduction cases because they involve domestic problems which they believe are best handled by a family court judge and not by the criminal justice system. They recognize, and rightly so, they do not have the expertise, nor is it their job to decide who's a good parent or who the child should reside with. But ironically, when prosecutors refuse to enforce the criminal laws against unlawful parental takings or detentions, they are, in effect, deciding these matters.

The message often transmitted to investigators is that the DA places a low priority on parental abductions and custody disputes. In those locales where the DA refuses to file charges or to see parental abductions as a criminal matter, investigators feel it is hardly worth it to put much effort into documenting the situation or collecting evidence.

Sometimes prosecutors issue a warrant for the absconding parent's arrest based on the report prepared by the investigator. But the goal in taking this action is not necessarily to bring the parent to trial for punishment. Rather, some DAs use this recourse to induce the parent to return to the jurisdiction with the child. Once the offending parent realizes the seriousness of the situation and delivers him- or herself to the local authorities, the DA may drop the criminal proceedings in exchange for a promise that the parent will deal with custody problems in the proper forum. The main objectives—getting the child back, and getting both parents to bring their problems to the family court for proper resolution—have been accomplished. While many investigators accept these outcomes as appropriate, others believe prosecutors should follow through on the appropriate criminal action, particularly if police personnel have taken the time and energy to prepare a solid criminal case.

By far, stranger abductions are the rarest type of missing children cases, yet they command and receive the highest mobilization of resources. Many jurisdictions, particularly smaller ones, have not encountered such a case in years. Even in larger cities, kidnaping or abduction by a stranger is a relatively rare event. One big-city investigator, for example, estimated that only one or two stranger abductions occur in a year and most have a quick resolution (that is, the youth is recovered unharmed). Many investigators believe that their jurisdictions do not have a kidnapping problem. Many officers feel the problem of stranger kidnappings is blown way out or proportion.

Unless there are witnesses to the abduction or clear evidence of foul play, the patrol and investigative units handle the case like that of an ordinary missing person. However, when it is determined that an abduction has taken place, the case is generally handled by a special investigative unit. When this unit becomes involved, all investigative personnel redouble their efforts—they reinterview witnesses, repeat a physical search, gather evidence, and the like. Investigators of kidnapping cases may encounter the same limitations to establishing leads and building a strong case that investigators of other crimes face—their case depends on the nature and quality of the evidence. If there are witnesses and the police can get the license number of the kidnapper's car, for example, the case may be relatively easy to solve.

But if there are no witnesses and no physical evidence, the police face a difficult, and sometimes impossible, task of finding the child and the kidnapper. This problem can be illustrated many times over. A seven-year-old, hearing-impaired girl, Amber Swartz-Garcia, was playing in her front yard one afternoon in 1988. When her mother went out to check on her, she had vanished. No clues, no witnesses, no physical evidence. She has not been seen since. Similar circumstances surround the disappearances of youngsters in many of the well-publicized cases, such as Etan Patz in New York and Kevin Collins in San Francisco.

Follow-up Activities

In most jurisdictions, once a child has been located or reunified with the family, police procedures for following up the case are minimal. Normally, an investigator with the juvenile unit interviews the youth or the parent over the telephone to verify that the youth has returned. Face-to-face interviews are rare in most jurisdictions, unless the youth has been located by law enforcement personnel and is in custody. When the investigator speaks directly with a runaway who has returned home, he or she makes an effort to find out why the youth ran away or at least recommends a counseling agency to the youth or parents.

A few departments make interviewing youths who have been found or returned home a routine function of the juvenile unit. For example, each precinct of the New York City Police Department has a designated youth officer to "debrief" returned runaways and their parents. Parents sometimes are asked by the youth officer to bring the child into the station house for a talk. The officer will ask the youngster why he or she ran away and what happened to the youth while away from home. The officer will also look for signs of child abuse or neglect. The debriefing includes questioning the parents. The officer asks them about the youth's school performance, about discipline at home, and about the youngster's moods and personality. In short, the officer tries to identify root problems and suggest solutions for them.

A few police departments offer programs to prevent repeat runaways. The police department in Lincoln, Nebraska, is one law enforcement agency that has developed an innovative follow-up service, called the Coping Program, to help returned runaways and their families address their problems. The Lincoln Police Department's Youth Aid Unit (the juvenile bureau) started the program in 1985. The program tries to short-circuit the cycle of running away from home as a way to cope with family problems by offering counseling sessions to parents and their runaway children, once the children have returned home. Headed by Lieutenant Erv Portis, the program is run by sworn officers who have received special training from psychologists at the nearby University of Nebraska. Counseling sessions are led by an officer who serves as a facilitator in putting group members through various communication exercises. All parties get the opportunity to vent their feelings. The communication exercises give parents and children specific tools for discussing difficult or emotional issues and for resolving them.

Closing the Case

All departments use the same general criteria for closing a case; that is, the youth is located and it is determined that the youth is no longer in danger. This does not necessarily mean that the youth has been reunited with the parent or parents before police personnel close the case. For example, a missing youth may be found in detention for alleged criminal activity. Sometimes, though, it is unclear when to close a case under these criteria. If the youth leaves the state and takes up residence with a friend or relative in another state, investigators are sometimes unsure what to do. On the one hand, the youth has been located and seems to be safe, but on the other hand, the youth is not with his or her parent or legal guardian, or there is no clear determination of which parent is legally authorized to have custody of the child.

In cases where a missing juvenile has not been located as a result of an initial search and investigation effort, the case will remain open until the missing youth reaches the age of majority. At this point, some departments close the case. Other departments automatically transfer the case to the adult missing persons unit. And still other departments notify the reporting party that if they want the case to remain open, they must come to the station and file a new report for a missing adult.

Conclusion

How law enforcement agencies handle reports of missing children varies enormously across the country. This variation has several bases. One is the size of the different law enforcement agencies. Some police departments have hundreds of officers and others have only a handful. Another is a department's internal structure and case management—whether police personnel are assigned to specialized units (such as juvenile, missing persons, homicide, and so forth). The law enforcement and crime control problems of the surrounding community as well as its political leadership are also important determinants of a department's priorities and resources.

The biggest reason for differences in handling missing children cases rests in the nature of the cases. As we have pointed out, there is no legal category of a missing child. The cases that fall within this rubric are quite different; the differential responses by the police follow from this variation. The circumstances presented by the different types of cases or categories of missing children call for different interventions and follow-up. Moreover, expertise and training equip police with particular resources and capabilities to deal with a set of circumstances. For example, the circumstances surrounding runaway and parental abduction cases tend to involve interpersonal conflicts that have a long history and individuals that are highly emotional. Police either feel ill-equipped to deal with these situations or assume their expertise in criminal matters is irrelevant; what is needed to resolve the situation is a social worker or a family counselor.

Police are most willing to investigate and follow-up cases that involve a clear-cut violation of the criminal law, behavior universally regarded as dangerous, a victim that has suffered or will suffer physical harm unless the police intervene, and an offender who is blameworthy and deserves to be caught and prosecuted. Stranger kidnappings involve all of these elements. From the perspective of the police, they call for and receive zealous police investigation and follow-up. Runaway cases, on the other hand, involve almost none of these elements, and receive little police attention.

Many of the differences in police responses to missing children cases make sense from the point of view of police operations and expertise. To the extent policymakers, missing children organizations, and affected parents want police to treat missing children cases differently, or want police to treat all missing children cases as if they were serious and life-threatening, they must take into account the organizational, legal, and ideological environment in which law enforcement personnel operate.

9

Issues in Law Enforcement and Missing Children

WHEN police officers respond to a report of a missing child, their actions are shaped by factors such as the type of case, the likely impact of police intervention, organizational constraints, and legal mandates. Police officers rely on departmental policies and written or unwritten procedures for direction on the appropriate course of action. They also rely on individual and department-wide perceptions, attitudes, and assumptions about different types of missing children. These factors explain why police deal with missing children cases the way they do. They can also tell us something about the obstacles that limit how proactive or effective law enforcement personnel can be in recovering missing children.

Police Perception of Missing Children

The famous American sociologist W.I. Thomas once observed that whatever people believe to be real can be real in its consequences. How law enforcement officers perceive the problem of missing children has a direct relationship to their actions. To the lay public and the media, the term *missing children* has come to be a short-hand reference to children who, because of having been abducted by a stranger or by a parent, or having run away or gotten lost, are not where they are supposed to be and are assumed to be in need of help.

To the police, the term *missing children* has no such meaning. To the extent the phrase conjures up any image, it is the image of a child who has wandered away and is lost. In the eyes of most police officers throughout the country, the social, legal, and criminal phenomenon popularly coined as the "missing children problem" does not exist. Rather, the police tend to think in terms of specific cases—situations in which children are missing because they have been kidnapped by a stranger, they have run away from home, they have been abducted by a parent, or they have gotten lost. Each of these situations presents a particular set of legal, investigative, and management requirements. And for each of these types of cases, law enforcement agencies have developed a standard method for responding. Some types of missing children cases are easier to solve than others, some warrant more intense or longer-term investigations than others, and some invoke a greater sense of alarm and urgency than others.

But, by a large, from the perspective of most police personnel, none of these cases constitutes a unique problem—in terms of the number of cases police are expected to respond to, the investigative resources available (or not available) to solve them, or the responses actually given the different types of missing children cases. Generally, police feel they respond appropriately to the different categories of missing children cases.

The problems police do encounter are generic problems that can affect all the cases the police are assigned to handle. Each police department has a finite set of resources; supervisors have to set priorities and cannot devote equal time and attention to reports of rapes, burglaries, thefts, runaways, and traffic violations. As a community grows, the number of crimes and other community problems reported to the police are likely to increase. If the deparment's budget and staff expand at the same pace, crime continues to be manageable; if not, finite resources have to be stretched even further. In addition, whenever a crime has been committed, the police must depend on the amount and reliability of the evidence to arrest the perpetrator and to help the local district attorney successfully prosecute the case. If the evidence is poor or there are no witnesses, the police may be unable either to catch the perpetrator or make the case against him or her stick in court. These factors are a problem for police whether they are dealing with a homicide case, a rape case, a drug dealing case, or a stranger kidnapping case.

Type of Missing Children Cases

Police officers generally do not think of missing children as some generic law enforcement concern; nor do they perceive missing children to be a problem, and certainly not a serious problem for law enforcement. When they think of specific categories of missing children, they assess their seriousness in terms of the harm posed to the child, the number of cases in the category, as well as the number and dangerousness of the other cases they handle. To all police officers—from the cop on the beat to the chief of police—stranger kidnapping is one of the most serious crimes that can be committed. Even when the restraint is temporary and the child returns home after a short period of time, many stranger kidnappings involve some sort of sexual or physical assault and psychological trauma. And some kidnappings end in the death of the child. Because of the likelihood of harm and the seriousness of the harm, no resources are spared to investigate a stranger kidnapping. Law enforcement agencies do all they can to find the child and prosecute the criminal. From the perspective of potential or likely harm alone, stranger kidnappings are a serious type of missing children case.

However, when this crime is compared with other serious crimes, such as homicide, officers have a different perception. In the overall crime picture, stranger kidnappings of children are not a serious crime problem—they do not happen often and they do not affect a large number of children. For example, in San Francisco in 1986, there were 114 reported murders and only one report of a child kidnapping by a stranger. This ratio of homicides to kidnappings is similar in most jurisdictions. Officers ask, rhetorically, "Which is the more serious problem?"

Recent empirical data confirm police perceptions that stranger kidnappings of children are rare and do not pose a serious problem to the safety of the community. The U.S. Department of Justice (Office of Juvenile Justice and Delinquency Prevention) recently sponsored a large study of law enforcement practices regarding missing children and homeless youth. This multiphase and multiyear study was jointly conducted by the Research Triangle Institute of North Carolina and the URSA Institute of San Francisco. The first phase, undertaken by Research Triangle Institute, consisted of a mail survey of 791 randomly selected law enforcement agencies throughout the country. Thus, the sample of agencies was fairly representative of all American law enforcement agencies. One of the questions asked if the agency had handled any stranger kidnapping cases for the year of 1986. *Ninety-five percent* of the agencies responded that they handled *no such cases* the entire year. Moreover, the median number (similar to the average) of stranger kidnappings of all departments was zero for that year. In all probability, 1986 was not significantly different from other years.[1]

Parental abductions are generally viewed by law enforcement personnel as far less serious than stranger abductions. In those few instances when there is strong evidence that the abductor is likely to harm (physically or sexually abuse) the child, police do view the case as serious; it warrants rigorous efforts to recover the child and prosecute the offending parent. Such cases are, however, comparatively infrequent. They are a small proportion of all crimes that involve assault or some other crime against a person. Although parental abductions appear to be on the increase, most likely due to the increasing divorce rate, they are still not as common as robberies, rape, aggravated assault, and so on. As will be discussed in greater detail later, the problems with this type of case are the vagueness of the criminal statutes, the perception that parental abduction is a civil matter rather than a criminal one, and the lack of cooperation and prosecution by the district attorney, even if the police do make an arrest.

Most police officers to not perceive runaways as a particularly serious problem—at least not in terms of the seriousness of the harm most runaways face or the likelihood of the harm occurring. While many more youths run away than are abducted by strangers or their parents, most of these youths return home after a short period of time, completely unharmed. And while they are away from home, they are in the company of known friends, they are by themselves but in an area in their hometown or neighborhood that is familiar to them, or they are hanging out on school grounds. Only a small portion of all runaways travel to unknown cities or towns to take up life on the streets. These youths do risk being harmed and exploited. But they are the minority of cases and for most police officers, they do not represent the typical runaway case.

The Research Triangle Study also addressed police perceptions of the seriousness of the runaway problem. The mail survey questionnaire asked law enforcement personnel in the 791 agencies to rate the "seriousness of the runaway/homeless youth problem" in their jurisdiction. Over 50 percent of the agencies claimed that the runaway/homeless youth problem was "not very serious" or "not at all serious."[2]

In the past, law enforcement and juvenile court officials had legal authority to incarcerate youths who were truants, runaways, incorrigible, beyond the control of their parents, or who violated curfew. Being subject to the coercive measures and sanctions used against individuals who did violate the criminal law gave running away the status of a quasicriminal act. Police had a clearer law enforcement mandate to intervene in runaway cases. To the extent they acted to prevent harm, it was to protect the runaway from doing harm to him- or herself or from falling into a harmful or dangerous situation. With the deinstitutionalization of status offenders movement, running away was no longer viewed as behavior warranting police intervention for the protection of the public or the youth—in fact, police lost their authority to use conventional law enforcement measures for crime fighting or public protection to deal with these cases.

Because there are few legal recourses for dealing with runaways, police officers view these cases as a matter for social and family service agencies, not law enforcement. To the extent police officers think of runaways as presenting problems to community safety or law enforcement, they do so when, out of economic circumstances, runaways commit criminal acts in order to survive on the streets. Then they are no longer simply runaways—they are criminals.

In sum, police officer perception of case seriousness is in direct proportion to the perceived danger of the child. Any case in which the child is in physical danger—for example, a stranger abduction or a lost, small child—is taken with utmost seriousness. Police departments mobilize all resources for such cases. Those cases in which the police believe the child is not in danger receive little attention. In fact, the older, habitual runaways are often viewed by the police as the "victimizers" of the community, rather than the "victims," because these juveniles are sometimes picked up for criminal activity while they are away from their residence. In many jurisdictions, essentially nothing is done to recover chronic runaways.

Duties Shape Officer Perceptions

In addition to the type of case, the attitudes and actions police take with missing children cases are influenced by their duties. Those officers who do not specialize in juvenile work have somewhat different opinions from those officers who do specialize in working with juveniles, except in stranger kidnapping cases. Officers at all levels of the department universally view kidnapping as an extremely serious offense—although not necessarily a significant law enforcement problem because the crime is so rare.

Officers who do not regularly work with juveniles (or who have not worked in the juvenile bureau) tend to see missing children cases both in terms of the exigencies they present for crime control and law enforcement and the most common outcome. The patrol officer, particularly in the larger jurisdictions, is confronted with an enormous number of calls for service of varying degrees of seriousness. The officer is often faced with finding immediate solutions to complex problems, and then moving quickly to the next call. These concerns are illustrated by the following parental abduction case. On being dispatched to respond to such a call, the patrol officer is told by the reporting party that an ex-spouse took the children, and the whereabouts of all parties are unknown. Compared with all of his or her other calls for service, what is the officer to think? On the one hand, the case is serious because a child is involved and the child may suffer emotional distress. On the other hand, the officer believes these cases are not particularly serious, in part because based on feedback from investigators, the officer believes the child is unlikely to be harmed. Moreover, the officer "knows" (based on personal and vicarious experience) that the district attorney rarely prosecutes such cases, even if an arrest is made. In other words, judging from the world view of the patrol officer who works with high-volume cases (such as burglary and larceny) and with violent crime (homicide, robbery, assault, rape), parental abductions do not represent pressing or threatening crimes that require intensive follow-up to protect the safety of the community.

Runaway cases present another good illustration. Although this type of "missing" juvenile is by far the most common, there are many factors that tell the patrol officer this is not a serious type of case. What officers commonly see is a situation in which a teenager cannot get along with his or her family and decides to leave the house. In the vast majority of cases, the youth returns home, unharmed, within a matter of days (or hours). Another common situation is the youth living in a group home who decides, as he or she has several times before, to go into town for the night with friends. These youths, too, normally return to their residences after a short period. Given the other demands of the job and the high volume of cases, most officers believe there is little they can do in such cases.

Officers, of course, know from experience that runaways often do not have enough money to survive on the streets for long without turning to illegal activities. Even when this occurs, the offenses committed by such youths are relatively minor—for example, larceny, prostitution, and selling small quantities of drugs—and are given less attention than other types of criminal activity. It is uncommon, in the patrol officer's experience, for a runaway to become involved in armed robberies or aggravated assaults. In short, the typical patrol officer is likely to view the runaway not as a serious problem, but as a "pain in the neck" or a troublemaker. The "generalist" police officer does not tend to consider runaways as victims of family abuse or conflict, or victims of exploitation on the street.

By contrast, officers who work with juveniles on a regular basis seem to have a broader and more sophisticated view of the nature and seriousness of runaway and parental abduction cases. Having had more time to delve into the details of the case, more time to understand the causes of the youth's behavior, and more time to reflect on the entire situation, juvenile specialists are more likely than patrol officers to look beyond the immediate crime control issues. They are aware of the other dimensions of runaway cases—family and social dynamics triggering the behavior, experiences runaways encounter on the streets, and interventions that are needed to address a youth's individual and family problems.

Juvenile specialists, particularly in large cities, are much more likely to believe that runaways, especially chronic or long-term runaways, present a serious problem. They have pressing medical, psychological, and physical needs that, when left unaddressed, can lead to criminal behavior (with the runaway being either the victim or the perpetrator) and other social problems. Juvenile specialists view out-of-jurisdiction runaways, in particular, as a problem because there are so many of them and few cities have resources to deal with them. Local social service agencies would like to help nonresident runaways, but they simply do not have the funds to do so. Moreover, there are relatively few private facilities to care for such youths. Far away from friends, relatives, and other sources of support or aid, these runaways often turn to illegal means to secure money and find a place to live.

Unfortunately, this means that such youths may be exploited or become involved in crimes such as prostitution, selling drugs, or theft. A scenario frequently cited by juvenile specialists is for a youth to start out in prostitution, be taken home by an unscrupulous adult, given affection as well as drugs, and end up in child pornography.

The police officer on the beat attempts to have minimal interaction with these youths because they do not present any immediate crime or law enforcement problem, and there seems to be little the police officer can do to or for them. Juvenile specialists, on the other hand, see police intervention as a way to bring runaways in contact with the facilities, services, and personnel that can address some of their needs. The juvenile specialist understands that the beat officer's strategy of minimizing or avoiding interactions with runaways is practical and cost-efficient given the other cases he or she is expected to deal with. Juvenile specialists also acknowledge that realistically, while the police have a general responsibility for protecting child welfare, there is little police personnel can do to help runaways; the most effective intervention for addressing the needs and problems of runaway cases must come from social services, not law enforcement.

Unlike other police officers and the lay public, the juvenile specialist does not dwell only on the one big tragedy that makes the headlines—the stranger kidnapping. He or she sees hundreds or even thousands of little tragedies of the missing children who are runaways. They are the tragedies of child abuse and neglect, family dysfunction, child prostitution and pornography, drug abuse, and unwanted pregnancies. In short, the juvenile officer sees runaways as presenting social and legal problems that are both more subtle and more damaging to the community's well-being than the stranger kidnapping. Unlike stranger kidnappings, with runaways (as well as parental abductions), there are few happy endings. In these cases, solving the crime or reuniting the child with the family does not bring an end to the family's or the community's distress. The immediate crisis of the missing child is over, but the underlying family problems are likely to continue.

The juvenile specialist sees runaways as a problem for the future as well. The chronic runaway of today has a good chance of becoming the adult criminal of tomorrow. It makes much more sense, in the specialist's eyes, to deal directly with the runaway youth's family and personal problems before they mushroom into serious criminal behavior that must be dealt with by imprisonment for extended periods of time. Moreover, not only can running away and associated street life lead to future law enforcement problems, they can also lead to serious future health care problems. As mounting evidence is showing, runaways who engage in unsafe acts of prostitution and substance abuse are more likely to contract and transmit the AIDS virus.

The juvenile specialist's "broader" view of the missing children phenomenon is beginning to encompass parental abduction cases as well. While the juvenile specialist realizes that few children are *physically* abused by their parent during an abduction, they are coming to realize that parental abduction can leave long-lasting emotional scars on its victims. For this reason alone, parental abduction cases are beginning to be viewed as more serious by the juvenile specialist. As we have repeatedly suggested, however, the types of missing children cases vary enormously in the degree of potential harm to the youth, and officer attitudes toward these cases vary accordingly.

Organizational Constraints on Law Enforcement

Law enforcement officers face many legal and organizational obstacles that limit their ability to resolve missing children cases. These obstacles often prevent law enforcement officials from doing everything possible in working the case; they also create disincentives that discourage individual officers from trying as hard as they can. Some of these obstacles affect all types of missing children cases, but some have direct relation to specific case types—for example, runaways.

Limited Department Resources

Many officers point to a lack of resources as limiting their ability to investigate every missing child case thoroughly. As one officer put it, "the bottom line is money." Although in smaller communities, the numbers are low and manageable; in large cities, missing children reports—largely of runaways—overwhelm the system. It is not uncommon for an investigator in medium to large cities to carry two-hundred to three-hundred open cases of missing juveniles each month. Given the volume of cases, patrol officers and investigators only have time enough to perform cursory investigative and follow-up activities. As one detective from a large midwestern police department stated. "We, quite frankly, do not provide the follow-up we would like on these cases and probably not what most people think they get."

Officers are pessimistic, given tight budgets and the low priority of runaway cases, that anything can be done to increase resources. Some departments have undertaken some internal reorganization to use existing resources more efficiently. Some officers have found that by reorganizing the department, there has been a significant decrease in the caseload juvenile detectives carry. For example, departments that have separate missing persons units are able to handle runaway and routine parental abduction cases more efficiently than a juvenile bureau because of case specialization. Whereas the juvenile bureau normally concentrates on child abuse cases and crimes committed by juveniles, a missing persons unit devotes all of its energy and expertise exclusively to missing person cases.

Unfortunately, reorganization and specialization may only be options for larger departments. Because the vast majority of police departments are small (fewer than fifty officers), and most department personnel do not believe a significant missing children problem exists in their community, it would not be cost effective to create and support a separate missing persons unit in smaller departments.

Some police departments have been able to stretch limited resources by employing civilians to assume some of the duties previously assigned to sworn officers. For example, the Seattle Police Department uses civilians to handle some runaway cases. These civilians, called community services officers (CSOs), primarily work cases of repeat runaways. They do more than simply take a report. They advise parents about their legal options, provide crisis intervention and short-term counseling, and make referrals to longer-term counseling programs to help families solve their problems. With these interventions, they hope to break the cycle of running away from home.

Inadequate Community Resources

Officers frequently mention that their communities do not have adequate shelter and counseling programs to help address the personal and family problems that frequently cause children to run away or that often lead to parental abductions. This obstacle is most often mentioned in larger cities because they are "magnet" cities—that is, they attract runaways from across the nation.

Unfortunately, even when the community is willing to pay for additional shelter space for runaways, often the services are only provided for youths residing *within* the jurisdiction, not for those who come from other parts of the state or country.

The scope of this problem is enormous in some cities. For example, Los Angeles County has fewer than one-hundred emergency beds for homeless or runaway children, yet it is estimated that on any given day there are ten-thousand or so juveniles within the county needing shelter and services. Many of these are youths who come from outside the Los Angeles area, and even outside California. This obstacle exists, to a lesser extent and in various degrees, throughout the country. Some cities have adequate shelter space, but the shelters are located miles from the law enforcement agency; consequently officers do not use the facilities that are available. They do not like to be used as a "taxi service" for runaways or street kids. When a sixteen-year-old juvenile approaches a patrol officer in a downtown area and says that he or she needs a ride to the runaway shelter on the other side of town, the officer has two options. He or she can drop everything and spend forty-five minutes as a taxi driver or tell the youth to take the bus. Most officers, particularly in larger cities, choose the latter alternative, because they feel they have more pressing matters to attend to.

Inadequate shelter space is an obstacle for law enforcement agencies because juveniles who do not have their material needs provided for are more likely to become involved in criminal activities, as victims or victimizers. Law enforcement officers and shelter staff alike believe there is a tremendous need to provide more short-term shelter care and services for runaway and homeless youth. Yet short-term care alone is not a solution. Shelter workers, in particular, would like to see longer-term programs. Most youths, particularly "street kids," stay in shelters for only a few days, on the average, just long enough to re-group or make plans to go home or back on the streets. What is also needed are long-term shelter programs that offer runaways housing and training in survival skills—sexual hygiene, problem solving and communication skills, job training, and employment. In the absence of programs that address the immediate needs of runaways and prepare those who refuse to return home for self-sufficiency, there are few actions police alone can take to help runaways.

Poor Follow-up and Prosecution of Parental Abductions

There are a number of obstacles that limit the effectiveness of police intervention in parental abduction cases in particular. When the abductor leaves the local jurisdiction, local officers must rely on authorities in other jurisdictions to track down or effect the return of the child and abductor. Detectives often state that private investigators (if one can be afforded) do a better job in these situations, and they sometimes recommend this option to the reporting parent. Officers also frequently cite poorly written or hard-to-interpret court documents (that is, orders or decrees) as an obstacle. The reporting parent is often unfamiliar with the document, and what might appear to be a violation of the custody order turns out to be within the legal framework of the agreement. Sometimes the reporting parent does not have a current custody order, sometimes there is joint custody, and sometimes there is a common law marriage. All of these situations cause great confusion to patrol officers as well as to investigators. Officers also complain about the lying and deception among the parties in parental abduction cases, including the parent making the report. Parents lie, on occasion, to make their case look better when they attempt to modify the custody order in civil court. To get more police interest in their case, parents make claims and counterclaims that the other is sexually or physically abusing the child. These claims are often not substantiated when investigated further by police and children's protective services personnel. When officers encounter these problems in responding to individual cases, they become frustrated and lose their interest.

One solution to making parental child snatchings a less ambiguous situation for law enforcement officers is to have parents work from more specific and detailed custody orders. Custody schedules and arrangements that are highly structured and detailed are easier to enforce, or rather, provide a clearer basis for police to determine when a term of the custody order has been violated.

Another frustration law enforcement officers encounter in dealing with parental abduction is the reluctance of the district attorney to prosecute, even when the cases have been thoroughly investigated by the police and there is a clear violation of the criminal law. Because the DA's office often has more serious cases to deal with, the elements of the crime of parental abduction are difficult to prove, and custody questions ultimately have to be referred to civil court for resolution, DAs do not like to prosecute such cases. As a consequence, law enforcement officers feel as if they are being used as an adjunct of the civil court simply to bring the child back—and are not serving in their crime-fighting capacity. In addition, law enforcement officers feel demoralized because they do not get any positive feedback after they clear these cases. From the police officer's perspective, the purpose of the criminal justice system is to arrest and prosecute violators of the criminal law. If DAs are unwilling to prosecute parental abductors, it is difficult for the police to see why they should work so hard to make an arrest.

Law enforcement agencies would like to see more aggressive action taken by the district attorney in parental abduction cases. There is a growing awareness among law enforcement personnel that parental abductions can and do inflict harm on the victim child as well as parent. In addition to psychological trauma, abducted children and left-behind parents are sometimes subjected to force or the threat of force when the abduction occurs.

Some law enforcement officers support the step taken in California to encourage active involvement of the prosecutor in parental abduction cases. There the legislature has authorized the local district attorney to handle the investigation of parental abduction cases and to locate and recover the abducted child. However, as we noted in chapter 6, this statutory change has not had the desired results—district attorneys in some counties continue to avoid dealing with parental abduction cases. In many counties, district attorneys still do not assign staff to investigate parental abduction cases and they do not file criminal complaints against the offending parent.

Lack of Cooperation and Poor Communication

Officers in smaller jurisdictions—jurisdictions where the missing and runaway problem is "manageable"—have complained of poor communication and lack of cooperation from other law enforcement agencies. Officers feel they do a good job recovering runaways and returning them to their homes throughout the country. But they find that other jurisdictions, usually larger cities, often do not reciprocate. Officers in other locales do not pay adequate attention to out-of-jurisdiction teletypes on runaways. Officers investigating parental abduction cases encounter similar problems in getting personnel in another jurisdiction to cooperate with their efforts to locate the absconding parent and to hold the parent for extradition.

Juveniles who run across jurisdictional lines create problems for law enforcement as well. Juvenile officers often know who their "own" repeaters are (that is, those who stay in the home jurisdiction), but do not know about the activities of youths who come from other jurisdictions. There is a lack of shared intelligence among jurisdictions concerning runaways involved in illegal activities—either as victims or victimizers—while on the run.

Aside from their uncooperative relations with law enforcement agencies in other jurisdictions, a number of departments have poor internal communication about missing children cases. This weakness stems in part from the fact that missing children cases constitute a low departmental priority. Officers often do not know how other units in their agency handle missing children or they refer to written policies and procedures that run counter to the way cases are actually handled. Many law enforcement agencies also have poor communication with local service providers or departments of social services. Such poor communications result in misunderstandings: either social service staff refuse to provide information to resolve cases or missing children reports are filed when the child is actually not missing (that is, the child was taken into custody by child protective services and is already under court supervision).

Lack of cooperation sometimes exists in parental abduction cases, particularly if the child is taken across state lines. Notwithstanding the requirements of the Uniform Child Custody Jurisdiction Act and the Parental Kidnapping Prevention Act, courts in the host (new) state still do grant a new custody order when the original order continues in effect in the home state. And sometimes states refuse to extradite known parental abductors to the original state because parental abduction is not a felony in their jurisdiction and officials of the host state do not want the parent to be subject to prosecution in the other state.

Moreover, some state officials will only enforce the custody orders issued by their state's family court. They insist left-behind parents in other states travel to their state to have their custody matter adjudicated. For example, the officials in Arkansas have taken this position, notwithstanding the fact that the Arkansas state legislature adopted a version of the UCCJA.

Law enforcement officers would generally like to see greater national uniformity in laws pertaining to missing children, and runaways in particular. An example of this would be the requirement that all jurisdictions must enter the names of missing children into the NCIC system. However, the federal system of government limits the extent to which uniformity can be imposed; states have the right to address their local problems in ways their elected representatives deem fit. When states choose to adopt policies contrary to the wishes of the federal government or the prevailing wisdom of other states, there are few recourses open for other states to dissuade or sanction them.

Officers would like a greater sharing of intelligence and case data on youths who run away or are taken across jurisdictional lines. But this costs money, which is in short supply at all levels of government. Officers would also like to see more cooperation and better communication with social service providers. This would, presumably, allow law enforcement to keep better track of children, decide who is responsible for them, and determine what services have and have not been provided.

Limitations of the NCIC System

Most officers state that the National Crime Information Center (NCIC) system is good in theory. On occasion, it helps identify missing children and return them to their homes. One such successful recovery involved two girls, ages twelve and fourteen, and a sixteen-year-old boy who were reported as runaways from Indianapolis. The police suspected that they might leave the city, so the names of all three juveniles were entered into the NCIC system. A few days later, police in London, Kentucky, noticed three juveniles hitchhiking. The police stopped the kids and questioned them, ascertaining their names and dates of birth. When the police entered this information into the NCIC system, they discovered that the kids had been reported as runaways from Indianapolis. The Kentucky police took the youths into temporary custody and then called the Indianapolis police. The juveniles were returned home safely.

In spite of successes like this, many officers express a lack of confidence in the NCIC system to identify runaways. The problem is several-fold. First, many states do not have mandatory NCIC reporting requirements. Although many departments automatically enter names into the system, other departments may be selective as to which names are entered and when they are entered. Second, even in those states that have NCIC reporting requirements, some jurisdictions ignore the mandate and either do not enter a child's name into NCIC or delay the entry for several days, or even weeks. In either situation the result is the same: if another department picks up a suspected runaway and his or her name is not listed in the NCIC system, officers have a hard time verifying the child's status. They therefore must release the youth because, in the absence of alleged criminal activity, they do not have a legal basis for detaining him or her.

Third, in order for the system to work, an officer needs the child's true name and date of birth. However, street-wise kids often have no identification or carry false IDs. Both situations produce the same result: inability to determine if the youth is a runaway. There are other practical problems with the system. If a youth's name is misspelled or entered in an alternative way, there may not be a "hit." Few officers claim that they have actually solved runaway cases by using the NCIC system.

One solution to some of these problems would be federal legislation mandating the entry of names of missing children into the NCIC system within a short period of time. But this is hardly a panacea, because runaways rarely come in contact with the police in the first place, and when they do, the more sophisticated youths will not supply the requisite information to make the system work. Moreover, based on the effects of other legal mandates relating to the handling of missing children, law enforcement attitudes and practices resist externally imposed change, particularly if it requires additional work without additional resources.

Legal Constraints

Inability to Detain Status Offenders

The inability of law enforcement to detain runaways (and other status offenders) for more than a few hours discourages police action in such cases. Police officials frequently complain that the youths are back out on the streets before the ink is dry on their reports. The perception that nothing is done by the courts or the social service agencies as follow-up to police intervention causes enormous frustration for most police officers. Slowly they learn that it is easier to do nothing—they turn a blind eye to possible runaways on the streets. As long as a youth does not commit a crime, he or she is pretty much free from police intervention.

Most officers would like to resume the practice of detaining status offenders, particularly runaways, although they may be selective in the use of this measure. Many law enforcement officers feel that the lack of secure detention for runaways only creates a revolving door where the youth runs away, gets caught and taken home or to a shelter, and runs away again shortly thereafter. Selective detention would give law enforcement officers another tool to use in dealing with runaways. But the ability to detain a youngster would do little to change a youth's reliance on running away as a coping method to deal with problems at home.

Some states allow for limited detention. Florida authorities, for example, can hold a youth for three hours before they must release him or her, while California may detain in-state runaways for twenty-four hours and out-of-state runaways for up to three days. In most cases, however, this is not enough time for parents—particularly out-of-state parents—to be notified and arrange for the return of their children.

Most law enforcement officers would like to be able to hold runaways in secure confinement in order to help the children with their problems, or at least protect them from getting themselves into more dangerous situations. Most officers realize that "going back to the good old days" when runaways could be detained up to eighteen years of age is not likely. Officers would prefer, when appropriate, a short period of secure confinement for runaways; many feel that three to five working days would be desirable. This amount of time would be sufficient to stabilize the situation, keep the youth out of high-risk situations (victimization and exploitation), and arrange for the youth to return home or to an adequate alternative placement. Even if state statutes were changed to allow for secure confinement, however, jurisdictions with large numbers of runaway youths, such as Los Angeles, New York, Chicago, and San Francisco, would, under present circumstances, not have the resources to house all such youths anyway.

A return to detention is also advocated by many others, including Alfred Regnery, the former administrator of the Office of Juvenile Justice and Delinquency Prevention. It also appears to have been advocated by the U.S. Attorney General's Advisory Board on Missing Children, appointed in 1984. The idea, evidently, is that juveniles would be better off detained rather than on their own.

But detaining status offenders clearly has its problems. It was deleterious to youth before 1974 and it would be again if it were reinstated. Personal testimony to that effect was given before the U.S. Senate by Mr. Lyonel Norris, whose testimony was related, in part, in the chapter on runaways. Mr. Norris, twenty-six years old at the time of the testimony, had run away from home when he was fourteen years old and spent some time in shelters. He got his life together and went on to become a successful lawyer.

> Mr. Norris: Thank you for inviting me to address this committee, Senator [Specter]. The first thing I would like to touch on . . . is to direct your attention to . . . the administrator's [Alfred Regnery's] statement . . . wherein [he] alludes to the fact that the . . . JJDP Act on runaway youth(s) has been to effectively emancipate them or to allow those who would leave home a free hand.
>
> I would contend that this statement is a gross misstatement of fact. Some twelve years ago, I was a runaway, and I turned to law enforcement agencies, which apparently the administrator believes will provide troubled youth with services and assistance.

> I was returned home with not so much as a question as to why I had left home. I do not quite understand how that fits into his overall statement, but it troubles me to think that some twelve years after the Runaway Youth Act was passed, the administrator is now taking the position that law enforcement can, in fact, do what they have never been able to do, which is to service children and to provide aid and assistance while they are away from home.[3]

In his testimony, Mr. Norris pointed to the negative connotation to a runaway of being placed in a secure facility, regardless of the intent to provide help.

> MR. NORRIS: When I was sixteen and on the street, detaining in a secure facility meant to be going to jail, whatever it was called. And I would submit to this committee that this is even more true than it was then.[4]

How to deal with runaways is an important policy issue related to child and youth welfare that will continue to require attention from public officials. It is not simply a current policy problem. There are hundreds of thousands of runaways each year. Most of these youths will grow up and try to survive in American society. If their needs and problems are simply ignored—either on the streets or in detention—as they have been in the past, they will not go away or resolve themselves. Based on the generational and familial patterns of abuse, alcoholism, drug addiction, and the fatal consequences of contracting the AIDS virus, the problems of today's runaways have a society-wide impact that is likely to worsen in the future. It seems penny wise and pound foolish either to ignore these youths, or to detain them in secure facilities. Providing shelters, social, remedial educational services, and family counseling will not only save money now, but money, social turmoil, and human misery in the future.

PRIVACY LAWS

Law enforcement agencies often encounter obstacles with state privacy and confidentiality laws that exist to protect clients of various social service, shelter, or mental health agencies. Officers in some departments, moreover, complain that they cannot secure information readily from mental health or social service agencies even when state law permits information-sharing. One example is of missing juveniles who may go off their medication or need treatment; the police frequently have a difficult time securing information about juvenile patients that are missing from state, local, and private mental health facilities. Sometimes the necessary information can be secured with a warrant, but it is not possible to get a warrant without probable cause, and probable cause is difficult to obtain without more information from the facilities. Securing a warrant from a psychiatric facility to find out if a youth has been treated there takes considerable police officer time and effort.

Obtaining social security information on a parent who has abducted his or her child—specifically the address to which the Social Security Administration is sending the alleged abductor's check—can be difficult and time consuming for police officers as well. State and the federal parent locator services are available to assist a police search for the abducting parent, but the information these agencies maintain is dated. Police can only turn to these sources after the absconding parent has been gone for several weeks or months and public authorities have begun to acquire records of transactions involving the parent—registration of a motor vehicle, application for a driver's license in a new state, application for welfare or other social services, and so forth.

Returning Children to Their Homes

Law enforcement officers in both large and small communities state that they often encounter problems returning missing children to their homes. This is particularly true for runaways. In some sites the problem is coordinating the child's return trip. Specifically, some law enforcement agencies, rather than local social service agencies or shelters, are responsible for contacting the child's parents and securing a bus or plane ticket if the parent is unable to pick the child up. Officers do not relish this task because it requires a lot of effort and is frequently a waste of time.

If the police apprehend a runaway from out of state, for example, the officer may put the child on a bus home. But if the child does not want to return home, he or she can simply get off the bus at the next stop.

A related, and more serious, problem concerns who will pay for the return transportation of the child. In theory, the parents should pay for their child's return. But many parents cannot afford cross-country transportation expenses, particularly if the child runs away frequently. Presumably one of the agencies involved could pay. But this is a major financial burden. The transportation bill for thousands and thousands of runaways would be millions of dollars a year. Local agencies can ill-afford such expenses.

Payment for return transportation may also be provided under provisions of an interstate compact (an agreement entered into by the states to authorize the means of detention and transportation of runaways). According to most compacts, the state to which the juvenile is returned shall be responsible for payment of the transportation costs. But there are problems. If a jurisdiction has a large number of juveniles who run to a nearby magnet city in a neighboring state, then the home jurisdiction will encounter huge transportation costs. Moreover, these compacts do not mention anything about intrastate runaways. For example, Dallas and Houston have runaways who regularly migrate between cities. The costs of continually returning these children are prohibitive when the funds come from the budgets of individual law enforcement agencies.

The costs of recovering a child who has been abducted by a parent are also prohibitive to many law enforcement departments. As a result, parents are expected to either pay for the travel expenses—usually air fare—of a district attorney investigator or a police officer to pick up the child, once located, or they are expected to make the trip and recover the child themselves. While police personnel generally believe it is safer for all of the parties involved to have sworn officers retrieve the child, fiscal limitations make this course of action unavailable most of the time.

Policy Issues

The foregoing discussion points out a number of specific procedural or policy issues law enforcement agencies have attempted to resolve internally or with direction from public officials and legislators. However, there are a number of other, larger organizational and philosophical issues that affect how police departments handle, or should handle, missing children cases. The issues relate to how agencies process information and take action. They also concern the legal and social status of children in our society.

Case Classification and Department Action

People who work in organizations find it necessary to make shorthand statements about cases to save time and trouble. This shorthand, coded communication develops in part to have a common working vocabulary about experiences in the organization and to save time explaining things in detail whenever a similar situation occurs. It is not possible, for example, for a dispatcher to go into enormous detail about a case with the patrol officer. The dispatcher may not know all that much about the case, and the dispatcher must get the officer to the scene with a minimum of time and effort. Dispatchers, therefore, use capsulized descriptions of cases, which take on special meaning to the patrol officer.

A common case situation is the following. The dispatcher calls a patrol car and says, "Respond to (such-and-such address). . . . Take a report on a sixteen-year-old repeat runaway from a group home." Those few words about this "missing child" convey a host of images and experiences. The term *runaway* tells the officer that the youth left home voluntarily and was not abducted, by a parent or a stranger. The fact that the youth is sixteen years of age tells the officer that the youth can probably take care of him- or herself. The word *repeat* tells the officer that the youth has made it back home (or to a group home) safely at least once in the past. This means, at least to the typical patrol officer, that chances are good that he or she will make it back safely this time. *Group home* means to the officer that the juvenile has probably been in trouble with the law in the past and may be a ward of the court. The youth may therefore be viewed as "trouble" or "no good." It means, if anything, that officers should be on the lookout for the youth because he or she may *victimize* people in the community. All cognitive assumptions tell the officer that the case is not an emergency. Responding to the call with urgency is not necessary.

A different example would be a dispatcher's call to a police officer about two hours before sunset with the following directive, "Proceed to (such-and-such location). . . . A three-year-old child is missing by the river." These few words convey a completely different set of images and assumptions to the patrol officer. The fact that the child is only three years old means that he or she is vulnerable to injury. The fact that the child is near a river means the officer has to act quickly, or else the child may drown. The fact that it is only two hours before dark also means that time is of the essence.

Informal classifications are well ingrained in the minds of most law enforcement personnel, from call-takers and dispatchers to top administrators. Because this informal classification system appears to work for law enforcement agencies *most* of the time, the question is: How can federal and state level policymakers, through passing laws, affect the everyday operations of law enforcement agencies regarding missing children?

Assumptions, Evidence and Decision Rules

The decision rules law enforcement agencies use both to formally classify cases and to direct agency action raise a variety of important issues. When police personnal classify a case, they are determining, in effect, what subsequent actions will be taken, and by whom. For example, in many departments a runaway case is investigated by the juvenile bureau and a missing juvenile is investigated by a missing persons unit. Of greater importance is the categorization of stranger kidnap cases because these cases are often investigated by some other specialized unit that has particular expertise, training, and resources to follow up serious crimes such as homicides. The initial circumstances of a case usual dictate how law enforcement personnel will classify it. Most circumstances present evidence that suggest the child is missing because he or she has run away from home or has been taken or detained by a parent or other relative.

The decision rule typically used by law enforcement agencies in classifying missing children cases that do not readily fall into these two situations is that in the absence of clear and convincing evidence of a stranger kidnapping, the case is classified as an unknown missing. The criteria for clear and convincing evidence are quite rigid. There must be an eyewitness to the abduction or some other obvious indicator such as, as one investigator put it, "there is blood all over the floor." This decision rule is very restrictive and may lead to situations in which kidnap cases are not vigorously investigated because the initial classification is incorrect. It may also lead to delays in the start of an investigation because the police anticipated that the situation would be resolved—as many runaways and parental abductions are—without police intervention.

One example of this restrictive decision rule is found in a case that took place in a west coast city. A three-year-old girl was playing in her front yard while her mother was taking a nap. When the mother awoke and went outside, the girl had disappeared. The mother called the police who responded immediately. Backup units were summoned and a thorough search was conducted. One of the girl's shoes was found on the sidewalk in front of her house. Some neighbors who were interviewed by the police claimed they had seen strangers driving on the street, but no one had seen a car stop near the child's house and no one had seen the child being pulled into a car. The police eventually classified the case as an unknown missing, because there were no witnesses to any crime. Although this case was investigated thoroughly, there are suggestions that it was not investigated as aggressively as it would have been if it had been classified as a stranger abduction.

The consequences of erronesoulsy applying this restrictive decision rule were pointed out in the testimony of Pearla Peterson, discussed at the beginning of chapter 8. Ms. Peterson was frustrated because the police would not respond to her pleas for help (her thirteen-year-old daughter was missing). The authorities felt there was no evidence of foul play. They expected the daughter would return home within a short period of time, so they did not begin an investigation and advised the mother to just wait. They were wrong. The daughter did not return.

For the police, evidence is an important factor in making decisions. They are trained to examine the evidence and to make conservative spekulations about the meaning of the evidence. With no clear or obvious evidence of any wrongdoing or foul play, police are reluctant to assume the worst. In their responses to the Research Triangle Institute's survey, law enforcement personnel emphasized the importance of evidence in stranger kidnappings. In their report on the survey results, researchers noted that "in the case of stranger abductions, the main obstacles (to recovering the child) were the difficulty in securing witnesses, obtaining physical evidence, and classifying the case."[5]

Police are like most people. They make decisions based on their experience. The most common type of missing child case is the runaway, and in the vast majority of these cases, the juvenile returns home on his or her own volition in matter of hours or days, usually within twenty-four hours. That is why some police departments have a waiting period before taking a report. From experience, police personnel have found that it is a waste of time, money, and personnel to thoroughly investigate a case that will solve itself in a matter of hours.

When individuals are required to process and digest vast amounts of information, they find cognitive shortcuts to help them. When dealing with similar categories of phenomena, individuals develop special code words to help them make sense of the world. Based on experiences with large numbers of cases, people begin to generalize. Gordon Allport, the famous American psychologist, calls this the process of "overgeneralization."[6] Individuals *assume,* based on a few key bits of data, that new situations will be the same as previous case experiences.

For many police officers, the tendency to overgeneralize missing children means that a new case will be treated like the most common case they have encountered in the past. If they handle a few hundred cases, and in all instances the youth returns on his or her own in a matter of hours or days, the officer assumes that the next case will probably be the same. This decision-making logic works most of the time for most departments, so it continues.

It is unclear, however, whether this decision-making logic is the best for the investigation and recovery of missing children. To ensure that police take the steps that will increase the likelihood of a missing child being found, it may be necessary to explore alternative decision rules.

In the criminal justice system, for example, the decision rule regarding the conviction of defendants requires that guilt be proven by the prosecutor beyond a reasonable doubt. This standard is intended to ensure that innocent persons are not convicted. In effect, this decision rule is designed to prevent harm to innocent persons. Perhaps law enforcement could use a similar decision rule and objective for decision making. Making the prevention of harm to innocent persons the goal of decision rules used for missing chldren cases seems particularly appropriate because most of our social and legal policies toward children are concerned with promoting their well-being and safety. Thus, it might be more desirable to have law enforcement personnel assume a child is the victim of a stranger kidnapping unless there is clear and convincing evidence to the contrary. Obviously, this assumption has signficant cost implications for police departments. Because they have a crucial impact on how missing children cases are ultimately viewed and handled, the decision rules used by police department warrant further exploration and discussion.

Many states have modified their laws to force police departments to be more responsive to reports of missing children cases. For example, following the Adam Walsh case in 1981, Senator Paula Hawkins (R-Fla.) and Mr. John Walsh were istrumental in lobbying the Florida state legislature (as they did in Congress) to enact specific reporting responsibilities. Florida became one of the first states to require all law enforcement officials to receive training in the investigation of missing children. Florida's new reporting statute eliminates the police waiting period to file a missing child report and requires immediate dissemination of missing children information to all law enforcement agencies in surrounding areas. In addition, Florida has established a state-operated missing children computer file and a state missing children clearinghouse.

Many other states followed suit. They adopted statutes requiring law enforcement agencies to take a report of a missing child immediately after the incident is brought to their attention. California's law is typical:

> All local police and sheriff's departments shall accept any report, including any telephonic report, of a missing person, including runaways, without delay and shall give priority to the handling of these reports over the handling of reports relating to crimes involving property.[7]

But not all states have enacted such laws. For example, the Research Triangle Institute study found that by 1986, 9.2 percent of the law enforcement agencies throughout the country still had a waiting period for taking a report of a missing child.[8]

Departmental Action and the Recovery of Children

Law enforcement agencies can conceivably take an enormous number of investigative actions and invest substantial amounts of time in every reported missing child. In those few cases when a child clearly is in imminent physical danger, most agencies do just about everything that can be done. In the vast majority of cases, particularly teenagers who run away from home, law enforcement agencies do relatively little. The level of investigative intensity thus varies significantly.

The relationship between law enforcement actions, including investigative intensity, and the recovery of various types of missing children, remains unclear. To the extent there is a connection, it appears to be related to the type of case. The greatest investigative intensity is manifested in stranger kidnapping cases. Ironically, in these cases, luck, rather than a systematic search and investigation, is the determining factor. Officers need viable physical evidence or witnesses, without which a case is extremely difficult to solve. Officers can put out teletypes or APBs or broadcast a picture of the missing child on television, but unless the officers are fortunate enough to have a citizen spot a child or a suspect, they cannot locate a child.

Police intervention in runaway cases presents a contrasting

situation. Although the activities vary somewhat by jurisdiction, most police departments give teenager runaway cases the slightest investigative intensity. Officers simply make a few telephone calls to determine if anyone has seen the missing youth or knows where he or she might be. Yet despite minimal law enforcement actions, the vast majority or runaway youths are reunited with their families. Reunification appears, however, to have little to do with any efforts made by law enforcement. Thousands of youths around the country run away every day. They are gone for a few hours or a couple of days, on the average, and then they go home. Exactly what happens to these youths when they are gone remains subject to speculation. But what is clear is that in the vast majority of cases, law enforcement have little to do with their return.

Part of the formula for the recovery of some missing children, particularly runaways, relates to actions not of investigative specialists but to officers on the street. For example, there may be differences in recovery rates between jurisdictions that have proactive law enforcement practices and those that are more reactive. A few of the large jurisdictions could be characterized as having strongly proactive policies regarding youths on the street. In some cities, there is local political pressure to keep the downtown area looking clean and safe, so officers are more likely to enforce runaway, truancy, and curfew laws. As a consequence, officers do not hesitate to take any youth into custody who is on the streets during school hours or at night after curfew. It is unclear whether this proactive police work is related to apprehending runaways or the reunification of children and parents.

How law enforcement officers deal with juveniles on the street must also be viewed from the context of state laws regarding the detention of status offenders. Because a few states still allow the secure detention of status offenders, including runaways, law enforcement agencies in these jurisdictions can be more proactive in their duties. This does not necessarily mean that children are less likely to run away from home in those jurisdictions that allow secure detention. Children in crisis will run from home no matter what the state's legal structure.

Secure detention may be related to the number and types of

transient youth in a jurisdiction. It appears that the word is out that it is unwise to run to those cities that allow secure detention. Youths seems to know that it is much better to run to a comparably sized city in a neighboring state, where police officers are not as proactive and state law prohibits the secure detention of status offenders.

The larger political and legal context must also be considered to understand the position of law enforcement officers on the street. State appellate court decisions regarding runaways in particular affect the actions taken by juvenile justice officials at the local level. One interesting example pertains to the sanctions local juvenile court judges can impose on status offenders. Most states, as mentioned, do not allow the secure detention of status offenders. Juvenile court judges in some jurisdictions try to get around this obstacle by making a status offender a ward of the court. If the ward violates a specific court order not to run away (or not to run away again), the youth can be detained for violating the valid court order. In California, this process was originally found illegal by the state Court of Appeals. The court held that "bootstrapping" a status offense into a criminal offense was improper simply because a youth failed to comply with a court order. Recently, however, the California Supreme Court held that the detention of a status offender found in contempt for violating a court order was legal. In Washington state, the courts have taken an opposing stance. The state legislature passed a truancy law, requiring youths to attend school. However, the Washington Supreme Court ruled that it was unconstitutional to impose any sanction—fine or detention—for the violation of that truancy law. In Seattle, therefore, police feel that their hands are tied, because they know that nothing of consequence will happen to truants if they are taken into custody.

In parental abduction cases, police involvement can make a big difference in case outcome. Mere threats by police officers of formal action and criminal prosecution has motivated fugitive parents to return to the state they fled in order to deal with their custody complaints in the appropriate forum. Many parents who abduct their children are otherwise law-abiding individuals with jobs and ties to relatives and friends. When they are confronted with the fact that their conduct constitutes a criminal act and criminal prosecution would hurt their employment and personal relations, such parents will often cooperate with law enforcement officials.

In those cases involving abducting parents who are desperate or who have committed crimes in the past, law enforcement interventions may provide the left-behind parents the only chance they have of tracking the offender and child down. State and federal law enforcement agencies can be quite effective in using their investigative intelligence and communications to locate and apprehend fugitive parents and abducted children. Police interventions in these cases may make the greatest difference in whether a child is located and returned.

Competing Philosophies of Juvenile Rights

One of the central issues facing policymakers at the federal, state, and local levels is how intrusive the government should be in the lives of juveniles, particularly in the lives of juveniles who have not committed any criminal offense. Put differently, a central issue is the extent to which the rights of juveniles should mirror the rights of adults and the extent to which juveniles should be free from state intervention in the absence of a criminal law violation. This issue has greatest relevance to governmental policy toward runaways.

The range of opinion about the basic rights of juveniles and the family, as well as about the role of the government in intruding into the lives of status offenders, is quite wide. On the one end is the view of child's rights advocates, who favor little or no governmental intrusion. When specifically discussing status offenders, for example, child advocate and lawyer Mark Green believes, essentially, that runaways should be able to travel wherever they please without state interference—just as adults can do. He bases his position on three constitutional principles that he believes apply equally to juveniles and to adults: it is a serious infringement of personal freedom to be compelled to live with undesired company (presumably including parents); individuals, including juveniles, have the right to be let alone; and thirds, individuals, including juveniles, have a constitutionally protected right to travel.[9]

A contrasting position is that parents have a right to be with their children and that children have no rights to live away from the family. This position is most recently exemplified by the Attorney General's Advisory Board on Missing Children. "We (the advisory board) believe that children have a right to custody with parents or legal guardians who provide care, support, discipline, and love. They do not have a right to freedom from custody."[10] If a child violates the sanctity of the family by running away, this position holds, then the state is justified in apprehending and detaining the youth until the family is reunited. This view seems to harken back to feudal conceptions of the family and the father's property rights in his wife and his children.

The issues of juvenile rights and governmental intrustion are obviously complex. Confusion among scholars and policymakers exists, in part, because it is unclear which policy direction will result in doing the greatest good or preventing the greatest harm. The philosophical and legal debates will likely continue for years. But one thing is clear now. The ambiguity of state and local policymakers in this area trickles down to the officer on the street who is most likely to come into contact with runaway and homeless youths. The officer is aware of the ambivalence in society and among various levels of government about what to do about runaways. The officer senses that there is something wrong when juveniles are left to their own devices—particularly when that means they become victims of crime or become victimizers. Yet, particularly since the deinstitutionalization movement, officers also receive the message that they are not supposed to crack down too hard on runaways and homeless youths. These youths cannot be kept in secure detention, even after they have run away on numerous occasions. These juveniles are also unlikely to be made wards of the court.

The message that these legal developments send to the officer in the field is that society does not really know what to do with runaways. Even stronger, the officer may feel that society does not care what happens to runaways. And if society does not care what happens to runaways and homeless youths, then neither should the officer. This attitude contributes to the situation in which the officer on the street avoids encounters with potential runaways—in fact, in all too many instances, the officer turns his or her back and ignores youths who might be in danger.

Conclusion

How the police—and all of society—deal with the various types of missing children cases remains problematic. Laws have been passed at the national and state levels that are supposed to aid the police in the recovery of missing children. But the issues are complex. There are also laws and organizational policies that work against the investigation and recovery of missing children.

Sometimes it is simply not clear what policy to follow. Sometimes taking a course of action that attempts to solve one problem creates other problems. It might be better, for example, for family courts to write extremely specific custody decrees, outlining in detail exactly when each parent can have custody of his or her child. But such specificity is frowned on by some family court judges, because they like to give parents flexibility to arrange their own lives. Moreover, many parents resist such rigid arrangements. And it might be better from a law enforcement perspective to be able to detain runaways for as long as is necessary. But detention was proved a failure in the past, and as Mr. Lyonel Norris pointed out in his Congressional testimony, there is no reason to doubt it would be so again.

Organizations—and the people who work in them—follow a course of action for reasons that are quite rational from their perspective. Some law enforcement officers may, for example, like to be more proactive in picking up runaways and taking them into custody. But officers soon learn there are few rewards to such efforts. The juveniles cannot be held for long. They resist being placed in custody. They do not feel helped or protected by such measures and do not see (let alone appreciate) that this action is for their own welfare. They are soon back out on the streets, cursing the police for the harrassment or embarrassment. Much of the lawmaking on missing children has failed to take into account the social and organizational realities of police work with missing children. On paper, the new laws promised to make a difference. In operation, they did not.

10

Conclusion

A Reappraisal of the Missing Children Problem

In the past decade, the topic of missing children has received heightened attention from the media, from private citizens and organizations, and from public officials. The media first alerted the public to the issue with sensationalized accounts of a few children who had disappeared never to be seen, or seen alive, again—Adam Walsh, Etan Patz, Kevin Collins. Media coverage transformed the personal tragedies of these children and their families into a public concern for millions of Americans. The media took up the claims made by parents and spokespersons for different missing children groups about the numbers of children who had disappeared. They claimed that there were thousands of children like Adam, Etan, and Kevin missing throughout the country; and that there were thousands of parents desperate to find them.

Treating these claims as facts, the media coverage helped to create the impression that the United States was experiencing an epidemic of disappearing children. In response to demands for action to do something about this epidemic, federal and state lawmakers accepted missing children as a political cause. After all, who could be against helping or recovering missing children? The real challenge was not to take up the cause, but rather to figure out what should or could be done to address the problem.

Much political posturing occurred on the issue; a few pieces of legislation were passed. The new laws increased the penalties for crimes against children (specifically kidnapping and sexual exploitation) and made parental abduction and the violation of child custody orders criminal offenses. Some of the new legislation also provided for the exchange of information among law enforcement agencies about missing children's identities and required law enforcement departments to take specific actions with missing children cases.

While it may be too soon to pass judgment on the long-term consequences of the missing children campaign, it appears that much of the rhetoric about missing children and the policy changes prompted by this rhetoric have led to few significant changes in the numbers of children who are either reported missing or are recovered. The rhetoric and the new policies appear to have had little impact on the procedures law enforcement officers actually follow to solve various types of missing children cases; nor have the new policies resulted in significant improvements in the health or welfare of children or in reducing the risks to children of sexual or physical abuse or neglect—particularly in the home where it is most likely to occur. How could a cause that captivated the media, the American public, and the political agenda produce so few significant effects?

What follows are some final thoughts about the course the missing children cause took, the symbolic significance of the cause, and the limits of the law and the political process to transform rhetoric and concern into meaningful action and social change.

The Missing Children Campaign
The Construction of Missing Children as a Problem

When people hear the term *missing children,* they visualize a small child kidnapped by a stranger—someone who has been lurking around a school yard or park. In this conception, the child is either murdered or never seen again.

Those types of cases are extremely rare. Although a hundred or so cases per year do constitute tragedies in and of themselves, they do not reach the dimensions, at least in terms of volume, of a social problem.

Of those children who are abducted, the majority are snatched by their own parents, normally as part of a custody battle. And of all missing children, the vast majority are runaways—juveniles fleeing from abuse, neglect, or conflict at home.

As a political strategy, lobbyists and spokespersons for different types of missing children joined forces to bring attention to their clientele under the more general rubric of *missing children.* The most frightening type of case—stranger kidnapping—became the vehicle to promote attention to and action on issues relevant to other types of missing children cases—child protection, social services to children, and law enforcement assistance to parents.

In associating the missing children cause with victims of stranger kidnapping, activists limited the definition of the problem and, therefore, the issues they could address. The problem of missing children was defined, first and foremost, as a *crime* problem, as opposed to a *family* problem. Second, it was defined as an information problem—specifically of law enforcement agencies not having enough information to solve crimes. Third, it was defined as the victimization of children and parents by external evils beyond their control. And last, it was defined as the problem of children being forcefully torn away from the families they wanted to be, and should be, with. These characteristics of the problem of missing children applied most aptly to stranger kidnapping cases; they were less relevant to and only partially descriptive of the problems associated with parental abduction and runaway cases.

Casting the problem of missing children as a crime prevention and law enforcement issue had important consequences for the policy solutions debated and adopted. Not surprisingly, the political mandates for "doing something" about the missing children problem focused on expanding the responsibilities of criminal justice agencies; police were to intervene in missing children cases by accepting reports and investigating them as if they all involved criminal conduct; they were to arrest and sanction parents who abducted their children; they were to severely penalize individuals who kidnapped, molested, or exploited children; they were to disseminate the description of missing children to other jurisdictions so that law enforcement agencies elsewhere would be prepared to apprehend the offending stranger or parent. The point of criminal justice agency intervention in runaway cases was less clear, particularly when youths did not want to be found or returned to their families and their behavior had no criminal status.

By constructing the missing children problem and strategies to solve it, along these lines, spokespersons and activists were unable to bring sustained attention to perhaps more important aspects of missing children cases. The reality was that different types of missing children cases involved different sets of issues. For parental abduction and runaway cases, the problem was not strangers lurking around shool yards and preying on innocent victims. The real problem was (and continues to be) family conflict and an inability to solve individual or interpersonal problems in nonabusive, nonviolent, and nondemeaning ways. In cases of parental abduction, both parents and the child are the victims of a disintegrated family, caught up in bitterness and rancor over the failure of one or both parents to sustain a satisfying or committed relationship. Although divorce is the immediate solution to incompatible or destructive marital relations, it creates new problems for family members, especially children. The new conflicts emerge over child custody, child support, and child rearing. Judicial and law enforcement interventions, alone, do little to resolve such interpersonal and family problems.

In cases of children who have run away from home, a dysfunctional (and perhaps a disintegrating) family is often the problem. Children who are loved, cared for, and respected rarely run away from home. Children whose parents love, care for, and respect each other rarely run away from home either. However, as studies of youths on the streets, in shelters, and juvenile facilities suggest, children who are physically or sexually abused or neglected are the ones that resort to running away. They cope with family dysfunction by leaving home; once away, some have little desire to return. Others return, only to run away again at a later point. Still others stay at home, but cope with their unhappiness in other ways.

For those youths who leave home and try to survive on the streets, running away has merely meant they have exchanged one set of problems for another. The immediate problem for them is no longer their debilitating family life, but finding shelter, food, clothing, companionship, protection. For the runaways who return home voluntarily or who are brought home through the interventions of law enforcement authorities, being home again does not solve the problem of an abusive, loveless, or chaotic family.

In the 1980s, U.S. Senator Arlen Specter concluded as much, as did other policymakers concerned with missing children. As chairperson of the Subcommittee on Juvenile Justice of the Senate Judiciary Committee, Senator Specter heard much testimony about children's problems, including missing children. He published an article in 1987 in the *Yale Law & Policy Review,* in which he states that children "are society's victims." He specifically states that "tragically, many of the most serious threats to children arise not on the streets, but in their own homes."[1]

Yet this awareness and concern did not get translated into measures to correct the situations that threatened the welfare or safety of large numbers of children. Policymakers continued to be preoccupied with crime control measures to prevent and punish abductors and with law enforcement interventions to get children back home. They did not seriously discuss or consider strategies that would create social supports to families in crisis.

Lawmakers did not adequately address the need to provide short-term shelter programs and social services for runaway youths, or the need to provide youths who refused to return home with long-term shelter and assistance for emancipation. To most child welfare experts, these measures were viewed as more appropriate to alleviating the problems most missing children faced. Having law enforcement and juvenile court officials hold these youths in secure detention failed to address more fundamental child welfare and family issues. But these more basic programmatic strategies were either ignored in the legislative and policy proposals that were ultimately adopted or, when they were enacted by federal and state lawmakers, were grossly underfunded.

As mentioned in chapter 5, in 1984 Congress created the United States Attorney General's Advisory Board on Missing Children. About two years after its creation, following many hearings and the collection of information, the advisory board issued its report, entitled *America's Missing & Exploited Children: Their Safety and their Future.* In the introduction to their report, the advisory board stated:

> We believe the first step [to helping children] is to bolster family values and to stop the continued disintegration of the family. Caring parents or legal guardians who give children love, discipline, and support can be powerful influences. We have outlined special roles for the family and government in an effort to prevent children from being out of their homes unlawfully.[2]

The advisory board then set forth a variety of recommendations. Ironically, the recommendations had little to do with addressing the family issues so vital to the health and safety of children. Notwithstanding the acknowledgment that families needed help, the board's policy proposals still treated missing and exploited children as if they were crime control and law enforcement problems or responsibilities, rather than social or family matters. Most of the board's recommendations involved criminal procedures or technical law enforcement measures—for example, having Congress amend the Juvenile Justice and Delinquency Prevention Act to ensure that each state juvenile justice system had the legal authority to take into custody and safely control runaways; modifying privacy laws so that police, courts, and other agencies receive cooperation and information when investigating cases of missing children; having all states give the crime of parental abduction a felony status; extending the statute of limitations on prosecution of child sexual abuse crimes; and providing child victims with legal representation in criminal proceedings.

The specific proposals of the advisory board did not address the needs of families or children, or measures to meet these needs. Rather, as its final recommendation, the board suggested such an undertaking be made the responsibility of yet another commission that the President should establish to deal specifically with issues of policy affecting families. Unfortunately, while policymakers realized the "bogey man lives at home," the actions they took encouraged the public to believe that it was strangers who threatened their children and that stronger crime control measures would provide the necessary protections.

Although the political pressure to do something about missing children has waned, missing children are still in the public eye. Stories of missing children—largely limited to stranger kidnappings—are carried on television in dramatic form. For example, on November 4, 1990, CBS primetime aired "83 Hours 'til Dawn," starring Peter Strauss and Robert Urich. The show was about the real life 1968 case of a college-age woman kidnapped and buried in a box. She was rescued alive. The movie, *After Dark, My Sweet,* starring Bruce Dern was released in theaters in 1990 as well. Based on a 1955 novel of the same name by Jim Thompson, the movie is the story of the kidnapping of a small boy. Both the image of missing children as being victims of such crimes and the belief that law enforcement interventions will help prevent or recover missing children have persisted. Sadly, after ten years of hoopla and hype, the missing children problem continues to be misstated and misunderstood.

The Limits of the Law and the Political Process

Political Rhetoric

In recent times, politicians have paid a lot of lip service to the importance of family and children in American society. The idealism of the family associated with the Reagan and Bush administrations has made these presidents popular with the voting public. These leaders have hailed the family as the basic building block of society; and children as society's most precious resource. As part of their political fundamentalism, Reagan and Bush have charged the nation with the task of revitalizing social institutions that will promote the country's economic productivity, domestic tranquility, and national pride. Stable families, healthy and well-educated children, and safe communities have been the keys to their revitalization agenda.

Child health and safety have been rallying bipartisan issues for members of Congress as well. Senator Arlen Specter has articulated a governmental position on this issue for which Democrats as well as Republicans have voiced their support. "I believe that the government has many responsibilities to children, two of which are of primary importance. For children who are victimized, abused, or troubled, it must offer protection and aid."[3]

As noted earlier, the U.S. Attorney General's Advisory Board on Missing Children expressed a similar sentiment in its report to Congress on missing and exploited children. But like the advisory board, most members of Congress have dismal records. When it has come to translating their concern into political actions and making a positive difference in the quality of child welfare in this country, many lawmakers have done little more than posture and promise.

President Reagan presided over a ceremony at the White House on April 29, 1985, in which he participated in setting up a "public-private" partnership to coordinate corporate efforts to try to locate missing children. President Reagan stated, "The possibility of kidnapping or abuse to a child is one of the major fears that . . . parents now face." He made a commitment to address this "national problem." In 1985, Congress asked for $10 million for the next four years to fund programs under the Missing Children Assistance Act. In response, the Reagan Administration provided only half that amount. Moreover, in spite of the fact that runaways are by far the largest category of missing children and are in the greatest need of services, the Reagan Administration cut the 1983 – 1984 budgets for services to these youths.[4]

Political and Organizational Realities

The United States has earned a reputation for being a litigious society. An ethos of American political life—living according to the rule of law, not of men—has led many to look to the law to govern a wide range of personal, social, and political conduct. When Americans encounter problems, they often think such things as "there ought to be a law"; "the government ought to do something about that"; "that should be a crime"; or we "need stiffer penalities." And when Americans feel strongly enough about something, they bring the issue to the attention of elected officials; they organize; they lobby; and they pressure legislators to pass new laws or to rescind existing ones. At the least, lawmakers reward such activists with rhetorical commitments to the cause; at the most, they will make the sought-for change in policy or the allocation of resources.

Activists succeeded in making missing children a political cause and in generating a great deal of political rhetoric about the seriousness of the issue; they also succeeded in getting state and federal lawmakers to adopt new public policies. These policies were intended to promote the recovery of missing children and were specifically aimed at the behavior and procedures followed by criminal justice agencies. At the same time, law enforcement agencies, prosecutors, and criminal courts became the objects of the new mandates, they were also given the responsibility to enforce them.

To be implemented, the new criminal and reporting laws had to be filtered through the perceptions and operational exigencies of these agencies. Unfortunately, the legislature's perceptions of the missing children problem and the correctives it mandated conflicted with law enforcement's first-hand experience in dealing with various types of missing children cases.

For example, police know that most missing children cases do not involve stranger kidnappings. Those cases that do are already receiving the most rigorous investigation and follow-up possible. From their dealings with runaways, law enforcement officers also believe that the majority of these cases resolve themselves—the youths return home on their own. Police intervention or use of the NCIC system does little to increase the numbers of those successfully returned. Moreover, while police officers acknowledge that children abducted by their parents are harmed psychologically and sometimes physically by the abduction, they believe this behavior is ultimately a problem for the family courts. The most they can do is to enforce the law against parental abduction when it is violated; in many cases, from their perspective, the absence of custody orders, the existence of vaguely written custody orders or conflicting custody orders mean their intervention is not warranted—they are unable to determine if a law has been broken.

The legislative mandates on missing children also conflicted with the crime control mandates and law enforcement priorities of the communities that set the local agenda for law enforcement agencies. These are also the communities that foot the bill for police services and protection. In the 1980s and 1990s, governmental entities of all types and at all levels have been expected to do more with less. When they were given the additional duties of reporting, investigating, and recovering missing children, and apprehending abducting parents, law enforcement agencies were not given additional funds to support these activities.

Since the early 1980s and the advent of the missing children cause, other pressing crime control and safety issues have arisen to compete for law enforcement's attention. The "War on Drugs" has become a major law enforcement concern. In most large cities, drug dealing and gang activity associated with it dwarf other crime control problems. For example, Los Angeles law enforcement officials face an average of *one juvenile gang-related homicide every single day.* The nation set a record number of homicides in 1990—about twenty-four thousand, up from an average of twenty thousand. Much of this violence is related to wars over drugs and drug turf. As a practicality, missing children has taken (or rather remained in) a back seat.

The Symbolic Significance of Missing Children

A recent national study of more than seventeen thousand children nationwide revealed that one in five children under age eighteen has a learning, emotional, behavior, or developmental problem that researchers say can be traced to the continuing dissolution of the two-parent family. The survey, sponsored by the National Center for Health Statistics, showed that by the time youngsters enter their teenage years, one in four suffers from one or more of these problems. For male teenagers, the rate increases to nearly one in three.[5]

These facts merely confirm something most Americans are already cognizant of—the high rate of divorce and family disorganization due to larger social and economic forces is having serious consequences for child welfare.

Growing concern over domestic violence and child neglect has brought about greater governmental regulation of and intervention in family life. Criminal laws have been passed, or enforced, with greater regularity, against child abuse, child neglect, spousal abuse, and spousal rape. These measures have been designed to protect the individual rights and safety of family members. Treating parental abduction as a crime, with the child and the left-behind parent as victims, has been another measure to use legal protections to safeguard individual family members.

However, few governmental resources or interventions have been invoked to help stabilize the family or to help family members cope more effectively with changing social norms and the stresses of modern family life. Little has been done to help families make their home life and personal relations safer and more satisfying. Liberalized divorce laws have provided couples with a solution to marital conflicts. Full-time employment for both parents has relieved some of the economic stresses on the family. While these actions help adults cope with their personal and financial situations, they have had untoward consequences for children. For many children, they have created significant disruptions in the continuity, predictability, and security of their lives.

Single parents, divorced parents, and working parents have less time to spend with their children, and are able to exert less control over what happens to their children in their absence. In the 1980s and 1990s, parents are less able than ever to provide their children with the conditions that psychologists say are fundamental to healthy child development—a stable home environment, ongoing relationships with both parents, and large doses of love and attention to foster self-esteem.

Because of the declining stability of the family and increasing pressures to address the full range of their children's developmental needs, parents have cause to feel anxious. The fact that the issue of missing children has evoked a strong response of fear among parents suggests that parents in fact do feel anxious about their children's welfare as well as uncertain of their ability to properly protect and care for their children.

Indeed, for many parents and for society at large, the missing children cause provides an outlet for expressing a deeper and broader anxiety about family life and the ability to control the most intimate and important aspects of one's being—relations with loved ones. Unfortunately, by focusing such anxiety on recovering missing children and punishing those individuals who hurt or exploit children, policymakers, child advocates, and parents failed to consider seriously the sources of their fears or the measures that would actually dispel them. Missing children became a symbol for grappling with issues that could not be readily articulated or resolved. Moreover, seeing the problem of missing children as a crime control and law enforcement problem gave parents and policymakers false assurance. They believed that they could rely on something seemingly quite concrete, powerful, and unrelated to their personal lives—law enforcement authorities.

Americans have looked to law enforcement both to allay their personal anxieties over the safety of their children and to halt the growing social ills associated with abducted and runaway children. As we have suggested, however, given the limited capabilities of law enforcement to recover the various types of missing children, this reliance is misplaced. Moreover, it distracts attention from the broader and more difficult social and economic issues affecting the family. The hundreds of thousands of children missing as runaways and parental abductions come from families in crisis. Realistically, law enforcement interventions alone can only have minimal effect on their plight. Until policymakers and the American public take measures to address the stresses of modern family life, the missing children problem will persist.

Notes

Chapter 1

1. New York Penal Laws, Section 135.25(1).
2. Idaho Revised Laws, Section 18 – 4501(1).
3. California Penal Code, Section 209.
4. New York Penal Laws, Section 135.25(2)
5. *An Evaluation of the Crime of Kidnapping As It Is Committed by Nonfamily Members.* Washington, D.C.: National Center for Missing and Exploited Children, March 1986, p. 16.
6. Ibid., p. 6.
7. Idaho Revised Laws, Section 18.4501(2).
8. Federal Kidnapping Law, 18 USC 1201.
9. Arizona Criminal Code, Section 1301302.
10. Nevada Revised Statutes, Section 62.040(3).
11. California Welfare and Institutions Code, Section 601.
12. Daryl Bramall, Erlinda Jimenez, and Karen Zytniak, *Alliance for Children, Youth and Families.* Seattle, WA: King County Runaway Network, November 30, 1985, p. 11.
13. David Finkelhor, Gerald Hotaling, and Andrea Sedlak, *Missing, Abducted, Runaway and Thrownaway Children in America, First Report: Numbers and Characteristics, National Incidence Studies.* Executive Summary. Washington, D.C.: Office of Juvenile Justice and Delinquency Prevention, May 1990, p. vi.

Chapter 2

1. *Uniform Crime Reports of the United States, 1988.* Washington, D.C.: Federal Bureau of Investigation.

2. For examples of victimization surveys see *Criminal Victimization in the United States, 1987, A National Crime Survey Report,* Washington, D.C.: U.S. Department of Justice, June 1989; Murray Straus, Richard Gelles, and Suzanne Steinmetz, *Behind Closed Doors: Violence in the American Family,* NY: Doubleday, (Anchor Press) 1980; and Wesley Skogan and Michael Maxfield, *Coping with Crime: Individual and Neighborhood Reactions,* Beverly Hills, CA: Sage Publications, 1981.
3. *Newsweek,* October 7, 1985, p. 30.
4. Ibid.
5. Ibid.
6. *Time,* November 18, 1985, p. 47.
7. *Newsweek,* October 7, 1985.
8. For example, see *An Evaluation of the Crime of Kidnapping As It Is Committed Against Children by Nonfamily Members,* Washington, D.C.: National Center for Missing and Exploited Children, March 1986.
9. Ibid.
10. Ibid., p. 7.
11. Ibid., p. 8.
12. *Newsweek,* October 18, 1976, p. 24.
13. *U.S. News and World Report,* September 3, 1979, p. 57.
14. *National Statistical Survey of Runaway Youth,* Princeton, NJ.: Opinion Research Corporation, 1976.
15. Statement of Wade F. Horn, Commissioner, Administration for Children, Youth and Families before the Subcommittee on Children, Family, Drugs and Alcoholism, Committee on Labor and Human Relations, U.S. Senate; February 7, 1990, p. 3.
16. David Finkelhor, Gerald Hotaling, and Andrea Sedlak, *Missing, Abducted, Runaway, and Thrownaway Children in America, First Report: Numbers and Characteristics, National Incidence Studies.* Executive Summary. Washington, D.C.: Office of Juvenile Justice and Delinquency Prevention, May 1990, p. v.
17. Ibid., p. ix.
18. Ibid., p. xiii.
19. Ibid., p. xvii.
20. James Collins, Mary Ellen McCalla, Linda L. Powers, and Ellen S. Stutts, *The Police and Missing Children: Findings from a National Survey.* Research Triangle Park, NC: Research Triangle Institute, June 1989.
21. John E.B. Myers, "A Summary of Child Abuse and Neglect Reporting Statutes," *Journal of Juvenile Law* 10 (1986):1 – 72.
22. C. Henry Kempe, F.N. Sullivan, B.F. Steele, W. Droegemueller, and H.K. Silver, "The Battered Child Syndrome," *Journal of the American Medical Association* 181 (July 1962): 17 – 24.
23. California Penal Code, Section 11166.
24. *San Francisco Chronicle,* June 8, 1990, p. 3.
25. See "Family Violence and Child Abuse," Science Monographs #1, *Families Today.* Washington, D.C.: National Institute of Mental Health, 1979.

26. Diana Russell, *The Secret Trauma.* New York, New York: Basic Books, 1986, p. 74.
27. Comments, "Criminal Law—Incest—Illinois' Response to a Family Problem." *Southern Illinois University Law Review* 12 (1988): 658.
28. Diana Russell, "The Incidence and Prevalence of Intrafamilial and Extrafamilial Sexual Abuse of Female Children," *Child Abuse and Neglect* 7 (1983): 133.
29. Lucy Berliner, and Mary Lou Barbieri, "The Testimony of the Child Victim of Sexual Assault," *Journal of Social Issues* 40 (1984): 126.
30. Note "Abused Children and State-Created Protection Agencies: A Proposed Section 1983 Standard," *University of Cincinnati Law Review* 57 (1989): 1419 – 1442.
31. Ibid.
32. *Child Abuse and Neglect: Critical First Step in Response to a National Emergency.* Washington, D.C.: U.S. Advisory Board on Child Abuse, June 1990.
33. Janine Jason, "Child Homicide Spectrum," *American Journal of Diseases of Children* 137 (1983): 578 – 581.
34. Hotaling, et al., p. i.
35. See Peter Schneider, "Lost Innocents: The Myth of Missing Children." *Harpers* (February 1987): 47 – 53.

Chapter 3

1. *Reader's Digest,* July 1982, p. 60.
2. *U.S. News and World Report,* 24 October 1983, p. 63.
3. *Parents Magazine,* December 1985, p. 81.
4. Ibid.
5. Hearings, U.S. Senate, Committee on the Judiciary, Subcommittee on Juvenile Justice, "Child Kidnapping," 2 February 1983, p. 33.
6. Hearings, U.S. House of Representatives, Committee on Education and Labor, Subcommittee on Human Resources, "Missing Children's Assistance Act," 9 April 1984, p. 102.
7. Hearings, U.S. House of Representatives, Committee on the Judiciary, Subcommittee on Civil and Constitutional Rights, "Missing Children's Act," 18 November 1981, p. 10.
8. *Newsweek* (7 October 1985): p. 30.
9. Joel Best, "Rhetoric and Claims-Making: Construction of the Missing Children Problem." *Social Problems* 34 (1987): 103.
10. *U.S. News and World Report,* (11 February 1985): p. 12.
11. *Newsweek* (13 February 1989): p. 62.

Chapter 4

1. Hearings, U.S. Senate, Committee on Labor and Human Relations, Subcommittee on Investigations and General Oversight, "Missing Children" (6 October 1981): p. 1.
2. Ibid., p. 4.
3. Ibid., p. 18.
4. Ibid., p. 33 – 34.
5. Hearings, U.S. Senate, Committee on the Judiciary, Subcommittee on Juvenile Justice, "Exploited Children" (5 November 1981): p. 2.
6. Ibid., p. 18.
7. Ibid., p. 27.
8. Hearings, U.S. Senate, Committee on the Judiciary, Subcommittee on Juvenile Justice, "Exploited and Missing Children" (1 April 1982) p. 1.
9. Ibid., p. 2 – 3.
10. Ibid., p. 57.
11. Ibid., p. 59.
12. Ibid., p. 65.
13. Ibid.
14. Ibid.
15. Ibid., p. 68.
16. 28 USC 534(a).
17. Hearings, U.S. Senate, Committee on the Judiciary, Subcommittee on Juvenile Justice, "Child Kidnapping" (2 February 1983): p. 3.
18. Ibid., p. 10.
19. Ibid., p. 15.
20. Ibid., p. 14.
21. Ibid., p. 88.
22. Ibid., p. 66 – 67.
23. Hearings, U.S. Senate, Committee on the Judiciary, Subcommittee on Juvenile Justice, "Serial Murders" (12 July 1983): p. 10.
24. Ann Rule, *Small Sacrifices: A True Story of Passion and Murder.* New York, New York: Signet Books, 1987.
25. Hearings, 12 July 1983, p. 11.
26. Ibid., p. 28.
27. Ibid., p. 27.
28. Ibid., p. 29.
29. Ibid.
30. Ibid., p. 33.
31. Hearings, U.S. Senate, Committee on the Judiciary, Subcommittee on Juvenile Justice, "Missing Children's Assistance Act" (7 February 1984): p. 100 – 101.
32. Ibid., p. 11.
33. Ibid.
34. 42 USC 5771.
35. 42 USC 5772.

36. 42 USC 5773(a)(2).
37. 42 USC 5775(a).
38. 42 USC 5778.
39. 42 USC 7773(b)(1)(A).
40. 42 USC 5778(b)(1)(2)(B).

Chapter 5

1. New Revised Standard Version. Grand Rapids, Mich.: Zondervan Bible Publishers, 1987.
2. William Blackstone, *Commentaries on the Laws of England,* vol. 4. Chicago: University of Chicago Press (1979): p. 219.
3. Ibid.
4. Rollin Perkins "Non-Homicide Offenses Against the Person." *Boston University Law Review* 26 (1946): 144.
5. Robert Louis Stevenson, *Kidnapped.* Running Press, p. 53.
6. Hascal Brill, *Cyclopedia of Criminal Law,* Volume 2. Chicago: Callaghan and Co., 1923, p. 1213.
7. Ibid., p. 1217.
8. Note, "Kidnapping in Iowa: Movements Incidental to Sexual Abuse." *Iowa Law Review* 67 (1982): 776.
9. Connecticut Codes, Section 53a – 92.
10. Ibid., Section 53a – 94.
11. Idaho Revised Statutes, Section 18 – 4501.
12. California Penal Code, Section 209 (1933).
13. *State v. Dubina,* 318 A.2d 95 (1972).
14. Ibid., p. 98.
15. *Chatwin v. United States,* 326, U.S. 455 (946), p. 458.
16. 18 USC 1201.
17. *Chatwin,* p. 460 – 461.
18. *United States v. Chancy,* 715 F.2d 543 (1983), p. 544.
19. Ibid., p. 547.
20. *People v. Chessman,* 28 Cal.2d 166 (1951), p. 192.
21. Joel Bishop, *Bishop on Criminal Law,* vol. 2, 9th ed. Chicago: T.H. Flood and Company Law Publishers (1923), p. 571.
22. Note, "Kidnapping in Florida: Don't Move or You've Done It." *Stetson Law Review* 13 (1983): 197.
23. Montana Code Annotated, Section 45 – 2 – 101(59).
24. Ibid., Section 45 – 5 – 303(2).
25. *State v. Goodwin,* 679 P.2d 231 (1984).
26. Bishop, p. 576.
27. Hugh Fisher and Matthew McGuire, "Kidnapping and the So-Called Lindbergh Law." *New York University Law Quarterly Review* 12 (1935): 652.
28. Horace Bomar, Jr., "The Lindbergh Law." *Law and Contemporary Problems* 1 (1933 – 34): 435.

29. 18 USC 1201.

Chapter 6

1. David Finkelhor, Gerald Hotaling, and Andrea Sedlack, *Missing, Abducted and Thrownaway Children in America, First Report: Numbers and Characteristics, National Incidence Studies.* Executive Summary. Washington, D.C.: Office of Juvenile Justice and Delinquency Prevention (May 1990): p. xi.
2. Statements by Michael Agopian, Dr. Doris Jonas Freed, Andrew Yankwitt, and Sara Keegan at the Joint Hearing before the Subcommittee on Criminal Justice of the Committee of the Judiciary and the Subcommittee on Children and Human Development of the Committee on Labor and Human Resources, "Parental Kidnapping Prevention Action of 1979, S. 105," U.S. Senate, (30 January 1980), pp. 52, 64, 112 (Addendum), 113.
3. Arthur Young and Co., *Final Report on a Field Study of California's Law Enforcement Agencies.* Sacramento, California Department of Justice (15 February 1988): p. iii.
4. Andrea Charlow, "Awarding Custody: The Best Interests of the Child and Other Fictions," *Yale Law and Policy Review* 5 (1986 – 1987): 267 – 290, p. 289.
5. Statement of Congressman John "Jimmy" Duncan at the Joint Hearing (30 January 1980): p. 19.
6. Henry H. Foster and Doris J. Freed, "Life with Father: 1978," *Family Law Quarterly* 11 (1977 – 78): 321 – 363, p. 321.
7. *Helms v. Franciscus,* 2 Bland 544 (Maryland, 1830). See also Foster and Freed, Ibid., p. 329.
8. Pennsylvania Act P.L. 405, March 31, 1860, Purd. Dig. Ed 1883.
9. *Burns et al v. Commonwealth* (Pennsylvania Supreme Court), 18 A. 756 (1889).
10. *Bonis v. Bonis* (Fla. App.), 420 So2d 104 (1982). See also Marion C. Abram, "How to Prevent or Undo a Child Stealing." *American Bar Association Journal* 70 (May 1984): 52 – 55.
11. Victim's statement by Ms. Georgia K. Hilgeman to the Honorable Mark Eaton, Superior Court of California, County of Alameda on the Sentencing of Juan F. Rios, 13 January 1983, p. 1.
12. Testimony of Lawrence T. Kurlander, District Attorney, Monroe County, New York, at the Joint Hearing, 30 January 1980, p. 60.
13. Joint Hearing, 30 January 1980, p. 2.
14. Ibid., p. 8.
15. Ibid., p. 35.
16. Overight Hearing before the Subcommittee on Crime of the Committee on the Judiciary, "Hearing on the Implementation of the Parental Kidnapping Prevention Act of 1980," House of Representatives, 24 September 1981, p. 5.

Chapter 7

1. Mark Lipschutz, "Runaways in History." *Crime and Delinquency* 23 (1977): 321.
2. Benjamin Franklin, *The Autobiography of Benjamin Franklin.* New York, New York: Collier Books, 1962, p. 30.
3. Ibid., p. 31.
4. Thomas Minehan, *Boy and Girl Tramps of America.* New York, New York: Farrar and Rinehart, 1934.
5. George Outland, *Boy Transiency in America,* Santa Barbara, Calif.: Santa Barbara State College Press, 1939.
6. Lipschutz, p. 330 – 331.
7. Note, "The Incarceration of Status Offenders," *Memphis State University Law Review* 18 (1988): 713 – 740.
8. Ibid.
9. South Dakota Laws, Section 26 – 8 – 7.1.
10. California Welfare and Institutions Code, Section 601.
11. New York Family Court Act, Part 29A Part I, Section 712(a).
12. *Matter of Price,* 404 N.Y.S. 2d 821 (1978), p. 822.
13. *National Statistical Survey of Runaway Youth.* Princeton, N.J.: Opinion Research Corporation, 1976.
14. Hotaling et al., p. xvii.
15. Hearings, U.S. Senate, Committee on the Judiciary, Subcommittee on Juvenile Justice, "Exploitation of Children," 5 November 1981, p. 30.
16. Ibid.
17. Ibid.
18. Mark Twain, *The Adventures of Huckleberry Finn.* New York, New York: Dell Publishing Company, 1960, p. 51.
19. Samuel L. Clemens, *The Adventures of Tom Sawyer.* New York, New York: Lancer Books, 1967, p. 126.
20. E. Farber, "Violence in the Families of Adolescent Runaways," *Child Abuse and Neglect* 8 (1984): 295 – 299.
21. Joseph Ryan and Arthur Doyle, *Operation Outreach: A Study of Runaway Children in New York City.* New York, New York: New York City Police Department, April 1986, p. 12 – 14.
22. Hearings, U.S. Senate, 5 November 1981, p. 31.
23. John Goldmeier and Robert Dean, "The Runaway: Person, Problem or Situation," *Crime and Delinquency* 19 (1973): 543.
24. *Runaway Children and the Juvenile Justice and Delinquency Prevention Act: What is the Impact?* Washington, D.C.: U.S. Department of Justice, 1988, p. 2.
25. David Shouvin, "Preventing the Sexual Exploitation of Children: A Model Act," *Wake Forest Law Review* 17 (1981): 535 – 560.
26. U.S. General Accounting Office, *Sexual Exploitation of Children: A Problem of Unknown Magnitude.* Washington, D.C.: General Accounting Office, 20 April 1982, p. 4.
27. Shouvlin, p. 541.

28. Bruce Fisher and Sandy Wexler, *First Year Evaluation of the Larkin Street Youth Center.* San Francisco, Calif.: URSA Institute, May 1985.
29. *Runaway Children and the Juvenile Justice and Delinquency Prevention Act: What is the Impact?* Washington, D.C.: Office of Juvenile Justice and Delinquency Prevention, 1988, p. 2.
30. Hearings, U.S. Senate, 5 November 1981, p. 29 – 30.
31. Patricia Hersh, "Coming of Age on the Streets." *Psychology Today* 22 (January 1988): 28 – 37.
32. James Collins, Linda L. Powers, Mary Ellen McCalla, and Robert M. Lucas, *Law Enforcement Responses to Runaway and Abducted Children and Youths.* Research Triangle Park, N.C.: Research Triangle Institute, 1990.
33. Gary Yates, Richard MacKenzie, Julia Pennbridge, and E. Cohen, "A Risk Profile Comparison of Runaway and Non-Runaway Youth," *American Journal of Public Health* 78 (1988): 820 – 823.
34. Deborah Sherman, *Homeless and Runaway Youth: Health Profile and the Need for Action,* San Francisco, Calif.: U.S. Public Health Service, March 1991.
35. 42 USC 5601.
36. 42 USC 5711.
37. Hearings, U.S. Senate, Committee on the Judiciary, Subcommittee on Juvenile Justice, "Exploited Children," 5 November 1981, p. 33.
38. Joseph Ryan, "The Plight of our Modern Huckleberry Finns—The Runaways," *Missing/Abused* 3 (1987): 6.

Chapter 8

1. Hearings, U.S. Senate, Committee on the Judiciary, Subcommittee on Juvenile Justice, "Missing Children's Assistance Act," 21 February 1984, p. 69 – 70.

Chapter 9

1. James Collins, Mary Ellen McCalla, Linda L. Powers, and Ellen S. Stutts, *The Police and Missing Children: Findings from a National Survey.* Research Triangle Park, N.C.: Research Triangle Institute, June 1989, p. 43.
2. Ibid., p. 103.
3. Hearings, U.S. Senate, Committee on the Judiciary, Subcommittee on Juvenile Justice, "Missing Children's Assistance Act," 7 February 1984, p. 166.
4. Ibid.
5. *The Police and Missing Children: Findings From a National Survey.* OJJDP Update on Research, Washington, D.C.: U.S. Department of Justice, September 1988, p. 3.
6. Gordon Allport, *The Nature of Prejudice.* Reading, MA: Addison Wesley, 1954.
7. California Penal Code, Section 11114.

8. Collins et al., p. 48.
9. Mark Green, "Runaways on a Legal Leash." *Trial* 7 (1971): 28 – 29.
10. *America's Missing and Exploited Children: Their Safety and Their Future.* Report and Recommendations of the U.S. Attorney General's Advisory Board on Missing Children. Washington, D.C.: U.S. Department of Justice, March 1986, p. 1.

Chapter 10

1. Arlen Specter, "Overview: Children and the State." *Yale Law and Policy Review* 5 (1987): 262.
2. *America's Missing and Exploited Children: Their Safety and Their Future.* Report and Recommendations of the U.S. Attorney General's Advisory Board on Missing Children. Washington, D.C.: U.S. Department of Justice, March 1986, p. 1.
3. Specter, p. 261.
4. *U.S. News and World Report* (19 August 1985): p. 62.
5. John Van de Kamp, *Justice News and Notes.* Sacramento, Calif.: Department of the Attorney General, 17 December 1990, p. 1.

Index

Adam Walsh Resource Center, 77, 79, 94, 110
Agopian, Michael, 68
AIDS, 30, 201, 202, 204, 255, 266
American Humane Association, 48, 49

Battered child syndrome, 48
Bayh, Birch, 176, 205
Bell, Camille, 86, 87
Bennett, Charles, 170, 176
Best, Joel, 71
Blackstone, William, 118, 119, 149
Boren, David, 107
Bundy, Ted, 56, 57, 59

Chessman, Caryl, 135
Child Find, 77, 106
Children of the Night, 207
Children's Rights, Inc., 77, 78
Child-saving movement, 183
Chowchilla kidnapping, 3, 4
Code of Hammurabi, 115
Collins, Kevin, 58, 243, 281
Common law, 2, 116, 118–120, 124, 125, 126, 137, 148, 158
Community services officers (CSOs), 257
Computer-aided dispatch, 216
Coping Program, 243
Covenant House, 90, 193, 194, 204, 207, 208
Cranston, Alan, 171
Custodial interference, 11, 167

Davis, Gray, 24, 176
Denton, Jeremiah, 106, 107, 193
Dickens, Charles, 121
Differential police response (DPR), 220
Duncan, John, 148

False imprisonment, 116, 118, 119, 120, 123, 124, 135, 136, 146
FBI, 28, 31, 32, 34, 36, 38, 39, 71, 93, 96, 99, 100, 101, 111, 143, 144, 168, 170, 171, 174, 175, 215
Federal Kidnapping Act, 133, 134, 145
Federal Parent Locator Service (FPLS), 172, 173
Federal Transient Service, 185, 186
Felony murder rule, 126, 127
Find the Children, 78
Finn, Huckleberry, 15, 179, 196
Foretich, Eric, 12
Foretich, Hillary, 12
Franklin, Benjamin, 181, 182

Gacy, John Wayne, 57, 89
Gallego, Gerald, 6
Gelles, Richard, 50

Hall, G. Stanley, 183
Hatch, Orrin, 100, 101, 102
Hauptman, Bruno, 3, 61, 126, 127
Hawkins, Paula, 85, 93, 94, 95, 98, 99, 100, 101, 102, 103, 106, 107, 109, 176, 273
Hawkins, Yusef, 57
Henry, O., 122
High-Risk Youth Program, 202
Hilgeman, Georgia, 78, 164, 165, 166, 176
Hollywood, 17, 35, 207
Homicide, 6, 38, 39, 55
Horn, Wade, 35
Howell, Jay, 31, 53, 85
Huckleberry House, 207

Interstate Compact, 268

Juvenile Justice and Delinquency Prevention Act (JJDPA), 189, 205

Kempe, C. Henry, 48
Kennedy, Edward, 85
Kevin Collins Foundation, 77

Larkin Street Youth Center, 198, 209
Leopold, Nathan, 60
Lindbergh, Anne, 3
Lindbergh, Charles, 3
Lindbergh kidnapping, 3, 61, 81, 126, 142
Lindbergh Law, 141–144
Loeb, Richard, 60

Missing Children Act, 93, 95–99
Missing Children's Assistance Act, 36, 105–112
Missing Children Research Project (MCRP), 44, 45
Morgan, Elizabeth, 12

National Center for Missing and Exploited Children, 31, 32, 53, 68, 69, 76, 88, 109, 110–112, 139
National Child Safety Council, 73
National Crime Information Center (NCIC), 96–98, 168, 228–230, 262–264
National Crime Survey, 29
National Incidence Studies, 36–43, 53, 192
Nickles, Don, 107

Offfice of Juvenile Justice and Delinquency Prevention (OJJDP), 36, 53, 249, 265
Operation Home Free, 74
Operation Outreach, 197, 198

Parental Kidnapping Prevention Act (PKPA), 172–175, 262
Patz, Etan, 58, 66, 67, 85, 112, 243, 281
Patz, Julie, 58, 85, 112
Polk Gulch, 17
Pornography, 90, 91, 92, 111, 194, 197, 198, 199, 201, 202, 254, 255
Portis, Erv, 244
Prostitution, 16, 17, 61, 89, 90, 179, 193, 194, 195, 197, 198, 199, 200, 201, 202, 204, 207, 254, 255

Rabun, John, 88
Ransom, 3, 4, 38, 116, 122, 123, 126, 129, 131, 133, 140, 141, 145
Regnery, Alfred, 265
Research Triangle Institute, 109, 201, 202, 250, 272, 274

Revell, Oliver, 101, 102
Ritter, Bruce, 90, 193, 194, 195, 197, 199, 207
Robbery, 5, 6, 89, 126, 129, 135, 137, 187, 188, 250
Roman law, 116–118
Rule, Ann, 102, 103
Runaway and Homeless Youth Act, 189, 205–207, 266
Russell, Diana, 50
Ryan, Joseph, 212

Sawyer, Tom, 15, 196
Seattle Youth and Community Services, 208
Sharp, Margery, 123
Simon, Paul, 68, 101, 176
Specter, Arlen, 87, 89, 91, 98, 102, 104, 106, 176, 213, 214, 215, 265, 285, 287
Status offense, 14, 15, 89, 184, 187–189, 190, 227, 228, 264–266, 275, 276, 277
Stevenson, Robert Louis, 121
Stop Parental Kidnapping, 77
Sullivan, Louis, 49
Sullivan, Terry, 89
Sweet, Robert, Jr., 53

Thurmond, Strom, 107
Times Square, 17, 90, 200, 207
Twist, Oliver, 121, 179

Uniform Child Custody Jurisdiction Act (UCCJA), 161, 162, 261, 262
Uniform Crime Reports (UCR), 28, 29, 34, 38, 46, 47, 48
URSA Institute, 109, 200, 201, 202, 250

Vanished Children's Alliance, 77, 78, 80, 164, 176

Wallop, Malcolm, 170, 171, 172
Walsh, Adam, 58, 59, 65, 66, 68, 78, 79, 81, 85, 86, 103, 105, 107, 193, 273, 281
Walsh, John, 66, 68, 79, 83, 86, 94, 95, 98, 100, 101, 103, 104, 105, 109, 273
Walsh, Reve, 66, 79, 86, 94
Williams, Wayne, 57

Yates, Gary, 202, 203
Yerkovich, Gloria, 77, 106

About the Authors

Martin L. Forst received a bachelor's degree in psychology from the University of California at Berkeley, and later earned a master's and doctorate in criminology from the same institution. Over the past fifteen years, Dr. Forst has conducted research in all aspects of the criminal justice system. His most recent research efforts have focused on missing chidren and homeless youths, the medical needs of homeless juveniles, and white collar crime. Dr. Forst is the author of numerous journal articles and the author or coauthor of several books.

Martha-Elin Blomquist earned her bachelor's degree in political science at the University of California at Riverside. She received an M.A. and Ph.D. in jurisprudence and social policy from Boalt Hall School of Law, University of California at Berkeley. Her research interests include juvenile justice, family law, and public policy-making. Dr. Blomquist is currently a senior research fellow with the California attorney general's office where she is conducting research on parental abductions.